"...WE ARE THE LIVING PROOF..."

THE JUSTICE MODEL FOR CORRECTIONS

Second Edition

By

David Fogel

B.A., M.S.W., Dr. of Criminology

Executive Director
Illinois Law Enforcement Commission

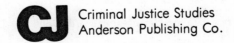
Criminal Justice Studies
Anderson Publishing Co.

"...WE ARE THE LIVING PROOF..."

for carl bingham

"The law must serve everyone, those it protects as well as those it punishes."

Article VI, *Declaration of the Rights of Man*, 1789

CONTENTS

FOREWORD

A rising tide of criticism challenges the prevailing policies and practices of criminal justice agencies throughout the United States. Public disillusionment and professional cynicism is widespread, fueled by the constantly rising crime rates which large, new appropriations of government funds seem unable to curb. These criticisms focus most sharply on the failure of the correctional agencies to reduce recidivism among convicted offenders. The climate of public opinion lends itself most readily to new demands for more repressive measures to increase the punitive and deterrent effect of correctional decisions. Advocates of more punitive sanctions are convinced that only more certain, more visible and more severe sentences of imprisonment for offenders will provide an adequate measure of deterrence and public protection.

Another group of critics espouse an opposing set of premises. They feel that it is not the underuse but the overuse of large maximum security prisons and uncontrolled administrative discretion in sentencing and parole decisions that constitute the failure of correctional policies to deal more effectively with the crime problem. These critics recommend the abolishment of the fortress prison, a moratorium on current prison construction, and the elimination of the indeterminate sentence and parole boards. They locate the failure of current correctional policies in the brutalizing and degrading effects of prison life and the destructive impact on offenders of unreviewable discretion by judicial, prison and parole authorities.

The position expounded in this book does not fit neatly into either of these opposing camps. On the one hand the author seeks to enhance both the certainty and the predictability of the operation of the criminal justice system. On the other he insists that the correctional system must be above all both humane and fair in its operation and conditions of confinement. In this book he is less interested in utopian solutions than in devising short-

vii

term and middle-range solutions to shape a rational and accept able set of correctional policies.

The issues the author must deal with are made no less difficult by this more limited and practical approach. If we do not place our confidence in the utility of fortress prisons, what types of correctional confinement or alternatives to imprisonment should we substitute instead? If our efforts to rehabilitate offenders and reintegrate them into law-abiding communities are ineffective, what principles and objectives should guide the management of prisoners? If the indeterminate sentence and parole board control over release decisions ought to be abandoned, how are we to maintain order in prison or to motivate offenders to change their lives? If the fortress prison is to be abandoned, how are we to identify and deal with that residual population of intractable, dangerous offenders from whom the public must be protected?

In this book the reader will find provocative, thoughtful and often iconoclastic answers to these and other questions. The author shows compassion and empathy not only for the prisoner but also for the neglected victims of crime and the harassed cus todial guard force trying to administer conflicting and irreconcil able objectives in the fortress prison. His proposals constitute an integrated system which deals with central features of the malaise that now afflicts current correctional policies and prac tices. His solution is built on the idea that "Justice-as-fairness represents the superordinate goal of all agencies of the criminal law," and the propositions which flow from this basic principle.

In considering the application of this overriding principle, Fogel deals with the appropriate role of legislative, judicial, and administrative discretion in the setting of sentences. He con siders the relative balance between the use of imprisonment and its alternatives, the role and design of maximum security facil ities in the prison system, the problems of maintaining prison dis cipline and order, the place of rehabilitation and treatment pro grams for offenders, the participation of prisoners in setting the conditions of confinement, and other problems of infusing the prison system, its conditions, and practices with "justice-as-fairness." In seeking answers for such fundamental questions, the author sketches the broad outlines of a philosophy and a design for a new system of sentencing and corrections. Inevitably, he leaves many details undeveloped while making it clear that the process and the problems of reform in different states will vary considerably. However, he attacks in uncompromising fashion hypocritical attitudes and defensive postures which obscure our capacity to devise realistic and rational alternatives. In short, he outlines a more constructive model of corrections and a new sense of purpose and direction for the future.

The author's proposals for change are fundamental and cut deeply into basic supports of a system long taken for granted. The system he describes is an integrated one which must supplant the present system in its entirety in order to be effective. There is always a measure of risk in proposing such major departures from existing practices. One of the greatest dangers is that parts of the new system will be adopted on a piecemeal basis without essential corrective changes in the existing system. This approach, for example, might result in more frequent use of confinement and for longer periods than is now the current practice. Will the older, outmoded fortress prisons really be closed as new model units are opened? Will the risk of arbitrary and discriminatory parole decisions be supplanted by equally arbitrary and discriminatory sentencing by judges? The proposals advanced here can only be properly tested if they are instituted as a comprehensive alternative to the present system of correctional policies and practices.

There is also a danger that the author's stress on "justice-as-fairness" might be adopted as a guiding principle for the development of a new model of prisoner rehabilitation. The author clearly intends that it should be the basic principle for organizing the correctional system itself in a manner that is both defensible and consistent with the ideology of a democratic society. He also believes that strict adherence to this principle will remove many of the sources of discontent with the present system. Will such a system also teach the individual offender to act more lawfully in his relationships with others? Will he learn better to understand and respect the rights of others in his future conduct? Though the author suggests at various points that this may in fact occur in some cases, this is not his prime objective. Adoption of the "justice-as-fairness" principle as a superordinate goal for corrections is justifiable in that it provides a more rational ground for the construction of correctional policies. He is not therefore proposing a new model for the rehabilitation of individual offenders so much as a set of principles for the rehabilitation of the correctional system itself.

In presenting the proposals advanced in this book, the author picks up where most critics leave off. Though he traces the evolution of the maximum-security fortress prison and identifies its many problems and defects, he also tries to answer the question, "Where do we go from here?" His long experience with the treatment of convicted offenders and his thoughtful and critical exploration of the failure of current correctional policies have generated a deep concern and understanding of the plight of both prisoners and correctional personnel caught in the irreconcilable conflicts of current correctional policy. His analysis of problems and his proposals for change do not yield a utopian formulation for reform. Instead they invite debate and creative contributions at many different points so that individual states may develop their own policies along lines consistent with the principles articulated here. Major change in our correctional systems now seems inevitable and this book helps us by proposing why, where, and how we might begin.

Lloyd E. Ohlin
Roscoe Pound Professor of Criminology
Harvard Law School

PREFACE

I have simply left the first four chapters intact (with a few minor corrections) since the history (Chapter I) has not changed much, the plight of the correctional officer (Chapter II) has changed less, and the case law (Chapter III) has, as projected in 1975, simply grown while no dramatic therapeutic breakthroughs have emerged. Chapter IV still contains the major theoretical underpinnings of the justice model and some practical program ideas for its implementation.

Chapter V has been revised and enlarged. It now updates some developments in case law and legislation affecting prison conditions, sentencing procedures and the abolition of parole as a release mechanism in three major jurisdictions. Lastly, I present a response to the "abandonment of rehabilitation" argument.

As with the first edition, the intent of this edition is not to present panaceas but to advance the debate in our continuing pursuit of justice.

David Fogel
Chicago, January, 1978

PREFACE TO FIRST EDITION

Following a series of Midwestern prison disturbances in the summer and fall of 1973, the Law Enforcement Assistance Administration (Region V Office°) invited each of its member state's criminal justice planning directors and correction department heads to a meeting in Chicago. Two years earlier I had attended a hastily convened session of the Association of State Correctional Administrators (A.S.C.A.) in San Francisco. This latter session was in response to the Attica uprising and a series of other less publicized riots throughout the United States. None of the 1973 Midwestern prison disturbances approached the horror of the 1971 Attica uprising. I attended the California meeting in my capacity as Commissioner of the Minnesota State Department of Corrections and the Chicago session as Director of the Illinois Law Enforcement Commission (the agency for L.E.A.A. state planning).

Outside of the meeting room of an elegant San Francisco hotel, the press clamored for admittance. We voted it down. We permitted silent TV footage, and our host had a press release prepared for the newspapers. Individual commissioners could be interviewed following the meeting. The meeting itself was to be a closed one. It did not make much difference. We didn't have much to say anyway. The agenda consisted of a parade of directors whose prisons or jails had recently experienced riots. Commissioner followed commissioner to the podium reliving anxious moments—Procunier at Folsom, Soledad, and San Quentin; McGrath at the New York City Tombs; Oswald at Attica; and others. Many would experience new disturbances in the months to follow. One was destined to himself be taken hostage, another was to offer himself in place of a guard hostage, and several others would negotiate the release of other hostages. Finally, a few would lose their jobs following new riots.

°Consisting of Illinois, Indiana, Michigan, Minnesota, Ohio and Wisconsin.

The San Francisco meeting was reactive. Most of us were still stunned by the New York tragedy, which has been described by the Attica Commission as the "bloodiest one-day encounter between Americans in this century." If America expected answers from its correctional leadership, the A.S.C.A. was not ready to offer them. Under the leadership of Bill Leeke, Director of the South Carolina D.O.C., and his assistant, Dr. Hugh Clement, a number of studies and action programs were developed (the series included a study on collective violence, grievance procedures, prisoner rights and a statement by the A.S.C.A. itself on guidelines for prison management), but all of this occurred later.

In 1973, following the most expensive prison riot in history (Oklahoma, $28 million°), the mood of the meeting in Chicago was less reactive and more deliberative. Each state represented had experienced some sort of violent disturbance between Attica and the L.E.A.A. invitation. The Chicago meeting was the first of six months' of regular sessions which moved from the directors' level down to the assistant wardens' level and was complemented by the presence of state planning agency corrections specialists. In 1971 the preoccupation, perhaps justifiably, was with riot suppression; by 1973 it was with violence prevention. The California session heard "evidence" of nationwide Black militant and Maoist revolutionary conspiracies to disrupt our prisons. A few of us had urged extended discussion on the problem of racism in the prison. The noise of Attica, however, was too loud to permit thoughtful deliberation.

In Chicago we tried to assess the meaning of the civil rights movement of the sixties, the erosion of the traditional "hands off" doctrine of the courts in relation to prisoner complaints, and the subsequent explosion of correctional case law, the student demonstrations, the women's liberation movement, the anti-war demonstrations, the ferment created in America by the War on Poverty, the Peace Corps, VISTA, Job Corps—all of these in

°National Clearinghouse of the Northwestern University Law School (July, 1973) said it was ". . . one of the most disasterous events in the American correctional history."

relation to a changing prison population. We did not come up with a conspiratorial theory; rather we found human dignity was reaching for a new plateau and both guards and prisoners were anxious to share in it.

The Chicago group was not a group of naive liberals. They had no illusions about prisons and the motivations of many prisoners. Contingency plans for violence suppression and new technological and hardware needs were examined. "Highlighting this committee's work was the need for preventive measures rather than riot control," reported Dr. Bennett Cooper, chairman of the group (and Director of the Ohio Department of Corrections and President of the A.S.C.A.). Michigan prepared a contingency plan which included continuous training of officers, pinpointed responsibilities for supervisors, and spoke to the need for negotiation as a model for settling disputes. Wisconsin developed a critical incident report that was shared with the other states and provided computerized feedback on how such incidents were resolved. It included ". . . reporting the action taken and . . . what policy change occurred after an incident was reported to prevent repetition."

A final action taken was to approve a grant to this writer providing for a three-month leave-of-absence to develop longer range thinking about prisons. This work is a part of the continuing Chicago Group's agenda. My charge was to develop an elaboration of what I have called the "justice model" of prison administration. It rests on the notion that justice—as fairness—is the pursuit we should be involved with in prison rather than the several treatment models to which we have given lip service in the past. My thesis is that the best way to teach non-law-abiders to be law-abiding is to treat them lawfully. My concern is less with the administration of justice and more (as Edmond Cahn suggested) with the *justice of administration.*

Lest there be any question of bias, the reader should be aware that I am identified with the movement that calls for the abolition of the fortress prison. It is before all else the task of this generation of administrators to lead in the demise of this medieval relic.

> ... if any person is addressing himself to the perusal of this dreadful subject in the spirit of a philanthropist bent on reforming a necessary and beneficient public institution, I beg him to put it down and go about some other business. It is just such reformers who have in the past made the neglect, oppression, corruption, and physical torture of the common goal the pretext for transforming it into that diabolical den of torment, mischief, and damnation, the modern model prison.
>
> George Bernard Shaw,
> *The Crime of Imprisonment*, 1922.

> Let us face it: Prisons should be abolished. The prison cannot be reformed. It rests upon false premises. Nothing can improve it. It will never be anything but a graveyard of good intentions. Prison is not just the enemy of the prisoner. It is the enemy of society. This behemoth, this monster error has nullified every good work. It must be done away with.
>
> John Bartlow Martin,
> *Break Down the Walls*, 1953.

My intended audience is the prison and corrections administrator. My charge evolving from the Chicago meetings is to elaborate the justice model. In order to accomplish this task I have found it necessary to take a few excursions.

Chapter One deals with our inglorious prison history. Prison administrators are notoriously ahistorical.

> In recent years a small group of radicals and naive nincompoops have adopted slogans like 'Tear down the walls!' and 'Prison are failures.' These slogans have become so popular

that I find myself discussing them as though we need to justify ourselves.

Warden Russell Lash,
Indiana State Prison,
New York Times, 1971.

It was once a truth so fully realized as to become proverbial that a criminal came out of a prison worse than he went in.

John Clay,
The Prison Chaplain, 1837.

Chapter Two will examine the plight of the "Keeper." When administrators have been given diametrically opposed tasks to undertake, they have always resolved custody-treatment disputes in favor of security. But this is not an attack on custody; it is quite the contrary. We will examine the inherent contradictions, the neglect and the fossilization of the role of the custodian, and we will suggest some new dignified roles.

Chapter Three will deal with two related phenomena: the rehabilitation (treatment) programs attempted in the last quarter of a century and the burgeoning correctional case law of the last decade. We will look at the failure of the former and try to assess the meaning of the latter. I have conceptualized both as a struggle by treaters and prisoners to gain power in correctional settings. Corrections' response to both processes has been to date largely unimaginative.

Chapter Four will propose an operational definition of criminality and suggest that the quest for a scientific unified theory is fruitless. It is not likely that our scholars will or even can produce such a theory. This will not stop the library shelves from filling up with volumes of attempts. In any event we cannot wait. The on-the-firing-line administrator lives in a rapidly changing field of action. In this chapter I will recommend viewing the criminal as largely volitional and propose an elaborated justice model for prison administration. A major point I intend to make is that justice requires the harnessing of discretion in sentencing, parole, and administration—not its elimination, but its narrowing. I will propose a new sentencing procedure and the abolition of parole. Finally, looking to the future, a short discussion of a new institutional environment will follow.

Chapter Five contains my doubts about the unintended consequences of proffered innovations. It will, however, mainly be concerned with the residual offender, that member of the elusive "irreducible minimum" who must be incapacitated. We will also look at the newest group of enthusiasts to come on the correctional horizon—the behavioral modifiers (a very loose term, broadly used to describe too many interventions) and their armamentaria (or what Matt Dumont describes, less charitably, as "technological fascism"). Finally, I will comment on our need to go the "high visibility" road with our constituency—the public, the legislature and the prisoner—in order to reduce distortions in practice. While the lessons of Watergate are still fresh, I will urge that we profit from the example of the high walls built around the White House which, as with prisons, kept the public out even as it imprisoned and corrupted its occupants.

I have no illusions about reforming the fortress prison. It has to go. Rather my intention is to help make it a safe and sane work and living environment (until we can quickly get out of it) for both the keepers and the kept—who, although they have a shared fate in prison, have invariably treated each other as natural enemies in the past. It is in this sense of modernizing our approach that I offer this work in fulfillment of the Chicago group's mission.

This project was accomplished in residence at the Harvard Law School Center for Criminal Justice upon the invitation of its Director, James Vorenberg. Located on the fifth floor of the Roscoe Pound Building, the Center provided the physical, and more significantly, the human resources for a stimulating experience. Lloyd Ohlin, as a consultant to the project, provided sustained encouragement and incisive criticism throughout the entire project. Without his guidance and assistance it would be difficult to conceive completion of this work. David Rothman of

Columbia University served as an historical consultant, generously sharing his thoughts, time and his Barnard, Vermont home with me. Irving Piliavin of the University of Wisconsin also served the project in his usual stimulating and challenging way. He assisted in focussing the work toward practical application, suggested innovative sentencing programs and inmate-staff self-governance models.

A number of people in the field also shared their as yet unpublished works with me. I gratefully acknowledge such magnanimous gestures on the part of: Richard A. McGee for his "A New Look at Sentencing: Part II" (since published in September, 1974 *Federal Probation*); David Greenberg of New York University for his research papers to be included in the Final Report of Senator Goodell's Committee for the Study of Incarceration; James B. Jacobs and Harold G. Retsky of the University of Chicago for their pioneering ethnographic study entitled the "Prison Guard," (since published in *Urban Life and Culture,* Vol. 4, No. 1., April, 1975); to Hans Mattick, Director, Center for Research in Criminal Justice, of the University of Illinois at Chicago Circle for his "Reflections of a Former Prison Warden" (forthcoming in *Essays in Honor of Henry D. McKay*); Stanley Griffith, a Chicago attorney, for his "A Training Experience as a Pseudo-guard" written for the Illinois Law Enforcement Commission; and Richard Wilsnack and Lloyd Ohlin of Harvard for their materials on "Prison Disturbances-(Winter 1973-1974)."

With the constraint of a tight schedule, three research assistants worked furiously to collect assigned information: Ann Morelli, a law student at Harvard, assisted in legal research concerning case law; Diane Gutman, a psychology student at Tufts, assisted in research dealing with experiments in correctional rehabilitation; and Toby Yarmolinsky, a political science student at Antioch, assisted with everything, even after the L.E.A.A. funds were depleted. Roberta Curtis, a recent Harvard graduate, must be the world's second fastest and most accurate typist (but I have not yet met the first). Finally, the Criminal Justice Center contains a number of people who provided unplanned but fruitful inputs into this study by way of chats, reading of drafts and a seminar (Walter Miller, Lloyd McDonald, Craig McEwen, Robert Coates, Alden Miller, Dale Sechrest, Arlette Klein, Dan Miller and Judy Caldwell). None of this would have been possible without the generous cooperation and assistance of Rosanne Kumins, who keeps the Center and its activities harmoniously orchestrated and in high spirits.

Since my return to the Illinois Law Enforcement Commission I have received much assistance from staff, commissioners and other colleagues, most notably from Chester Kamin, Hans Mattick, Norval Morris, Stephen A. Schiller, Richard A. McGee, Robert Schuwerk, Edmund Muth, Eugene Eidenberg, J. David Coldren and Lawrence Meyers. Special gratitude goes to Cheryl McLinden for her tireless effort in typing and retyping revisions in the manuscript on weekends.

There is no way, other than the actual publication of this book, to thank my wife for her assistance, confidence, and patience.

With all the encouragement and assistance I received, the responsibility for the biases and final content remains with me. I first conceived of the notion of operationalizing justice in corrections while waiting to testify at the U.S. House Select Committee on Crime in December 1971 as it inquired into the Attica riot. Inspiration came from watching (former Senator) Representative Claude Pepper of Florida preside over the Committee as it provided (in several volumes) this century's most sane legislative debate concerning the mission of corrections.

This project was funded by the L.E.A.A.'s National Institute of Law Enforcement and Criminal Justice (Grant No. 74-TA-05-0001).

August, 1975

DF

"On Change"

It must be remembered that there is nothing more difficult to plan, more doubtful of success, nor more dangerous to manage than the creation of a new system. For the initiator has the enmity of all who would profit by the preservation of the old institutions and merely lukewarm defenders in those who would gain by the new ones. The hesitation of the latter arises in part from the fear of their adversaries, who have the laws on their side, and in part from the general skepticism of mankind which does not really believe in an innovation until experience proves its value. So it happens that whenever his enemies have occasion to attack the innovator they do so with the passion of partisans while the others defend him sluggishly so that the innovator and his party are alike vulnerable.

Niccolo Machiavelli, 1513

1
Prison Heritage

Those who cannot remember the past are condemned to repeat it.

George Santayana

We will try to account for the emergence of prisons in America. In order to do so we must hazard an historical journey replete with its problems of selectivity and incompleteness. Institutions never arrive full blown; they are historical products of layer upon layer of custom emerging from the distant past into hesitant shapes. The modern prison is a product of such a process. In order to best understand our own prison development we must appreciate what was on the minds of the contemporaries who built them. But we need also to examine the influences pressing upon early Americans—namely, their English heritage.

There is no linear legacy to trace. We know only the problem our ancestors faced—how to control deviance in a strange wilderness. They would be astounded to see a modern fortress prison. They would not have understood the notion of rehabilitation. "You do not rehabilitate Quakers—you whip and banish them," a Puritan might have said. Quakers did not understand why practically all felonies upon third commission necessitated death. The Philadelphia Society for Alleviation of the Miseries of Public Prisons might have said, "Penance, labor and solitude will transform a criminal." But these Puritan-Quaker notions would have been anathema to Elam Lynds of Sing-Sing, who said, "Break the convict's spirit, whip him and he'll learn!" Zebulon Brockway of Elmira would recoil in horror. He was superintendent of America's first reformatory. "Habits of industry school, individual attention and an indeterminate sentenc ingredients of rehabilitation," he might have said. Ragen of Stateville, Illinois, preferred the iron-fisted discipline while his contemporaries in the West were putting together the most ambitious program of rehabilitation using the "medical model." California would develop medical facilities, intake and classification processes, and a host of therapies under an umbrella of the indeterminate sentence. Thomas Jefferson, who also had a prison plan, would be baffled to see Vacaville.

If there was no "grand scheme" for American prison development there were also few proud moments and fewer heroes. Our heroes do not leap out of the pages of history with any quality of instantaneous recognition. We have had no Isaac Newtons, no Albert Einsteins, and no Marie Curies. No one has ever won a Nobel Prize for prison work. With the exception, perhaps, of the ideas of an 18th century Italian Count (Cesare Beccaria, 1738-1794), the programs initiated by a Scottish sea captain and ex-prisoner (Alexander Maconochie, 1787-1860), and the vision of an American contemporary, a shoemaker and a court volunteer (John Augustus, 1785-1859), corrections has made very little progress beyond the prison walls.

There were some proud moments by several heroic types, but they were short-lived. It seems reforms never out-lived re-formers. John Haviland (1792-1852), the architect, set into con-crete the basic pattern of cellular confinement that was to set the parameters of correctional development to the modern day both physically and morally.[1] The cell is the legacy. From its crudest beginnings in castle dungeons through the concept of prison architecture as a "moral science," to its technological per-fection in a modern prison-hospital, the cell remains the legacy—the medium has always been the message. The message has, at the bottom line, always been the same. We have called the occupiers of the cell heretics, sinners, criminals, offenders, paupers, revolutionaries, defectives, and patients. "We are all brought up to believe that we may inflict injuries on anyone against whom we can make out a case of moral inferiority," ob-served George Bernard Shaw.[2]

IN THE BEGINNING WAS THE CHURCH

Gerhard Mueller said the prison "was inherited as an institu-tion from the medieval bushwhackers and highway robbers, who used imprisonment as a means of coercing cities to pay ransom for captured merchants."[3] Frederick Kuether believes that the church greatly influenced the history of prison development. He points out that Thomas Aquinas described penance as: "the pay-ment of temporal punishment due on account of the offense committed against God by sin."[4] Because the church did not allow its courts to impose death sentences, it developed institutions called "penitentiaries" where presumably one paid up his account. Kuether claims that the secular state copied this practice at first only to detain until trial and to hold for execution. Pope Clement XI had St. Michael Prison built in 1703, and it was described as a "house of correction for younger offenders" with a program of silence, work and prayer. Its punishments included: "isolation, bread-and-water diet, solitary work in the cells, floggings and the black hole."[5] William Nagel also speaks of church-government prisons in which "certain heretics having been spared death, were imprisoned for life, often in single rooms underground . . . a Portuguese religious prison . . . contained cells for witches, sorcerers, and sinners."[6]

> . . . Some of the monastic quarters provided totally separate facilities for each monk so that it was a simple matter to lock up an errant brother for brief periods. As 'mother houses' of monastic orders had satellite houses often located in less desirable places, it was also the practice to transfer monks for periods of time to such locations. There is some evidence that some of these satellites came to be regarded as punitive facilities.[7]

Nagel also agrees that when the feudal system began to crumble and social unrest increased, the church invented the "workhouse,"—the forerunner to the modern prison.

SOME EARLY PRACTICES

In Roman and early English law incarceration as punishment was unknown. While both used imprisonment for detention, the Romans had outlawed it as a punishment. As far back as the Saxon invasion castles are known to have been used as jails. In canon law, the Roman principle of custody, not punishment, was followed in spirit, but history records some English clergy spending years, even life, in early English institutions doing penance upon conviction of a crime.[8]

With the erosion of the feudal system (14th century) and the consequent disruption of the labor market, vagabondage greatly increased. In the 16th century the criminal law was used heavily to control the wandering unemployed, those who left their masters and the lawless.[9] A major departure (probably occasioned by the need to deal with increasing numbers of itinerant poor) was the establishment in 1557 in London of a workhouse for vagrants. Ironically, the site was an abandoned castle famous for its well that was said to produce water of medicinal quality—St. Bridget's Well. Bridewell is the currently surviving corruption of that name. Bridewell is still used to identify many municipal workhouses.[10] This type of institution also proliferated on the continent.

Imprisonment was then a "secondary" type of punishment—secondary to capital punishment—but was not as commonly used as transportation or exile to a colony. From the earliest days of colonization, America received about 2,000 convicts a year until the Revolution. During the years of American Revolution, England turned to Australia for transport. For eight decades to follow, Australia and other Pacific penal colonies received no less than 100,000 convicts, about the same number as had earlier come to our shores. Transportation was interrupted periodically by the American Revolution and later by the Napoleonic Wars. However, the English did not build a prison system during these respites, rather they imprisoned convicts on "hulks"—prison ships tied to piers. Transporting prisoners worked admirably for the English. It rid the country of criminals and provided the colonies with cheap labor. As Rubin points out, it takes a flight of the imagination to consider other more lofty motivations for transportation such as a reduction in punishment or as a rehabilitative opportunity for a new start in a colony, in light of the large profits awaiting shipowners and the treatment of "passengers."

Conditions in slow-going vessels were worse than even

those prevailing in the jails. The crowding, the vice, and the filth were unspeakable, and great numbers died on the voyage . . . [In the penal colonies, convict gangs] worked in irons and recalcitrant prisoners were subject to frequent lashing. [11]

The social cost of the mercantile and industrial revolutions and the great land discoveries were devastating to the poor. A labor market requiring stability and predictability could not tolerate roaming vagrants and thieves but neither did it provide a social program short of repressive control. The Renaissance and Enlightenment which produced:

great surges of human creativity . . . also produced . . . widespread impoverishment, [and] some of the grimmest chapters in the history of penology. Transportation, which killed and degraded many, was a by-product of discovery and colonization. Practically the entire law of theft was written in the eighteenth century, and it was routine to write the penalty of death in the laws. [Radzinowicz notes] 'Practically all capital offenses were created more or less as a matter of course by a placid and uninterested Parliament. In nine cases out of ten there was no debate and no opposition!'[12]

COLONIAL PUNISHMENTS

In trying to trace our own penal institutions we must have a picture of the frame of mind of our ancestors. The colonies operated under English criminal law standards and practices, although frequently modified in a rustic setting. Early penalties which may now shock our sensibilities were frequent, common and accepted. They changed only when the concept of man changed.

A stroll through Boston Commons today takes one through areas marked for colonial punishment for Sabbath-Breakers (wooden cages), the pillory, the stocks, ducking stools, the whipping post and the gallows. In Philadelphia, the City of Brotherly Love, Sellin described the practice of gibbeting as capital punishment followed by placing the carcass in an iron cage until it decomposed. The public presumably would take heed of such a ghastly sight in conducting its own affairs to avoid a similar fate.[13]

Americans were also widely accustomed to huge fines, ear clippings, mutilation, hanging, drawing and quartering, dismemberment, blinding, burning, branding and maiming. A nineteenth century account of punishments describes the temper of the colonial times:

> In these barbarous methods of degrading criminals the colonists in America copied the laws of the fatherland. Our ancestors were not squeamish. The sight of a man lopped of his ears, slit of his nose, or with a seared brand or great gash in his forehead or cheek could not affect the stout stomaches that cheerfully and eagerly gathered around the bloody whipping post and the gallows.[14]

If being unemployed or a vagabond was an offense in England, simply being a Quaker in Massachusetts was little better. The penalty for such "blasphemous hereticks" and any who read books of their "devilish opinions" was:

> . . . if male for the first offense shall have one of his ears cutt off; for the second offense have his other ear cutt off; a woman shall be severely whipt; for the third offense they, he or she, shall have their tongues bored through with a hot iron.[15]

New York and Virginia were no less ferocious. Church absence in Virginia was a capital offense. In Maryland and Virginia the hog occupied an unusually lofty place in the penal codes. Men of power were able to minutely define penal sanctions against their particular property. For hog theft:

... It was enacted in the New York Assembly that for the first offense the criminal should stand in the pillory 'four compleat hours,' have his ears cropped and pay treble damages; for the second offense he be stigmatized on the forehead with the letter H and pay treble damages; for the third be adjudged 'fellon,' and therefore receive capital punishment. In Virginia . . . 'twenty-five lashes well laid on at publick whipping-post;' for the second offense he was set two hours in the pillory and had both ears nailed thereto, at the end of the two hours to have the ears slit loose; for the third offense, death.[16]

Nor was "clerkly"—the exculpatory plea of "benefit of clergy"—available for hog stealers. For over five centuries the English permitted its use for some to avoid more savage punishments. Originally granted in the 12th century, it was a way of having the clergy escape secular punishment. Gradually, anyone passing the test of reading could escape the gallows. Since the ability to read was associated with the privileged classes, only they could avoid the heavier penalties. The "benefit" that replaced the gallow was branding, which was in force until the close of the 18th century in America. Branding was in ubiquitous use in the colonies; S L stood for seditious libel and was burned on the cheek, M for manslaughter, T for thief (usually on the left hand), R for rouge (and Quakers), F for forgery, B for burglary, H for heretic (and hog stealers). Other symbols, unless impressed on the skin, had to be worn as symbols of degradation on the "uppermost" garments. Hawthorne immortalized this practice in *The Scarlet Letter*. The real Hesters wore the letters upon pain of public whippings. This primitive classification system presumably recognized lesser offenses: A for adultery, B for blasphemy, V for viciousness and D for habitual drunks. Public aid recipients wore a color patch on their sleeves signifying the name of the parish that furnished relief. Other offenders stood on blocks with inscriptions detailing their transgressions: "A Wanton Gospeller"; "An Open and Obstinate Condemner of God's Holy Ordinances"; "A Defacer of Records"; "Public Destroyer of Peace"; "Lampoon-riter"; "False Accuser"; "Defamer of Magistrates"; and as many others as there were specific offenders.[17]

These were not colonial inventions. Labeling and branding were ancient English customs accompanied in the old country by a procession and trumpets. It is not clear how many of the spectators of this three-century-old practice could read, but they did understand from the fanfare that a solemn event was taking place when the offender mounted the block and stood there for hours with words scrawled on a sign around his neck.

Burdened with a barbarous English heritage in a frightening wilderness, the shadow of Calvin cast itself upon the deliberations of those meting out punishment to the "destroyers of the peace." And there were many of them. The search for order in isolated settlements produced all sorts of "deviants." Could it have been otherwise with witches stalking the land in Massachusetts, as they had in Europe a few centuries earlier, with boat loads of convicts arriving regularly (2,000 a year from 1607 to the Revolution until 100,000 had arrived*), runaway slaves, indigenous poor, red savages and Quakers.

Comprehension of the moral world view of the powerful, who could enforce the law in the early period, leads us to an understanding of the regimen they believed necessary for controlling the miscreant. Such an understanding will tell us something of the physical facilities they considered necessary to contain offenders. This is the major thrust of our quest. Although we will learn how prisons were rationalized, we will need to look to a more contemporary period—our own—to understand their persistence. But we begin in the colonial period.

---

*Little is known of the thousands of ex-convicts coming later to the west coast from Australia until 1867. H. H. Bancroft, the verbose chronicler of Pacific coast history, records a settlement in San Francisco known as the Sydney Town at the foot of Telegraph Hill. The ex-convicts were said to take advantage of fires they set which ravaged the city and in the confusion come out of Sydney Town to steal as much as they could carry off. They were a constant problem for the Committee of Vigilance of 1851. (H.H. Bancroft, *Popular Tribunals*, 1887, pp. 73-74).

If the colonists had elaborate punishments, they did not have elaborate views toward the deviant. The deviant was the pauper-criminal-stranger-defective. Rothman, in his remarkable *The Discovery of the Asylum: Social Order and Disorder in the New Republic,* says of colonial enforcement that it

> stood midway between poor relief and crime prevention measures, [it] was one basic technique by which colonial communities guarded their good order and tax money. Towns everywhere used their legal prerogatives to exclude the harmless poor, who might some day need support, and suspicious characters, who could disturb their peace.[18]

The escalation of penalties to death for third-timers, as earlier noted in the case of hog stealers, was built into the penal codes of the settlements as a response to recidivism. "The colonists' rationale was clear: anyone impervious to the fine and the whip, who did not mend his ways after an hour with a noose about him, was uncontrollable and therefore had to be executed."[19] The jail, not to be confused with the as yet undeveloped prison, was simply a place of confinement for debtors or those awaiting summary punishment. Self-preservation, not correction, was on the mind of the colonist.

> Given their [colonists'] conception of deviant behavior and institutional organization, they did not believe that a jail could rehabilitate, or intimidate or detain the offender. They placed little faith in the possibility of reform. Prevailing Calvinist doctrines that stressed the natural depravity of man and the powers of the devil hardly allowed such optimism. Since temptations to misconduct were not only omnipresent but practically irresistible, rehabilitation could not serve as a basis for a prison program.[20]

The colonists saw the deviant as willful, a sinner, immoral, a captive of the devil, simply pauperized or defective. Isolated settlements engendered xenophobic feelings; the stranger aroused natural fear. Internal transportation was in widespread use. The offender was marched to the town line and sent off to plague another community. Shame, banishment, and summary punishment, including mutilation and death, were the colonial deterrents. Yet the imagery of institutional confinement as punishment was invoked early by William Penn. It was short-lived and forgotten, and had to await the end of English dominion in America for its resurrection.

> The Great Law of 1682 drafted by Penn read in part that every County within Pennsylvania . . . shall build or cause to be built in the most convenient place in each County, respective, a sufficient house, at least twenty foot square, for Restraint, Correction, Labor and Punishment of all such persons as shall be thereunto committed by law . . .[21]

This was the first known statement in American history that spoke of imprisonment at hard labor in place of corporal or capital punishment as the prescribed punishment for serious crime.

POST-REVOLUTION DEVELOPMENTS

After the Revolution, it was Penn's idea that became operational, then failed and finally led to the notion of cellular confinement. With the end of the War of Independence there was a slow dismantling of things English in the new United States. Enlightenment ideas gained currency and the barbarities of the English sanguinary law gave way to the new Rationalism. "Enlightenment ideas challenged Calvinist doctrines; the prospect of boundless improvement confronted a grim determinism."[22] Beccaria's *On Crimes and Punishments* was already known to leaders at the time of the Revolution.

> . . . The essay was a tightly reasoned devastating attack upon the prevailing systems for the administration of criminal justice. As such it aroused the hostility and resistance of those who stood to gain by the perpetuation of the barbaric

and archaic penological institutions of the day. . . . It had the power to rally to the cause it pleaded, the energies and efforts of most of the enlightened minds of eighteenth-century Europe. . . . It is not an exaggeration to regard Beccaria's work as being of primary importance in paving the way for penal reform for approximately the last two centuries. The reader will find proposed in his essay practically all of the important reforms in the administration of criminal justice and in penology which have been achieved in the civilized world since 1764.[23]

Beccaria's ideas were quite fitting to the young Republic intent upon ridding itself of Old World ideas and practices. But it was more complex than a clash on the ideational level. America itself was becoming complex: travel, resettlement, new communication methods developed during the war, the sense of community transcending parochial local boundaries, social mobility, the beginnings of a factory system, urbanization, and immigration all combined to erode the Puritan methods of social control. We could hardly be expected to continue to rely on laws that had driven us to rebel. Probably more important was a congruity between a post-Revolutionary image of man in freedom and a keen sense of pragmatism which sensed that the old ways of social control would no longer work in a burgeoning new nation. Rationalism's main tenent was:

The first conviction that social progress and advancement was possible through sweeping social reforms carried out according to the dictates of 'pure reason' . . . so barbarous and archaic a part of the old order as the current criminal jurisprudence and penal administration of the time could not long remain immune to the growing spirit of progress and enlightenment.[24]

Thus in 1776 in Pennsylvania, under heavy Quaker influence, and probably with a fresh remembrance of their treatment in Massachusetts and elsewhere under colonial rule, the provisional state constitution read in part: 'The Penal Laws heretofore used shall be reformed by the future legislature of the State, as soon as may be, and punishment made in some cases less sanguinary, and in general more *proportionate to the crimes.*"[25] If it was shades of William Penn it was also the hand of Beccaria who a dozen years earlier had written "punishment . . . should be . . . *proportional to the crime.*"

Imprisonment was visualized as a substitute for capital punishment. The purpose of the penal law, stated the Pennsylvania constitution, is:

> To deter more effectually from the commission of crimes, by continual visible punishment of long duration, and to make a sanguinary punishment less necessary houses ought to be provided for punishing at hard labor those who shall be convicted of crimes not capital wherein the criminals shall be employed for the benefit of the public or for reparation of injuries done to private persons. And all persons at proper times shall be admitted to see the prisoners at their labour.[26]

But during the war years this law was not able to be implemented. However, by 1786, Rubin states that most crimes were punishable by imprisonment at hard labor. An Act in that year called for punishment to be: "publicly and disgracefully imposed . . . in the streets of the cities and towns, and upon the highways."[27] This system, which appears to be the embryonic chaingang (prisoners "dressed in motley and weighted down") of public works, failed because of riots, escapes, and as a result of public displeasure over degrading practices. The time for change was ripe. The war was now over, the old system was in a cycle of failure and a new enthusiasm for prison reform was beginning to emerge.

THE PHILADELPHIA SOCIETY FOR ALLEVIATING THE MISERIES OF PUBLIC PRISONS

Yet how might such a program come about? Dr. Benjamin

Rush, a signer of the Declaration of Independence, proposed a new method for treating criminals. At the home of Benjamin Franklin in March, 1787, a group of influential Philadelphians gathered to hear Dr. Rush's radical ideas. He read a paper proposing the establishment of a prison program that would:

1. Classify prisoners for housing.
2. Provide prison labor which would make the institution self-supporting.
3. Include gardens to provide food and outdoor areas for recreation.
4. Classify convicts according to a judgment about the nature of the crime—whether it arose out of passion, habit, temptation or mental illness.
5. Impose indeterminate periods of confinement based upon the convict's reformative progress.[28]

"So persuasive and logical," notes Bennett, "were the pamphlets and views of Franklin's group that the American penal system abolished the practice of mutilation and execution as a method of deterring crime."[29]

Armed with a plan, the Philadelphia Society for Alleviating the Miseries of Public Prisons (formed in May, 1787, but known as the Pennsylvania Prison Society since 1887) now went about organizing to implement its program. In January, 1788, the Society wrote to the Supreme Executive Council of the Commonwealth and in a month the latter recommended changes in the penal law to the Pennsylvania legislature

calculated to render punishments a means of reformation, and the labour of criminals of profit to the state. Late experiments in Europe have demonstrated that those advantages are only to be obtained by temperance, and solitude with labour.[30]

There had indeed been "late experiments" in this direction in

Europe (Belgium, Italy, England). But the great significance of these memorable years (1787-1790) in Philadelphia was the beginning of a continuous, systematic and permanent departure that would indelibly mark a change in the official methods of dealing with criminals in America.[31] The Legislature provided for the renovation of the old Walnut Street Jail in Philadelphia; the new facility (1790) would include a "cellhouse."

Yet it would be an oversimplification to suggest, as some have, that inside the Walnut Street Jail was born the present prison system of the civilized world. Sellin finds that Blackstone had earlier recommended—without the slightest reservation—a system of solitude and constant labour. "What can be more truly beneficial, he queried," . . . for the riotous, the libertine . . . the idle delinquent, than solitude? . . . Solitude will awaken reflection; confinement will banish temptation; sobriety will restore vigour; and labor will beget a habit of honest industry.°"[32] William Paley published his "Principles of Moral and Political Philosophy" in 1785, and in discussing reformation and deterrence as the goals of punishment concluded: "Of the reforming punishments which have not yet been tried, none promises as much success as that of solitary imprisonment, or the confinement of criminals in separate apartments."[33] Further evidence of British, not Quaker, beginnings for the solitary system is cited by Sellin, noting that John Howard had described the Bridewell at Petworth as a cellular facility: "The rooms are on two stories, over arcades [just like the Walnut Street 'penitentiary house'], sixteen on each floor, thirteen feet three inches by ten and nine feet high."[34]

On the basis of the facts it is reasonable to claim that the philosophy of solitary confinement, with cellular labor or

---

° Later Jeremy Betham spoke with equal enthusiasm about the possibilities of general reformation:

"Morals reformed, health preserved, industry invigorated, instruction diffused, public burdens lightened, economy seated as it were upon a rock, the Gordian knot of the poor laws not cut but untied." (Hermann Mannheim, ed., *Pioneers in Criminology*, p. 64)

with congregate labor insuring the non-intercourse of prisoners, had fully matured in England before the 'penitentiary house' in the yard of the Walnut Street Jail was even contemplated. Indeed, it is fair to assume that it was the ideas of Howard, Blackstone and Paley that spurred the members of the Philadelphia Society to action. We know that they were fully conversant with Howard's work and writings and acknowledged their indebtedness to him on more than one occasion.[35]

Thus, if we had earlier sought an escape from the sanguinary British penal practices, we were to begin a new era under the influence of British reformers, legal scholars, and theologians.

What made this new penology between 1790 and about 1830 possible was the post-Revolutionary image of the criminal. He was rational, willful in his behavior and repetitively criminal because of the evil British sanguinary laws. The treatment regimen called for was imbedded in Beccarian law reform; a reduction of penalties, particularly the barbarities of execution; flogging; branding; and maiming. Incarceration in place of the gallows would deter the prospective criminal. Just laws would cure criminality. Further, physical facilities were necessary to confine the criminal for purposes of useful work and good habit formation, and from his labor the prison would pay for itself. But this first reform thrust was to collapse in a decade "due to overcrowding, idleness and incompetent personnel."[36]

Until these problems overtook and defeated the Walnut Street Jail program, it apparently worked well.

Each male prisoner was paid for his labor at the same or somewhat lower wages than those paid for similar work on the outside and female prisoners had opportunity to earn small sums. All were debited with the cost of their daily maintenance. Some prisoners earned as much as a dollar a day. Moreover the prisoners were informed that good conduct would be rewarded by recommendation to the governor for a pardon, and many were pardoned. No chains or irons were allowed. Guards were forbidden to use weapons or even canes. Corporal punishment was unknown. The silence rule was enforced in the shops but prisoners could talk in the night rooms before bedtime.[37]

Slowly, as the population increased, housing classification gave way to overcrowding and personal attention yielded to mass care. In Massachusetts convicts began wearing half red and blue uniforms, while in New York only second termers could be so distinguished. Massachusetts later put "two timers" in suits of red, yellow, and blue and except on the Sabbath fed them bread and water as a third meal daily.[38] By 1808 Newgate (New York) was granting so many pardons as to make discharges equal to commitments, while Ohio simply pardoned convicts whenever the population rose above 120 in number, just enough to make room for newcomers.[39] Escapes, violence, indiscriminate housing of all types of offenders, corruption and idleness brought forth a report in 1820 from the Visiting Committee of the Philadelphia Society (that had earlier played such a key role in reorganizing the Walnut Street Jail) finding: (1) the present building unfit for a penitentiary; (2) classification non-existent; (3) the prison over-crowded; and (4) the prisoners idle. These conditions caused them to conclude: "It is with deep regret the Visiting Committee feel themselves obliged to state, they have not been able to perceive any reformation among the prisoners."[40] To overcome idleness the Walnut Street Jail administration introduced the tread-mill—which had failed at Charlestown the year before.[41]

At the very moment when the idea of imprisonment itself was in doubt,° indeed a near total failure, a new burst of enthusiasm came from New York and again from the Pennsylvania Society.

° "The decline of the early American prison was evident as early as 1800, and in 1817 it was a question whether the whole penitentiary system should not be abandoned in favor of a return to the former system of capital and corporal punishment. In a 'Report of the Penitentiary System,' issued in 1821, Daniel Chipman of Vermont wrote, 'the projectors of the penitentiary system were peculiarly exposed to an enthusiasm which led them to expect beneficial effects which could never be realized.' " (*The Attorney General's Survey of Release Procedures*, as cited in George Killinger and Paul Ciomwell, *Penology*, pp. 25, 34)

These new programs would become the celebrated Auburn and Pennsylvania systems. At the early signs of the collapse of the Walnut Street Jail, the Philadelphia Society for the Alleviation of the Miseries of Public Prisons had already put together ideas for a new prison.

> This plan called for complete solitude with labor in the cells and recreation in a private yard adjacent to each cell. Again the Pennsylvania Legislature embodied the Society's plan in an 1821 enactment. One prison would be built at Pittsburgh [The Western Penitentiary opened in 1826] and one in Philadelphia [The Eastern Penitentiary opened in 1829].[42]

Contact with the outside world was to be entirely eliminated. A Bible would be furnished each inmate for moral guidance.

The New York and Pennsylvania systems unleased a pamphlet war, each side proclaiming the virtues of their own systems; Pennsylvania's, total solitary isolation of the inmate, work in the cell and penance; and Auburn's, congregate work program in silence by day and separation at night—enforced seclusion from the contaminants of the outside community through silence, separation and work. Auburn's program simply had the virtue of being cheaper to operate and, as we shall see, developed the extraordinary will on the part of its administrators to organize a program of "calculated humiliation" to enforce non-communication between convicts. While the Pennsylvania Quakers relied upon penitence and seclusion, the New Yorkers relied upon the breaking of the convict's spirit. But Auburn itself did not initially set out with such a planned program.

It was becoming increasingly difficult to maintain order even after New York returned to legalized flogging of convicts and use of stocks and irons.[43] While the post-Revolutionary zeal took criminals out of society, it had also created a society of criminals inside the institutions.

> Faced with such a problem, New York prison reformers groped for an answer throughout the decade which fol-

lowed the war of 1812. Experimenting with ideas that had originated in Europe and were being implemented in Pennsylvania, which was experiencing penal difficulties at the same time, prison administrators in the Empire State eventually devised a system which, for all its borrowing from outside resources, possessed a high degree of originality.[44]

The key, as John Howard had earlier suggested, was seclusion. American reformers now proclaimed that the criminal was both a product and a victim of his environment.

THE FORTRESS PRISON EMERGES 1820-1870

The literature reflects a desperate attempt on the part of reformers to save the faltering prison system through a minute ordering of the relationships and environment of the offender. Jacksonian America was caught up in the ambivalence of a process which saw rapid movement away from colonial values of order and regularity but with a clinging nostalgia to restore them lest the republican experiment die.

. . . Assuming that social stability could not be achieved without a very personal and keen respect for authority, they looked first to a firm family discipline to inculcate it. Reformers also anticipated that society would rid itself of corruptions. In a narrow sense this meant getting rid of such blatant centers of vice as taverns, theaters, and houses of prostitution. In a broader sense, it meant revising a social order in which men knew their place. Here sentimentality took over, and critics in the Jacksonian period often assumed that their forefathers had lived together without social strain, in secure, placid, stable, and cohesive communities. In fact, the designers of the penitentiary set out to recreate these conditions. But the results, it is not surprising to discover, were startlingly different from anything that the colonial period had known. A conscious effort to instill discipline through an institutional routine led to a set work pattern, a rationalization of movement, a precise organization of time, a general uniformity. Hence, for all the reformers' nostalgia, the reality of the penitentiary was much closer to the values of the nineteenth than the eighteenth century . . . The prison would train the most notable victims of social disorder to discipline, teaching them to resist corruption. And success in this particular task should inspire a general reformation of manners and habits. The institution would become a laboratory for social improvement. By demonstrating how regularity and discipline transformed the most corrupt persons, it would reawaken the public to these virtues. The penitentiary would promote a new respect for order and authority.[45]

With the offender redefined from sinner (Colonial Era) to victim of bad laws (Post-Revolutionary Era), and now in the Jacksonian Period to victim of his environment—the wayward child—prison reformers and, incidentally, administrators (the latter were becoming estranged from the former, their spiritual godfathers), received a new lease on life. Pennsylvania and New York took different roads, but optimism pervaded both camps. The first generation of fortress prisons were built in the late 1820s. In Pennsylvania, separation was built in physically.°

°Sellin notes:

"But the philosophy of the system was a British importation and the 'penitentiary house' of the Walnut Street Jail was no innovation. English reformers gave us both the fundamental ideas that their application in practice to such an extent that no Pennsylvanians can lay claim to be the inventors of the Pennsylvania System.

Roberts Vaux in his Letter on the Penitentiary System of Pennsylvania addressed to William Roscoe, a British critic, in 1827.

'The treatment of prisoners,' he wrote, 'should be of such a nature, as to convince them 'that the way of the transgressor is hard;'

'In separate confinement, every prisoner is placed beyond the possibility of being made more corrupt by his imprisonment . . . In separate confinement, the prisoners will not know who are undergoing punishment at the same time with themselves . . . [Separate confinement will provide an opportunity] . . . for promoting his restoration to the path of virtue, because seclusion is believed to be an essential ingredient in moral treatment, . . .

In New York it was accomplished through a paramilitary program.°°The program and physical facility were both seen as being in the service of reformation. Once again an attempt would be made to transform the offender. But from this era forward, a century and a half of redefinitions would have to conform to the architecture of the fortress prison. Whatever notions of convict reformation were to prevail, most prisoners would have to be behind the high walls of the fortress prison designed in Jacksonian enthusiasm.

PIONEERS OF PENAL ADMINISTRATION

The 1820-1850 era produced the most extraordinary penologists. They carried the day, transforming any vestige of individual self-discipline to a program of compulsive, en masse compliance, enforced with the whip if necessary. It began with the strictest seclusion. No visits, letters or communication with

---

'In separate confinement, a specific graduation of punishment can be obtained. . .

'In separate confinement, the same variety of discipline [will be available].

'By separate confinement, other advantages of an economical nature will result; among these may be mentioned a great reduction of the terms of imprisonment. . .'

(Thorsten Sellin, "The Origin of the Pennsylvania System of Prison Discipline," *Prison Journal,* summer, 1970, p. 14-15).

°°Auburn first experimented with the Pennsylvania system of complete solitary confinement, but it collapsed in a series of self-mutilations, suicides and other deaths.

Eighty-three prisoners, classified as the most dangerous, were placed in solitary confinement. "In less than a year five of [them] had died, one became an idiot, another when his door was opened dashed himself from the gallery, and the rest with haggard looks and disparing voices begged to be set to work." (Paul F. Cromwell, Jr., *Auburn: The World's Second Great Prison System,* p. 69); and Lewis notes that "the stage was set for a new order, and a state that had already conducted two major penological experiments [Newgate and Auburn] now embarked upon another." (W. David Lewis, *From Newgate to Dannemora,* p. 80).

the outside world was tolerated. Rothman quotes an early Sing-Sing chaplain: "The prisoner was taught to consider himself *dead* to all without the prison walls," and, carrying the metaphor, a warden instructed new inmates in 1826: "It is true that while confined here . . . you are to be literally *buried* from the world."[46]

In order to fully understand today's elaborate maximum custody prison routines it is necessary to look to some of the "pioneers" who created them. There is little controversy that the dubious distinction of founder of "calculated humiliation" may be attributed to Elam Lynds of Sing Sing (and his disciples, John Cray and Robert Wiltse). W. David Lewis, in his history of New York's prisons *From Newgate to Dannemora*, has perhaps the most complete picture of Lynds. The following composite of Lynds and his proteges relies heavily on Lewis' work.[47]

Lynds was born in Litchfield, Connecticut, in 1784. He had trained and worked as a hatter in Troy, New York, for a time but chose a military career, first in the state militia and then as an infantry captain in the War of 1812. He settled in Auburn, New York, after the war and was later attracted to the prison, joining the Auburn staff in 1817. Lewis states that it would be "difficult to avoid concluding that cruelty was part of his makeup." Lynds saw all dishonest men as cowards needing to be ruled by fear and intimidation accomplished by breaking their spirits. The smallest infraction had to be followed by the whip as surely as thunder follows lightning. He saw the purpose of prison as punishment and terror, not reformation. The convict had to be reduced to a "silent and insulated working machine." If Lynds' makeup was cruel, it suffered not from uncertainty. He scorned his rivals. A request to bring in working convicts from a freezing rain was dismissed by him with the warning that the inmates "would want ruffle shirts next." He became legendary for his sternness and cruelty but also for his effectiveness. The visiting DeToqueville said of Lynds that his: "practical abilities are admitted by everyone, including his enemies." When a visitor asked how Lynds could identify a convict violating the silence rule in a cellblock, Lynds replied, "take out fifteen, twenty or twenty-five and flog them all, and you will be sure to get the right one." Once he heard of a plot by an inmate barber to murder him.° He took his place in the barber's chair demanding to be shaved and declared, "I am stronger without a weapon than you are armed." Lynds believed in no privileges whatsoever for inmates and did not like the idea of sentence reductions through good time or pardons. Since routine required that all inmates be treated alike, so too they were to be dressed alike in "black-and-white outfits which made them look grotesque and ridiculous," states Lewis. Although visitors were prohibited, spectators at a fee—as one might visit a zoo—were encouraged.°° A Bible and occasional prayer book were the inmates' only reading materials.

> At other times, however, [Lynds] . . . upheld the Auburn-style prison as a veritable model for free institutions; indeed, it is not too much to say that he wanted to convert individual American homes into miniature penal establishments . . . He recommended a plan for a Massachusetts school in which individual night rooms would be so placed in galleries as to be subject to close surveillance from a central location. In his view, the unceasing vigilance which characterized the Auburn system afforded a principle of very extensive application to families, schools, academies, colleges, factories, mechanics' shops.[48]

°Lewis points out, however, that another warden was also reported to have been the subject of such a plot and to have responded in a similar manner.

°°At Auburn, Lewis reports:

"From six to eight thousand people came through the prison yearly, and the revenue from the admission fees of twenty-five cents per head sometimes determined whether or not the institution showed an annual surplus or deficit. . .

. . . one inmate had been so overcome by the presence of a young lady in his shop that he could not restrain himself from throwing his arms around her and kissing her repeatedly until forced to desist. One can only speculate about the punishment which followed so serious a breach of discipline." (W. David Lewis, *From Newgate to Dannemora*, pp. 122, 124).

Enforcing silence led to bizarre, obsessive prison practices. John Cray, a Lynds assistant, had, it was rumored, deserted from the British Army in Canada during the War of 1812. It should be remembered that Lynds was in the American Army during that war. If they were former enemies, they now made a good team. Cray devised many techniques to enforce silence, to move men en masse, to feed them and to arrange congregate work in silence as if an "invisible wall" separated the inmate population. The lockstep was a modification of "the military march, crossed . . . with a shuffle to lessen its dignity, and pointed heads to the right, rather than facing straight ahead, to prevent conversation."[49] Shuffling while facing the guards permitted the latter to keep vigilant for the slightest lip movement. The lockstep was to endure until well into the 1930s. Non-verbal communication by way of gesture or facial muscles was prohibited.

When not in marching formation, the inmates were required to keep their eyes on the ground. At night . . . keepers noiselessly patrolled the ranges in their stocking feet, ready to report for punishment the slightest breach of discipline.

One reason for placing the original workshops along the prison's outer wall stemmed from the desire of administrators to watch inmates surreptitiously. Running through the rear of each shop was an enclosed passageway which extended for two thousand feet around the base of the wall. From this alleyway, which was only three feet wide, visitors and prison officials could peer through narrow slits at the laboring convicts . . . it permitted visitors to view the shops without disturbing the occupants . . . it provided a means of convincing suspicious citizens that the penitentiary had nothing to hide . . .

Within an atmosphere of repression, humiliation, and gloomy silence, the Auburn convict performed an incessantly monotonous round of activity. He arose at 5:15 in the summer, or at sunrise in other seasons when the days were shorter. As soon as his cell was unlocked, he marched out carrying three pieces of equipment: a night tub used for calls of nature, a can for drinking water, and a wooden food container called a 'kid.' Holding this paraphernalia with his left hand, he laid his right one upon the shoulder of the felon who occupied the next cell and marched in lockstep to a washroom where the kids and cans were deposited for cleansing. He then proceeded across the yard, emptied his tub in a sewerage vault, and rinsed it at the prison pump. After this he marched to his workshop, placing the tub against the wall of the building as he entered. . . [in the dining hall inmates] were placed at long tables, seating themselves on one side only so that there would be no opportunity for conversation or signals. If an inmate wanted more food, he raised his left hand; if he did not want all that he had, he put up his right. Convict waiters watched for such signals and provided hearty eaters with extra food taken from those who were less hungry. The prison steward looked over the men as they ate and rang a bell when he decided they had been given enough time . . . [Twenty minutes to half an hour.]

Dinner was served at noon, after which the men returned to the shops to work until six o'clock or sundown. When closing time finally came, they washed up in buckets provided for this purpose, marched out, scooped up their night tubs, and continued on to the prison, where they received kids and cans filled with food and water. Without breaking step they picked these up and proceeded to their respective cells, leaving their doors slightly ajar as they entered. After the turnkeys saw that the inmates were in their apartments they walked along the ranges and placed their keys in the locks. As each convict heard a key enter his lock he immediately slammed his door shut so that the keeper would know without looking that he was in his proper place. . . After eating his evening meal in solitude, the convict waited for a signal to take off his clothes and go to bed on his mat or hammock. Until this occurred he was positively forbidden to lie down. If light permitted, he could read his Bible or wait for the chaplain to come along and talk to him about educational or religious matters. . . Officers prowled stealthily throughout the ranges all night in accordance with a system designed to see that they were attentive to their duties. The guard stationed in the administration building placed a little ball in the doorway leading to the south wing, where another keeper picked it up and carried it to a window at the far end of the corridor. Here it was taken by another officer who carried it through the shops and yards to the other side of the institution, where a watchman patrolling the north wing received it and took it back to the starting point. Regulations specified that the ball must make a complete revolution once every twenty minutes; if it did not, a ten-minute grace period was allowed; after which the officer who should normally have received the ball reported to the principal keeper or his deputy.[50]

This was Auburn. If it was gloomy, repressive and humilitating, it was not the terror of Wiltse's Sing-Sing. Levi Burr was a prisoner who in 1833 published an account of his stay at Mount Pleasant (Sing-Sing) in a volume entitled *A Voice from Sing-Sing.*

The government of the Sing-Sing prison may be emphatically called, a *Cat-ocracy* and *Cudgel-ocracy* [regimens based upon the use of the whip or club for compliance]; that is, a Government instituted by a law of a free people, and entrusted in the hands of a single individual, over whose conduct there is no control; a Government, whose subjects are denied the power of life and death, without fear of censure or reproach; a Government where the subordinate officers are of that character and class of society, that for a miserable *hire,* they become the servile tools of the Autocrat, and with the Cat and Cudgel in their hands, as the representatives of their master's power, they exercise his pleasure on the subjects of his command, where there is no eye to pity, no tongue to tell, no heart to feel, or will or power to oppose.[51]

Legislative investigating committees uncovered scores of brutal flagellations. Some guards laced their whips with wire, others whipped convicts across the genitals, and, when there appeared to be no immediate reason to whip a man, reasons were invented, as in the case of incoming convicts: "for insults offered to such keepers, or alleged offenses committed *previous* to conviction."[52]

From the founding of Sing-Sing until the close of Wiltse's regime in 1840, therefore, convict life at the penitentiary was likely to be a phantasmagoria of wretched living conditions, poor food, incessant harshness, and brutalizing drudgery. That defects in the institution's construction, honest convictions about the abnormally depraved nature of the inmates confined there, and other special circumstances made the prevailing stringency understandable did not detract from the tragedies that sometimes ensued. Instead of making a felon more fit for human society . . . the rigors he experienced were apt to break him both physically and psychologically.[53]

Summing up the contribution of this period (from the Revolution to the Civil War) to the development of correctional progress, the *Attorney General's Survey of Release Procedures* (1940) states:

In the final reckoning, the fifty years which followed the opening of Auburn Prison, though years of great activity in prison development and administration, did not produce a single lasting contribution to penology. . . The greatest contributions of this period which persisted for nearly one hundred years were (1) a prison industries program, and (2) the interior cell block, and both of these have proved to be liabilities.

. . . as provision for the indiscriminate housing of thousands of prisoners who do not need tool-proof steel monkey-cages, it has no justification either economically or penologically.[54]

Howard Gill, with a style reminiscent of Agnewian alliteration, characterized fortress prisons as "massive, medieval, monastic, monolityic, monkey-cage, magnificent monstrocities."[55] The Attorney General discussed the Lynds-Cray-Wiltse legacy of punishment and silence, and with characteristic insights found throughout the "Survey," concluded that:

> With non-communication went a whole new 'prison discipline,' and so effectively did its advocates do their work during the second quarter of the 19th century that even today prison officers protest in horror against anything which might upset the discipline.
>
> As punishment for every violation of these non-communication rules was considered essential in maintaining discipline, soon all orders of the prison and especially those relating to industrial productivity were reinforced through the fear of punishment.
>
> This whole program of non-communication had another result: the public was less and less disturbed by prison problems and prison activities. . . Especially when the new factory system of production began to show an excess of receipts over expenditures, the legislatures were satisfied and the penitentiary system was assured its place in public administration.[56]

We will shortly turn to the problem of prison labor and industry, but in closing this commentary on the ante-bellum period we should note that there were some humanitarian programs introduced, sustained for a while, and then lost. Eliza Farnham, Matthew Gordon, and John Bigelow at Sing-Sing (with the support of Horace Greeley) introduced conversation (for the women's wing), a library, and prohibited the more brutal punishments during a short-lived radical period in the mid 1840s.[57] As political parties changed, prison administrators were swept in and out of office with them. Eliza Farnham's espousal of phrenology did not help her gain credibility with either party.* Yet it is a testament to her fortitude that she was able to establish Charles Dickens on the approved prisoner reading list.

---

*"John Quincy Adams said he did not see how two phrenologists could look one another in the face without bursting into gales of laughter. . ." Oliver Wendell Holmes had attacked phrenology as a pseudo-science. (Howard W. Chambers, *Phrenology for the Millions,* p. 151)

In the first half of the nineteenth century prison reform was a problem which drew to it the keenest intellects, the most influential leaders of the community. Prison reform was in the air. No effort—financial, legislative or philanthropic—was too great to apply toward a solution of the newly 'discovered' problem of the criminal and his reformation. Today prison reform finds itself in the backwaters of society's problems, receiving little attention except for brief periods following riots or scandals.[58]

The wave of democratic enthusiasm of the post-Revolution period now ebbed. The prison's future was now in the hands of the administrators. As the new professional prison administrator effectively displaced the volunteer, so, too, the *cause* which motivated the latter yielded to *function* guiding the former.[*][59] The John Howards and Elizabeth Frys would slowly become "outsiders" upsetting the function of the prison. The reformers would become battle-fatigued and, finding a new and more promising field in Abolition, leave the prison in the "backwaters." With thirty-some fortress prisons now operating with the contradictory and almost impossible tasks of providing seclusion, hard labor and moral training, administrators turned to their micro-worlds behind the walls to manage men against their wills. What difference could it make to a warden that offenders were sinners, had environmental disabilities or led indolent lives—they were now prisoners. Lynds had set the tone and provided some of the technology. The "old prison discipline," as Gill calls it, would endure for a century; and it "stood for some very specific things: Hard Labor, Deprivation, Monotony, Uniformity, Mass Movement, Degradation, Subservience, Corporal

---

[*] "The momentum of the cause will never carry over adequately to the subsequent task of making its fruits permanent. The slow methodical organized effort needed to make enduring the achievement of the cause calls for different motives, different skill, different machinery. At the moment of its success, the *cause* tends to transfer its interest and its responsibility to an administrative unit whose responsibility becomes a *function* of well-organized community life." (Porter R. Lee "Social Work: Cause and Function," Presidential Address, National Conference of Social Work 1929 as cited in Clark A. Chambers *Seedtime of Reform*, p. 86)

Punishment, Non-Communication, No Recreation, No Responsibility, Isolation, No 'Fraternization' with the Guards, [and] Reform by Exhortation."[60]

THE NEW PENOLOGY 1870-1930

A new wave of optimism swept through corrections following the Civil War. It was ushered in with a "mountain-top experience" in October, 1870, at Cincinnati. Here gathered the elite of the international correctional community presided over by James G. Blaine, a former Maine prison commissioner, then Speaker of the House of Representatives, and in 1884, the Republican presidential candidate. His good friend, James Garfield, who in ten years would be President of the United States, also addressed the Congress in his capacity as a Congressman from Ohio. Visiting administrators from Ireland, Prussia, Italy, Denmark, England, Canada and France exchanged views with prison officials from New York, Michigan, Pennsylvania, Ohio, California, Massachusetts, and other states. E. C. Wines, Secretary of the New York Prison Association and organizer of the Cincinnati Congress, presented an overview of prisons in the United States. Sir Walter Crofton presented the Irish System. Zebulon Brockway spoke of "The Ideal of a True Prison System." Sentencing occupied a major portion of attention at the Congress, with a great deal of interest in the indefinite sentence. M.D. Hill of England spoke of "The Substitution of Reformation Sentences for Time Sentences." T.W. Dwight, President of Columbia College Law School, warned of possible abuses. An ex-warden of Sing-Sing, G.B. Hubbell, suggested "Reformatory Discipline for Adult Prisoners." There were a few esoteric papers delivered on the subject of the "Nautical Reform School" and "The True Idea of a Reform School Ship" from eastcoast reformers in New York and Massachusetts, while landlocked reformers discussed "The Family Reform Farm" in Ohio. There was an undeniable momentum built up through papers on "The Strongest Wall of All" (a Wall of Confidence), "The Coming Prison," "Restitution as an Element in Criminal Punishment" (delivered by no less a personage than Florence Nightingale), "The Power of Religious Forces in Prison," the "Responsibility of Society for the Cause of Crime," a paper against "Vindictive Punishment," and a far-reaching attempt to end crime altogether in Edwin Hill's speech entitled "The Absolute Dependence of the Criminal Class on the Cooperation of Certain Capitalists, and the Possibility of Extinguishing the Criminal Class by Compelling the Withdrawal of Such Cooperation." On the Sunday before adjournment, Reverand James Murray of New York selected Matthew XXV:36 for his morning sermon: "I was in prison, and ye came unto me," while Rev. Frederick Merrick, President of Wesleyan University of Ohio, selected for the evening sermon the "Duty of Society to Neglected and Criminal Children—take this child away, and nurse it for me." Rev. James Wadsworth of San Francisco warned the conference group that all future reforms were tied to the transformation of the guard into a trained professional. All progress was dependent on the guard; and if he was transformed, prison reform would positively follow as surely as the oak is wrapped up in the acorn. Blake McKelvey captured the evangelical mood:

> The convention was in the hands of reformers who had arrived with prepared speeches while the traditionalists had no spokesman. Overwhelmed with inspired addresses, with prayer and song and much exhortation, even the hardheaded wardens were carried up for a mountain-top experience. In their enthusiasm for the ideal they rose above the monotony of four gray walls, men in stripes shuffling in lock-step, sullen faces staring through the bars, coarse mush and coffee made of bread crusts, armed sentries stalking the walls. They forgot it all and voted for their remarkable Declaration of Principles.*[61]

---

*Brockway, Elmira's first superintendent, looking back on the Cincinnati conference where he "had had an experience similar to that of the disciples on the Mount of Transfiguration and had felt himself strengthened by a . . . spiritual force with which he was going to have a grand success . . . but it did not work." (Negley K. Teeters, "State of Prisons in the United States: 1870-1970," *Federal Probation* (December 1969) p. 62).

The "new penology" was embodied in the 1870 Declaration of Principles. It stated, *inter alia,*

> Crime is an intentional violation of duties imposed by law. ... Punishment is suffering ... in expiation of the wrong done. ... Crime is ... a moral disease, of which punishment is the remedy. The efficiency of the remedy is a question of social therapeutics, a question of the fitness and the measure of the dose ... punishment is directed ńot to the crime but the criminal ... [in order to reestablish] moral harmony in the soul of the criminal ... his regeneration—his new birth to respect for the laws. Hence ... The supreme aim of prison discipline is the reformation of criminals, not the infliction of vindictive suffering. ... The progressive classification of prisoners. based on merit, and not on mere arbitrary principle, as age [or] crime.. should be established ... a penal stage ... a reformatory state ... a probationary stage. Since hope is a more potent agent than fear [we should establish] ... a system of rewards ... 1. A diminution of sentence. 2. A participation of prisoners in their earnings. 3. A gradual withdrawal of prison restraints. 4.. Constantly increasing privileges ... earned by good conduct. ... The prisoners' destiny, during his incarceration, should be placed, measurably, in his own hands. ... Peremptory sentences ought to be replaced by those of indeterminant duration—sentences limited only by satisfactory proof of reformation should be substituted for those measured by mere lapse of time.[62]

It also called for religious training, professionalization of staff, an end to political patronage and meddling, community action for crime prevention (and it even speaks of "warfare upon crime"[*]), after-care programs, special care for the mentally ill, and an end to the abuses of executive clemency. It spoke ap-

---

[*]In Principle XXXIII, one finds the contemporary military analogy: "Let it be remembered that crime is the *foe* against which we *war* ... and it is to lead the *battle* and suggest the methods of *assault,* that this bureau [a new national society] is needed. The *conflict* must be bold, skillful, sleepless, and with such *weapons* of love rather than vengeance. So *assailed* the evil will *yield* ... to the *attack.*"

provingly of Jeremy Benthams' (Panopticon) suggestion that "a prison should be so arranged that its chief officer can see all, know all and care for all." Costly materials were to be avoided. No prison should "exceed five or six hundred prisoners." Finally, it called for compulsory universal education, central state administration of institutions and better sanitation standards.

In a nutshell, this much heralded "new era" was in fact a rediscovery of Alexander Maconochie,* who a generation earlier had already practiced what the Declaration now preached** (although Sir Walter Crofton was largely credited for the "new thrust"). In Principle XXIV, Maconochie was quoted as having said: "Man is a social being; his duties are social; and only in society, as I think, can he be trained for it." The Congress simply suggested this thought as an amelioration of the regulation of solitude and non-communication. Maconochie was further invoked in a plea to wardens to permit their prisoners to speak to each other and give up the Cray's lockstep, which the Congress voted to be at "warfare with nature" (man is social).

American corrections was now to embark upon a path of reformation with a grander rhetoric than had previously been available. Now the criminal, with a focus on younger offenders, would be trained and reformed (in a reformatory—not a prison) through classification, education,*** and progression through a

---

* "There were earlier efforts in Europe, but chief credit for the establishment of parole for adult criminals belongs to Alexander Maconochie, who was in charge of the English penal colony at Norfolk Island [in the Pacific, about 800 miles east of New South Wales]. In 1840 he introduced the plan of passing convicts through several stages—first, strict imprisonment; then, labor on government chain gangs; next, freedom within a limited area; and finally ticket-of-leave, resulting in a conditional pardon ending with full restoration of liberty." (Sol Rubin, *The Law of Criminal Correction*, p. 33)

** . . . Justice Sir John Barry of the Victoria (Australia) Supreme Court wrote: "Most of the ideas in the 1870 Cincinnati Declaration of Principles were taken from Maconochie's writings, the language sometimes lifted bodily." (Negley K. Teeters, "State of Prisons in the United States: 1870-1970" *Federal Probation* (December 1969), p. 21.) Justice Barry is the author of *Alexander Maconochie of Norfolk Island*, 1958.

*** Blake McKelvey called this new era a period of "pedagogical penology" (as cited in *The Attorney General's Survey of Release Procedures*, p. 42).

system of marks based upon good behavior under indefinite (but with high maximum) sentences that could lead to parole short of the maximum if correctional progress so indicated. Great discretion now moved into the hands of correctional officials.

The first of these new programs, the Elmira Reformatory in New York (1876), with Brockway at the helm, became the model for several that followed. It was built like Auburn prison with interior cell blocks, providing solitary confinement at night and space for congregate work-shops. It differed from the typical state prison of this period in that (1) prisoners were now subject to indeterminate sentences—with a maximum—and early release on parole if prisoners showed progress; (2) inmates were assigned to three groups according to progress and deportment. New inmates were placed in the second group for six months and were demoted to the third for bad conduct, or elevated to the first as they gained their "marks." Within the next quarter of a century reformatories were built in twelve states.°

By the turn of the century, the reformatory movement began to decline. A half dozen states°° built more reformatories between 1908 and 1913 which were patterned after Elmira, but the rhetoric was muted and the reformatory idea moved into the

---

°New York (Elmira) 1876   Illinois (Pontiac) 1891
Michigan (Ionia) 1877   Kansas (Hutchison) 1895
Massachusetts (Concord) 1884   Ohio (Mansfield) 1896
Pennsylvania (Huntingdon) 1889   Indiana (Jeffersonville) 1897
Minnesota (St. Cloud) 1889   Wisconsin (Green Bay) 1898
Colorado (Bueva Vista) 1890   New Jersey (Rahway) 1901

Michigan did not adopt the Elmira 'frills' at its new reformatory at Ionia; Massachusetts merely turned over its new prison for a reformatory; and Indiana tried to make a reformatory out of an old prison. Similarly at a later date, 1907, Iowa tried to turn its new prison at Anamosa into a reformatory by statute and Kentucky changed the name of its ancient bastille at Frankfort from penitentiary to reformatory. (*The Attorney General's Survey*, p. 43)

°°Washington (Monroe) 1908   Wyoming (Worland) 1912
Oklahoma (Granite) 1910   Nebraska (Lincoln) 1912
Maine (South Windham) 1912   Connecticut (Chesire) 1913

(*Attorney General's Survey of Release Procedures*, p. 44).

prison system. The Reformatory Spirit which had been destined to imbue the prison with a new moral purpose was now simply a part of it. The prison system, however, was the recipient of a powerful new disciplinary tool—the indeterminate sentence.

During the period of the New Penology (1870-1930), deterministic thinking began to make strong inroads on the absolute volition of the criminal. Beginning with ethnic and biologic determinism, it was to lead to the modern era of the Rehabilitation Ideal based upon the "medical model." The deviant would be seen as sick and non-volitional, and therefore, in need of treatment. In the period from 1870 to 1930, close custody was still the mainstay of institutional life, but we see the introduction of libraries, recreation, schools, vocational programs, and good-time laws designed to help institutions run more smoothly. Classification schemes also led to the expansion of probation and parole services. Wisconsin enacted the first work release law in 1913 for misdemeanants.[63]

Bench-work in the cell of the Pennsylvania System could not compete with the Auburn workshop system in an age that was rationalizing congregate work into a factory system. Housed in maximum custody bastilles, the reformatory idea with all its innovation was now doomed to failure. The grading system became a reward for conformity. The regimen was as repressive as the routine prison, overcrowding did not permit individualization of treatment, and, coupled with the demise of contract labor, idleness was common.

The fundamental principle of the Elmira reformatory system was reformation, not expiation of guilt. It was hailed around the world as the greatest forward step in penology since the substitution of imprisonment for medieval maiming and execution, which indeed it was . . . [It] was dead by 1910. . . . It was swallowed up by the prison. Its residue remained the indeterminate sentence, parole, education and trade training, . . . but the reformatory idea itself, which was to revolutionize penology, failed. And there has been no new idea since. The prison remains essentially unchanged [1953].[64]

PRISON AND PRISONER POPULATION GROWTH

From 1870 on, prison population spiralled upward. In 1870, the Census Bureau could account for only 32,901 prisoners in state institutions. By 1890, the figure rose to 45,233 and by 1904 to 53,292, an increase of 62%; from 1904 to 1935 it increased again by nearly 140%.[65] Although the period from World War I to the Depression saw the introduction of many new programs and the construction of medium and minimum custody facilities, it was also one of the most retrogressive. The mailed fist was covered with a velvet glove. Howard Gill called it:

> 'bird shot' penology. We fill the old blunder-buss full of a little work, a modicum of education, a bit of religion, some medical care if necessary, a good deal of recreation—rodeos, baseball, bands, choral groups, and what not—and call it rehabilitation.[66]

Rubin states: "the decade from 1917 to 1927 is one of the blackest in American correctional law."[67] It was the period of the Great Red Scare and its accompanying Mitchell Palmer Raids. The Noble Experiment was being debated and soon adopted. The Sacco and Vanzetti case developed, organized labor was struggling for recognition, and immigrants were pouring into the country. Before World War I, five states had abolished the death penalty, but between 1917 and 1920 four states restored it.[68] Sentencing laws reflected increased severity. Sutherland found, for example, that in the median state in 1880, a concealed weapon charge was punishable by a $110 fine and 6.8 months in prison; by 1930 it had risen to $367 and 14.4 months imprisonment. The same was true for armed robbery; while only 12% of early laws (up to 1900) meted out as high as a five-year sentence, new laws enacted between 1922-1929 showed that 40% of them had a five-year *minimum*.[69] Increased severity of sentences was looked to, in a climate of national fear, as a solution for the increase in crime, judicial "softness," and "coddling" of prisoners. The American Friends Service Committee attributed increased median length of time served to the introduction of the reformatory idea and the indeterminate sentence; modifications of which found their way into the statute books of many states in this period.[70]

In the pre-depression era the prisons were custodial, punitive, and overcrowded. Non-communication was vanishing with the rise of the industrial prison.

> Except for changes in housing, imprisonment in 1900-1935 was substantially what it had been one hundred years earlier; custody, punishment, and hard labor. By the end of the period, in many prisons it reverted to custody and punishment.[71]

Fortress prison construction continued, with 16 states having built such facilities before the end of the century and six more between 1901 and 1920. Beginning in 1922 and culminating with Attica in 1931, an additional five were built. Jeremy Bentham's Panopticon ° concept, rejected in his own country, found a home in Holland, Cuba, Spain and Stateville, Illinois, after World War I. With the latter as the sole exception

> All of these prisons were of the Auburn type with nothing of special interest except improvements in construction through the introduction of steel cells with plumbing and running water in each, and ventilating systems. Still 77 prisons used the bucket system as late as 1900. . . . Except as modified by the indeterminate sentence and parole and the abandonment of non-communication, the old system of prison discipline and industrial production continued to govern [1939].[72]

SOME AIMLESS GROWTH

A few examples of haphazard, but sometimes politically motivated prison site planning, point to the nature of the

---

°Aldous Huxley referred to the Panopticon as a "totalitarian housing project." (Norman B. Johnston, "John Haviland," in Hermann Mannheim, ed., *Pioneers in Criminology*, p. 97).

accidental or aimless growth of American penal institutions. It is considered aimless, because it lacked professional calculation.

> The Bureau of Prisons operates a federal prison in Sandstone, Minnesota, in a virtual wilderness between Minneapolis and Duluth. The institution was authorized in 1933, when northern Minnesota was a center for the activities of bootleggers. Sanford Bates, who was at that time the Director of the Bureau of Prisons, decided to 'put one up there where they are coming from.' But by the time the prison had been built, prohibition had been repealed, and, according to the present Director, 'there we had an institution 16 miles from anywhere, where it gets pretty cold in the winter.'[73]

Sometimes the founding fathers of a state allocated functions by municipalities, naming the sites of the capitol, university, mental institution and prison in the state constitutions and codes. The prison in Minnesota was built in Stillwater in 1851. Its replacement was built about three miles away in Bayport. The old relic still exists; although unused since the end of World War I. Minnesota has not violated the constitution—there is a state prison in Stillwater. As a matter of fact, the Bayport prison has received its mail from a Stillwater post office for over half a century.

In Nevada, prison officials tell of the origins of the Territorial Prison at Carson City in 1861 (still in use). Apparently, the prison site is the result of a group of territorial legislators' drunken vandalism at a hotel spa near the capitol. The threat of public exposure by the hotel owner led to the purchase of the hotel and property on which today stands a decaying prison.

Alcatraz, an island without water in San Francisco Bay, once housed Geronimo's lieutenants until Al Capone and his associates arrived there in the 1930s. Now closed, it too is eroding under the pounding surf and the elements.

Site selection for California's largest prison was the result of a storm which tore a frigate-jail loose from its moorings in San

Francisco Bay. The frigate, loaded with Gold Rush ne'er-do-wells, ran aground on the coast of Marin County at a remote spot on the peninsula. The keepers and kept put up some shanties and awaited orders. That remote spot, named San Quentin Point, would eventually house 5,000 inmates.

Pennsylvania was among the first states to establish a state prison. Blake McKelvey notes that it occurred accidentally:

> The Pennsylvania legislature in 1790 ordered the erection of a cell house in the yard of the Walnut Street Jail for the solitary confinement of men convicted of felonies, designating the old building for the separate detention of suspects, witnesses, and misdemeanants. The act directed the Walnut Street Jail authorities to receive convicts from other counties until similar provisions could be made in their jails, thus providing a state prison without committing the legislature to that policy.[74]

Persistent effort failed to reveal why Lucasville Prison—which can only be described as instant pastoral obsolescence—was ever built in Lucas County, Ohio, on a remote marshland as far from any of the urban centers of Ohio as could possibly be found. (Located 100, 110, 150, 200, and 500 miles from each of the five largest cities.)[75] It is only known that Governor Rhodes, under whose first administration the project began, wanted to develop that area of the state.

In 1972, North Carolina opened another new-obsolete institution which is described by Nagel: "We could not, however, understand the reason for building a 16-story prison in the foothills of the Smokey Mountains on thousands of acres of open land."[76]

Farming is perhaps the most ubiquitous industry associated with prisons, although license plate manufacture may compete with it. Aside from the obvious benefits of growing and raising the prison's foodstuff, rural areas were recommended as sites of choice as late as the 1950s by the Federal Bureau of Prisons.

Robert D. Barnes, a Bureau Senior Architect, speaking to the importance of the site of correctional institutions, said that among the most fundamental elements was:

> As much remoteness as is practicable from any large population center ... Since most correctional institutions operate a farm—the ideal size of which is about an acre to each inmate—the institutional site should be one which is located on, or is immediately adjacent to, good farming land.[77]

It is not surprising that a 1971 nationwide survey by William Nagel found that, contrary to the leading thinking of penologists, practically all of the 23 newest correctional institutions for men were located in sparsely populated areas. Nagel reports that on the average, the institutions are 172 miles from the state's largest city (or a 344 mile round trip), with a low of 30 miles and a high of 455 miles (a 910 mile round trip!). The population of the supportive community averaged 9,900; with a low of 1,300 for a southern maximum custody prison and a high of 44,000 people for a midwestern medium custody facility. The average population of minority inmates was 45%; ranging from a low of 2% in an eastern medium security institution to a high of 65%. The average percentage of minority staff was 8%, with a low of zero in a southern maximum custody prison and a high of 20% in an eastern maximum-medium facility. Ten institutions had 5% or less minority staff and in three the number was "unknown."[78]

If many prisons accidentally or even as a result of political contrivance ended up in rural areas, that was not the whole story. Professionals believed that if the rural area had (morally) healthful qualities, perhaps of greater importance was the idea that the prison should pay for itself. This notion is supported by some, even today. In the early days mining, quarrying and farming were the principal guideposts for self-support. Auburn, Sing-Sing, Folsom, and many other institutions were built alongside marble or granite quarries worked frequently with convict labor. Many famous urban landmarks are the products of prison quarries.

Sing-Sing's principal industry in the early years—indeed, its chief raison d'etre—was stone-cutting. Out of its quarries came marble for Grace Church on Broadway, the Albany City Hall, the United States Subtreasury Building in New York City, New York University, and many fine residences.[79]

Dannemora, the New York State prison in Clinton County (1845), took its name from the well-known Swedish iron mining center.[80] Dannemora was built on the false premise of the availability of unlimited iron ore—hence prison productivity and profits. When the ore ran out, the prison and its mainly urban convicts were left on a wind and ice swept wasteland in a remote rural area of northern New York State.

Political tradeoffs using projected prison sites are not unusual. Rural areas are invariably the "beneficiaries" of prisons and mental hospitals. Rural Legislatures "buy" institutions with a promise to vote for some urban project in exchange for the urban legislator's vote for the rural prison. Many older prisons were built on the outskirts of a city only to find themselves confined eventually by urban growth (Baltimore, Columbus, Auburn). The newest facilities have undeniably chosen rural setting as locations. Nagel suggests the following among the reasons for rural site selection:

(1) powerful legislators demand that institutions be built in their rural districts especially if unemployment there has become chronic; (2) citizens' lobbies fight the establishment of correctional facilities in urban neighborhoods; (3) many states already own large tracts of land in the more isolated areas or land is cheaper in the country; (4) correctional administrators think they can get more desirable (code for white) staff in rural America; (5) some officials have an honest Jeffersonian belief in the curative virtues of bucolic setting; and (6) historical accidents.

. . . On the other hand, powerful rural legislators on key committees have frequently demanded as the price of their support that a proposed new facility be built in their districts if unemployment is chronic there. This is certainly a worthy reason, but we never once heard it advanced as a reason for selecting an urban site though there is severe black unemployment in the cities.[81]

It is not unusual to be driving through a prairie area and suddenly come upon an enormous prison sprawl. Several prisons in the United States are in one-industry towns—the prison being the industry. Nor is it uncommon to meet second or even third generation prison guards. Father and son (guards) combinations are frequently seen. It is not difficult to understand why many of the local folks feel deeply that the prison is "theirs." Sometimes the prison population exceeds the host town population.

Some institutions were built for one purpose, but by the time of their completion had their missions changed. It usually takes years of planning, legislative scrutiny, scores of appropriation hearings, site selection, drawings, scale models, and a myriad of detail with contractors, real estate owners, local government, environmental protection agencies, etc. (to say nothing of program planning within the department of corrections in partnership with the architect), to achieve the physical treatment appropriate to the program purpose announced and justified. Corrections, however, occupies no high priority in state (or Federal) government. Hence it is possible to understand how, as Nagel points out,

> Many institutions have been conceived to serve one purpose, but because of the exigencies of the everchanging world, end up performing an entirely different function. Bordentown in New Jersey, for example, was designed as a medium-security farm for older and more stable offenders but was converted to serve a youthful escape-prone, acting-out population. Marion, the federal penitentiary, has gone the cycle from maximum security prison (replacing Alcatraz) to correctional center for youthful offenders back again to maximum security prison. Caught in this process of change, correctional officials learn to 'make do.'

Morgantown, North Carolina was first designed, we were

told, after a riot at the old state prison at Raleigh. It was to serve as a maximum security prison for the western half of the state. Later, after construction was well along but before occupancy, its purpose was redefined to serve the state's youthful felons. [16 story high-rise prison in the Smokey Mountain foothills.][82]

Sandstone Federal prison, originally intended for bootleggers, was leased by Minnesota as a mental institution for awhile and then returned to the Federal Bureau as a prison. Wisconsin, in response to citizen pressure, did not occupy a new prison it recently built. The Federal Bureau acquired this new facility for its own use. There are numerous examples of second-generation use of facilities that were presumably carefully thought out for an entirely different purpose at another time.

Quite aside from the obvious drawbacks remote locations present for those interested in rehabilitation (or even humaneness) such as the scarcity of professional services, inaccessibility for the families of prisoners, and few resources for study or work release, we are now confronted with "a divided house dominated by rural white guards and administrators unable to understand or communicate with inmates who are often [and increasingly] black, Chicano, Puerto Rican, or from other urban minorities."[83] While the guards as a group get older, frequently because of the absence of dignified mandatory retirement plans, the inmates are typically younger. Differences in life styles, symbols, dress, hair, music, dance, literature, and language barriers (even when both presumably speak English), all combine with the normal burdens of compressed life in a prison to produce and maintain high levels of mutual distrust and fragile tensions—not unlike a latent volcano.

PRISON LABOR

American prison history cannot be fully understood unless one understands how work was woven into the treatment regimens. In the beginning, work was naturally assumed to be beneficial.

No one supposed, however, that vocational training would result. Work was simply a way of repaying the state for the expense of the prisoners' stay. Prisoners earned money for themselves and their families. The 1790 prisons paid more than many of our current ones do. Hard labor in solitude, it will be recalled, was continually extolled from the days of John Howard. It was not rationally justified—it was simply proclaimed as virtuous. With the advent of the workshop factory system at Auburn, labor was transformed from any moral beneficence it may have contained for guiding the indolent into an exploitive revenue-producing program for state legislatures. But it also gave the faltering prison system a new lease on life. If the prison did not reform the criminal, it could at least pay for itself. Prison labor produced other fringe benefits for administrators. Richard McGee found that: "As the contract system of labor was introduced in the prison system, their [administrator's] power increased. Prison labor was a highly coveted prize, and the opportunity to dispense patronage and favors became increasingly important."[84] Yet it was becoming impossible to operate at a breakeven point, much less at a profit in a contracting market, even if books were occasionally juggled.

The fate of prison labor has been tied to four market systems. Under the *Lease System*, the state turned prisoners over to an entrepreneur who exploited their labor and paid the state for the service. This system persisted into the 1920s when public outrage ended it. The *Contract System* saw the state retain custody of the prisoners, but market their labor to a contractor for an agreed-upon daily sum. The Federal government finally eliminated this system with restrictive legislation. Next came the *Piece-Price System*, which simply substituted the stipulated sum a contractor paid to the state for finished *products*, rather than for each prison *worker*. This, too, ended. Finally, under what was to become the mainstay of American prison industries, the *State Account System* came into use. The state itself became the entrepreneur: it developed prison industries by purchasing raw materials, it manufactured products, sold them to a restricted market, and assumed the risks.[85] At first the prisons operated in "open market" systems. As outside pressures from free labor and employers grew, the prisons—with no effective lobby—withdrew to a narrower market. This was called the "sheltered market" system. Under it, prisons had to content themselves with *state use* and *public works* for the sale of their products. With the chief exceptions of farm commodities and goods, prisons could sell their products to the state and its political subunits.

As early as 1801, protests by free labor against the "unfair competition" of prison-made goods were heard from New York mechanics, and later from cabinet makers.[86] Employers' associations were able to obtain legislation in 1801 to have prison-made boots and shoes labelled "State Prison."[87]

From the 1820s through the 1840s, contractors exploited the prisons and prisoners. Legislative committees uncovered many cases of excessive contractor profits, corruption, unauthorized inducements, brutal prisoner working conditions and punishments.[88] Workers marched on prisons to halt stonecutting operations and rallied in the streets of New York City, collecting 4,500 signatures to restrict prison labor.[89] With non-communication lost, profit became the main goal of prison administrators. Enoch Wines reported in 1865 that: "communications . . . takes place among convicts continually and in most prisons to a very great extent . . . one string is harped upon ad nauseum—money, money, money."[90] With sheltered market conditions, prison production went up in value for about twenty years. But, under the Bentham notion of lesser eligibility, the prison worker was not seen as a legitimate competitor with the freeworker. In all legislative clashes for jobs, despite the need to remain self-supporting, prison-worker interests lost. There was a constant retrenchment of the open market system, and eventually profits plummeted downwards.

TABLE I
STATE PRISONS: PERCENT OF PRISONERS EMPLOYED AT PRODUCTIVE LABOR UNDER DIFFERENT SYSTEMS IN SPECIFIED YEARS

System	1885	1895	1905	1914	1923	193:
Prisoners employed at productive labor under—	%	%	%	%	%	%
Lease system..............	26	19	9	4	0	0
Contract system	40	34	36	26	12	5
Piece-price system.......	8	14	8	6	7	11
State-account system...			21	31	26	19
State-use system..........	26	33	18	22	36	42
Public works and ways systems............			8	11	19	23
TOTAL..............	100	100	100	100	100	100°

By 1940, Flynn records only 12% of prisoners on the open market system (mostly in state accounts) and 88% working in sheltered market.[92] But Flynn cautions that it would be misleading to think that all prisoners were at work in the 1940s: "The latest official data showed 44% of all prisoners productively employed in 1940, but this was a gross exaggeration of the true state of affairs."[93]

The southern prisons did not conform to shifts in the market systems earlier described. Southern and border states put a great premium on "the most primitive kind of penal slavery." Continuing, *The Attorney General's Survey of Release Procedures* reaches the conclusion that:

. . . in the development of American prisons, these southern prisons represent a large and special group which did not conform to the general pattern set by the Auburn or Reformatory type of prison ... On the whole, these southern prisons during this period offer only examples of the depths to which modern civilized states can sink in the punishment and custody of criminals. Their contribution to penology was chiefly a negative one.[94]

By 1940, private industry had emerged successfully in its struggle to end the sale of prison made commodities on the open market. In 1887, Congress prohibited the use of Federal prisoners in leased or contracted labor. There was no Federal Bureau of Prisons yet, thus violators of Federal statutes were prisoners in state institutions at a boarding rate. (The states promptly began charging a higher rate.) As a result of the continuing agitation against "unfair competition," a series of Federal acts succeeded in driving prison-made products from the market. The *Hawes-Cooper Act of 1929* (which was to become effective in 1934) declared that prison products were no longer to have a status in interstate commerce; they became subject to laws of the states. This was followed by a companion piece of legislation in 1935, the *Ashurst-Sumners Act*. It prohibited the transportation of prison products into a state which had barred such transport and required the labeling of such goods as "prison made" when they moved between states.[95] The *coup-de-grace* was administered when, after the Supreme Court unanimously upheld these acts, Congress passed the *Prohibitory Act of October 14, 1940*, banning virtually all prison-made products (except some agricultural commodities) from interstate commerce.[96] For all intents and purposes, prison industry was now confined to the state-use system and public works. During the emergency conditions of wartime, President Roosevelt, by an Executive Order in 1942, lifted the ban on interstate commerce. President Truman reinstated the prohibition in 1947.[97]

Testimony to the aimlessness of prison industry is found in the *Attorney General's Survey of Release Procedures*. In response to inquiries of 88 prisons as to the purpose of correctional industries, prisoner training was selected by 22; simply giving employment to prisoners was chosen by 11; 21 gave profit as their chief motive; while 34 never reported a purpose.[98]

The industrial program of the Reformatory Era placed great emphasis upon work and production and inadvertently caused the collapse of the Lyndsian and Pennsylvanian silent systems; but as a result of the low level of personnel, a lack of training, and depressed salaries, it could not reach other professed reformatory goals. The reformatory became a prison; and the prison became an inefficient factory with widespread unemployment inside the walls. This did not impair the rhetoric which now turned the factory into a vehicle for "vocational training." When it was discovered that the factory tools, machinery and products were either obsolete or inferior and that ex-convicts with such training could not fairly compete in the free world job market, the elastic rhetoric maintained that prisoners could learn "habits of industry" [in anachronistic shops using outmoded tools. When it was discovered that over-assignment of prisoners to jobs produced slow-motion "habits of industry,"] the rhetoric began to talk of work's "therapeutic value."

WOMEN IN PRISON

Women have consistently been treated shabbily in corrections. W. David Lewis' book on New York prisons contains a chapter on women aptly entitled "The Ordeal of the Unredeemables." [In the early part of the 19th Century the courts were lenient in the prosecution of women; even more so in the case of white women. The prisons, however, were not.] A "fallen woman" was not a category lending itself to a classification of "first timer": placed upon a pedestal as long as she lived a virtuous life, she was a victim of an inflexible double standard if she fell.[100] In 1844, New York prison officials said:

> The opinion seems to have been entertained, that the female convicts were beyond the reach of reformation, and it seems to have been regarded as a sufficient performance of the object of punishment, to turn them loose within the

pen of the prison and there leave them to feed upon and destroy each other.[101]

Yet women like Elizabeth Fry in England, Sophia Wyckoff and Sarah Hawxhurst of New York; Rachael Perijo of Baltimore; and the previously mentioned Eliza Farnham of Sing-Sing; among others, were able, after dogged efforts, to bring humaneness to women's units of several institutions.

Indiana was the first state to fully segregate women from men prisoners. The Indiana Women's Prison opened in Indianapolis in 1873. Nationally, the female prison population has remained between 3.4% and 5% of the total for the last quarter of a century. In 1961 it was 7,878 out of 220,329, and in 1972 the National Prison Statistics counted 6,594 women in a population of 196,007.[102] Fifty percent of the women in prison are either in a federal facility or in a facility in one of eight states. Housing is usually of the cottage system type; but cells, including strip-cells, are also to be found. Most women's institutions are depressing and have an aura of monotony about them. Domestic sciences training programs are ubiquitously found, and, quite frequently, office machinery and cosmetology are available. Women are usually not paid the same as men for the same work.[103] In Maryland, a large group of women sew mountains of American flags for forty cents a day.

The usual discipline routines and problems found in men's prisons are also found in women's. Lesbian behavior is rampant, although it takes a different turn in a cottage environment—usually it is organized around a contrived, make-believe family with women taking male roles (husband, father, son, boyfriend, even nephew). Custody is not of the maximum grade in most states. There are 28 separate women's state institutions.[104] The women's liberation movement through various magazine articles has (in the last few years) begun to expose women's prison life to the public view.

Starting with a 3.4% population in American prisons in 1972, there is now some evidence to plausibly predict a rise in the future. The 1971 Uniform Crime Report showed an 83% increase for men arrested for major crimes, but a 219% increase for women in the last decade. While prostitution increased 87%; robbery increased for women by 227%. Ten years earlier only 2 in 17 arrests included women, but by 1971, 2 of 9 were women.[105] Although the rate of commitment remains low, Nagel reports an interesting phenomenon:

> Probably the best institution that we visited in America was the new, handsome one, the Purdy Treatment Center for Women, at Gig Harbor, Washington. In our view, both its architecture and its leadership are inspired. Before it was opened, however, only 69 women were imprisoned in the state of Washington. In less than two years of its opening, the population at Purdy has soared to 153, very close to its capacity of 170.[106]

It seems to violate the whole present thrust of the community-based corrections movement that, at a time when male prisoners are moving to the community, a second round of "better" prisons for women is being built. This is especially ironic because there already exists a tolerance for women offenders, which has yet to flourish for men.

THE REHABILITATION MODEL

By a model, we mean a conceptualization of a problem and an accompanying strategy to deal with it. The rehabilitation model (although still vague in implementation) has a powerful rhetoric about it. Rehabilitation, or treatment as it is more widely referred to, is the result of two historical movements: (1) the ascendency of democracy with its new hopeful view of the nature of man and (2) the development of the behavioral sciences leading to the positivist school of criminology.[107] Tracing a line of thinking from Gall (Phrenology) to Rush (crime is a disease of the moral faculty) to the Lombrosians (criminal types, moral insanity, atavism) we perceive a deliberate shift of concern from the crime to the criminal. If Becarrian classical thought was a victory for political democracy, equality, and legality; it was also contrary to the individualization theories (with a focus on the criminal rather than the crime) being espoused by the behavioral scientists.[108]

The treatment movement begins in the early 19th century when case studies of criminals in prisons were used to demonstrate that the offender was a victim of his environment. The early definers did not believe individual (prescriptive) treatment necessary. They merely changed the offenders' environment from the corrupting influences of the community to the antiseptic prison. Later, as behavioral science began to develop and needed both subjects for study and a setting for salaried work, the experts discovered that delinquents and criminals were divisible into all sorts of subgroups.*

Later a treatment strategy would be proposed for each. Howard Gill and others credit Dr. William Healy with being the pioneer of individual study in 1915.[109] Others followed in his footsteps—Dr. Bernard Glueck, Dr. W. T. Root, and Dr. W. J. Ellis. They studied criminals and found *inter alia*, body types, intelligence, glandular dysfunction, feeble-mindedness, neurosis and other factors "related" to crime and suggested different classification schemes for institutional treatment.

The prison gates were now flung open to let clinicians in and, as a result of the ascendency of the indeterminate sentence so necessary for treatment, inmates were kept in longer. Several professions saw the opportunity and took advantage of the open gate. Speaking of social work, Kenneth Pray, a former Dean of the Pennsylvania School of Social Work, wrote (1943):

------

*Dr. R. L. Jenkins at the Illinois Welfare Association annual meeting in November 1934 suggested an example of such: the asocial aggressive, the socialized aggressive, the defective delinquent (Maryland now has a facility with 500 such patients called The Patuxent Institution for the Defective Delinquent), the situational delinquent and the psychiatric delinquent. (Frederick C. Kuether, "Religion and the Chaplain," in Tappan, ed., *Contemporary Corrections*, 1951).

A system of almost unmitigated and undifferentiated mass treatment was converted to a regime of constantly increasing individualization. From a place of isolation, idleness, and silence, where inmates were expected to abandon all their accustomed social obligations except obedience, the prison became, increasingly, a busy, productive, responsible, and real-though narrowly enclosed—community. . . . In the otherwise unfamiliar environment of the prison, they provided a setting in which social workers could feel quite at home.[110]

On the question of casework in an authoritarian setting, Pray continues:

This disciplined skill in helping individuals make an adequate and satisfying social adjustment within relatively narrow limits is the distinctive potential contribution of professional social work to prison administration. It is precisely the same problem with which social case workers are engaged outside and to which their whole professional training and experience is geared. . . . Such a worker can bring to the helping of the individual prisoner something which goes beyond the incidental, intuitive service of untrained officers. . . .[111]

With the granting of and the preparation for parole, Pray also saw a role for social case work.

If parole is granted only when the individual has proved its capacity and his willingness to take that kind of responsibility for his own plans, it can be justified, not otherwise. This demands of the prisoner something more than barren conformity to prison rules. It demands of the administration something more than acquiescence in a sponsorship, or approval of a job, that meets the bare minimum requirements of the law. . . . This can only come from a case-work program that rests on a professional relationship with the individual inmate, which steadily and firmly holds him to the obligation of putting purpose and will into the process of preparing for citizenship outside, which helps him muster his own powers and resources to that end, and which faces him steadily as a test of his readiness for parole.[112]

Dr. Ralph Brancale, as head of the New Jersey State Diagnostic Clinic, identified psychiatry's role in prison as necessarily meeting two conditions; and spoke enthusiastically about its future (1951).

First there is the need for the phychiatrist and coworkers realistically to adjust to the peculiarities and traditions that characterize the institution. Second, institutions which would have good clinical facilities must accept the values and the need of clinical psychiatry. . . . The problems of diagnosis are yielding to increasing knowledge and better techniques, and in consequence the outlook for therapy is more optimistic. Another favorable sign is that the polemics which have so long existed on the problems of defining what the 'psychopath' is are now gradually yielding to a much more emphatic interest in doing something therapeutic about offenders.[113]

Educators were also quick to come into prison; pointing to the earlier benefits education provided farmers and complaining about oldline wardens. Price Chenault, Director of Education for New York State's prisons, said (1939):

. . . Education as a contributing force to a complete program of rehabilitation has never been fully tried. There is still so much resistance that the education enthusiasts are lucky if they get half a loaf in most correction systems. Today there are still those in positions of authority who resist every effort to expand programs of correctional education. It is difficult to prove the value of education in any specific instance. However, those who tend to question its merit as one means of rehabilitating inmates of correctional institutions should draw some lessons from a study of what agricultural education has done for rural communities throughout America.[114]

Religionists, who were relegated to passing out Bibles and delivering Sunday morning sermons by custody-oriented wardens, found a new promising arena for their continued labors in "pastoral psychology" and joined the team. Rev. Frederick Kuether, Director of the Council for Clinical Pastoral Training sums up this development (1951):

> The conduct of the Sunday worship service was often the only obviously 'religious' duty of the chaplain. More than one warden or board was willing to settle for a part-time chaplain or a rotating chaplaincy on a fee basis.
>
> Clinical pastoral training was introduced as an experiment in the chaplain's department of the Worcester, Massachusetts, State Hospital in 1925. Its founder, Dr. Anton T. Boisen, held that 'service and understanding went hand in hand.' He saw it as a device both to study the relationship between the experiences of certain types of functionally ill psychotics and the 'religious conversion experience' and to adapt the message of the church to the needs of the institutionalized mentally ill. Within five years, clinical pastoral training had spread to the correctional field. . . .
>
> In 1934, the Federal Bureau of Prisons, wanting to improve its chaplaincy service, requested the Federal Council of the Churches of Christ in America to train and nominate for appointment chaplaincy candidates who would be able to join the projected 'treatment team,' modeled after that of the child guidance clinics, and composed of psychiatrist, psychologist, social worker, and others. The Federal Council turned to the Council for Clinical Training as having the only facilities adequate for such training, and in 1936 the first provisional appointment was made. . . . For the first time, that same September, was a full-time, permanent, resident Protestant chaplain with adequate training appointed to any penal or correctional institution in the United States. Within a few years, the first full-fledged 'in-service' training program was established, and all the major institutions of the system were staffed with trained chaplains. The chaplain had joined the 'team.'[115]

The reader will recall that the traditionalists did not react negatively to these developments, because they were given powerful new weapons of control. Writing in 1951, Frank Loveland, the Assistant Director of the Federal Bureau of Prisons, recalls that diagnostic clinics were never really a part of the basic prison organization.

> A few prison administrators in the 1920s began to point out that individualized treatment was not possible without more knowledge of the individual offender, his background, his abilities and limitations, and some attempt at a prognostic evaluation. . . . The diagnostic clinics had developed as more or less autonomous units. They had been superimposed upon the prison organization and were not truly a part of it.[116]

Charles McKendrick, a former Sing-Sing warden, further pointed out that (1951):

> The professional staff fails to realize the essential totalitarian structure to the prison. . . . Professional personnel fail to accommodate their techniques to the prison . . . and seek to adopt the prison to their own specializations, conflict always results. The professionally trained . . . often underestimates the intelligence of custodial employees . . . and [the latter] often looks upon . . . [the former] with suspicion. The professional frequently approaches his prison assignment with a deterministic theory of behavior. This leads to an impractical emphasis on positivism unsuited to the classically constructed prison community. . . The pattern of custody is the oldest and first essential element of confinement. It is as much a part of the prison environment as the presence of inmates. All of the relationships in the prison community take place within the atmosphere of custody, and treatment processes cannot take place apart from it.[117]

The treaters, however, did not read history and arrived in the prison to convert it into a hospital or at least a therapeutic community when the former failed. But there were enthusiastic visions (Kaysman, 1949):

> We have to treat them psychically as sick people, which in every respect they are. . . . It is the hope of the more progressive elements in psychopathology and criminology that the guard and the jailer will be replaced by the nurse, and the judge by the psychiatrist, whose sole attempt will be to treat and cure the individual instead of merely to punish him. Then and then only can we hope to lessen, even if not entirely to abolish crime, the most costly burden that society has today.[118]

McKendrick had pointed out the fruitlessness of such *ad hoc* schemes.

> The representatives of many disciplines have entered the arena of penal reform. Economists have advanced ideas about productive labor; biologists—hereditary defect; moralists—systems of silence and reflection; psychologists—mental defect; psychiatrists—psychopathy and mental disease; and educators—vocational training. Each has altered the structure of the prison community and each, in turn, has felt the impact of conflict with the representatives of custody, who, however much they are willing to move in one direction, cannot move in all directions equally well.[119]

The same criticisms exist today. At the core of the problem is that the prison cannot be non-puntive if imprisonment—the central fact of a prisoner's life—is itself punitive. Clinicians, justifying their methods, seek a mitigation of some of the more onerous aspects of incarceration, but also make grander claims.

The three key goals of the rehabilitation model are: (1) classification into a limited number of types with prescriptive treatments for each; (diagnosis is therefore of central significance); (2) continued evaluation of the prescribed treatment's progress to determine the point of recovery called "parole readiness"; and (3) all of this must occur in an indefinite time sequence lest a sentence expire before the optimum therapeutic time for release.[120] But, correctional therapists argue, they have not had a chance to really prove what they can do because the proper resources have never been made available. This is indeed true; but probably of more importance are the facts that treatment and punishment do not mix and that the public will never invest the necessary dollars in such programs behind walls for "lesser eligible" criminals. A national commission found the following pauperized clinical staff ratios in American corrections (1968):

TABLE II

Position	Number	Ratio of Staff to Inmates
Social Workers	167	1:846
Psychologist	33	1:4,282
Psychiatrist	58	1:2,436
Academic Teachers	106	1:1,333
Vocational Teachers	137	1:1,031
Custodial Officers	14,993	1:9 [121]

We will, in Chapter Three, turn to an examination of the pay-off of the rehabilitative model in practice. We wish here only to account for its historical entry and identify its place in corrections today. The latter is still elusive. Although corrections continues to pay lip-service to rehabilitation (particularly at legislative budget hearings), at other times it is denigrated. Raymond Procunier, Director of the California Department of Corrections, probably the earliest and most professionalized department in the world, told a 1971 prisoner rights' conference: "There is no one in this field of any consequence at all that believes prison is the place to send a person for rehabilitation."[122] Gerhard Mueller, the former Director of a Criminal Law Research Institute at New York University, states: "I know of no American criminologist or lawyer who does not subscribe to resocialization as a foremost aim of our correctional approach."[123] The American Corrections Association's *Manual of Correctional Standards* (1966) states that:

> Today with few exceptions correctional administrators subscribe to the philosophy of rehabilitation as opposed to the old punitive philosophy. . . . Punishment as retribution belongs to a penal philosophy that is archaic and discredited by history. . . .
>
> Penologists in the United States today are generally agreed that the prison serves most effectively for the protection of society against crime when its major emphasis is on rehabilitation. They accept this as a fact that no longer needs to be debated.[124]

However, it also states that "the fundamental responsibility of prison management is the secure custody and control of prisoners."

The treaters and treated however seem to be in different worlds. The modern treater says (1973):

> If we are to persist in our treatment metaphor, we must see crime as *disease,* not as *a* disease. Just as there are many different treatments which we apply according to the nature of the sickness and the requirements and condition of the individual suffering from it, so must we apply, by analogy, this diversity theory to the problem of criminal behavior and design our treatments accordingly. We must think exclusively, of individuals who have offended against established precepts and of the treatment appropriate to the individual case.[125]

While the treatment strategies occupies the mind of the treater, getting out is uppermost in the mind of the treated. A convict recently said: "If they ask is this yellow wall blue, I'll say of course it's blue. I'll say anything they want me to say if they're getting ready to let me go."[126] Perhaps more elegantly, another inmate makes the same point in a poem entitled "Rehabilitation":

> Five months have passed since I came here,
> To me, now it's quite clear,
> I'll have to adjust to the institution
> Then I'll be ready for restoration.
> I'll have to erase my emotional needs,
> Make new habits, and take new leads.
> Hide my hates in my subconscious mind
> And give the Board a good stiff line.
> Everything we do we have an expression,
> To retreat to childhood, that's regression.
> To get angry, or peeved, a word was created
> And that word we titled as frustrated.
> When we get frustrated, we become aggressive. . . .
>
> But I should be happy and sing a cheer,
> If I get out in less than a year.
> My sentence was stiff with an unjustly bout,
> But the point is, I'm here, and gotta get out.[127]

A recent book by Judge Frankel may be a forebearer of a changing judicial view toward rehabilitation; although probably most judges have yet to move through the rehabilitation phase before the disillusionment, as expressed by Frankel, can overtake them.

Another facet of the case, abstractly separate but not easy to keep always separate in fact, is the severely limited character of our ability to treat the supposedly sick criminal. As to the theoretical separability of this point, there is no strain in distinguishing the idea of disease from that of cure. We know of identified diseases, some deadly, for which we know no cure. In the field of criminology, however, where ignorance reigns so nearly absolute, the distinction is blurred. The apostles of rehabilitation and indeterminate sentences posit 'sickness' without identifying its character and then urge 'treatment' no better defined or specified. The absence of treatment or facilities—is by itself a fatal defect for purposes of the present discussion. However useful it may be elsewhere to identify incurable diseases, there is no justification for a regime of rehabilitation through indeterminate sentences unless we have some substantial hope or prospect of rehabilitating. Our subject is, after all, the confinement of people for long and uncertain periods of time. It is an evil to lock people up. There may be compensating goods that warrant it. But a mythical goal of rehabilitation is no good at all.[128]

Yet the image of a fully financed, rehabilitative prison, albeit smaller, still persists with influencial leaders. A former Director of the Federal Bureau of Prisons, James Bennett, looks ahead:

Individualized discipline, care, and treatment of these people will be wholly.possible.

The prisons of the space age will be small—federal, state and local—with populations of no more than six hundred men. They will be equipped to serve as diagnostic centers to advise the courts on sentencing—and this might well become standard operating procedure. Because it will pay, correctional facilities will be able to program and manage rehabilitation schedules for each individual prisoner almost on a tutorial basis. They will organize work for every man, in and out of the institution, on the same individual basis.[129]

Finally, a note on the black convicts' view of rehabilitation and treatment brings to a close commentary on the erosion of credibility of the rehabilitation model:

The convict strolled into the prison administration building to get assistance and counseling for his personal problems. Just inside the main door were several other doors, proclaiming: Parole, Counselor, Chaplain, Doctor, Teacher, Correction, and Therapist. The convict chose the door marked Correction, inside of which were two other doors: Custody and Treatment. He chose Treatment, and was confronted with two more doors, Juvenile and Adult. He chose the proper door and again was faced with two doors: Previous Offender and First Offender. Once more he walked through the proper door, and, again, two doors: Democrat and Republican. He was a Democrat; and so he hurried through the appropriate door and ran smack into two more doors; Black and White. He was black; and so he walked through that door—and fell nine stories to the street.[130]

The prison monolith was basically unshaken by the entry of professionals; rather, it absorbed social workers, psychologists, psychiatrists, teachers, chaplains, and others to help insulate itself from criticism after the demise of the industrial program. This is vividly demonstrated in a *New York Times* (9/26/69) story about a Pendelton (Indiana) Reformatory convict demonstration:

On the other side of a chain link fence were eleven white guards [the inmates were black] and *at least one vocational teacher,* dressed in riot helmets and carrying loaded shotguns. . . . The guards fired warning shots and then, at the Command of the Captain . . . began firing through the fence. . . . One witness said that some of the men were trying to rise from the ground, raising their hands in a gesture of surrender but were told by the guards, 'You've had your chance,' and were shot down. . . . They killed one and wounded forty-six. [A second died later.][131]

Until the advent of the Cincinnati Declaration, there were very clearly defined programs in corrections; spoken about openly, even by the most brutal. The Puritans shamed, banished, mutilated, and executed the sinner-criminal. The Quakers secluded and worked the offender urging penance. The Auburn penologists regimented and worked convicts in non-communication, while the Sing-Sing heritage was openly calculated brutality and the breaking of the spirit. Whatever misgivings may arise today, our early brethren were explicit in what they said and did.

The New Penology, above all else, successfully delivered enormous discretion to prison officialdom. Private citizens were displaced by professionals and a long slow unsuccessful process of clinicizing the cell blocks got underway. But the innovation was merely rhetorical. Some of the most brutalizing years were experienced coincidentally with the rise of the rehabilitative ideal. Most convicts paid little serious attention to the clinicians. If the treaters had paid attention to Maconochie in the mid-19th century, they would long ago have realized

a man under a time sentence thinks only how he is to cheat that time, and while it away; he evades labor, because he has no interests in it whatever, and he has no desire to please the officers under whom he is placed, because they cannot serve him essentially; they cannot in any way promote his liberation.[132]

THE PARIAH-PENITENT-PRISONER-PATIENT-PLAINTIFF-CONTINUUM

Correctional history may be analyzed as a series of conflicts centering on successful and unsuccessful efforts on the part of the inmate to change his correctionally ascribed status. Each status brought with it roles for the keeper depending upon how the kept was then defined. When the offender was a *pariah,* the then embryonic correctional apparatus operated as *banisher, mutilator* or *executioner*—its least complicated roles. After the Revolution, the offender was deemed to be a *penitent* (and thus in need of a place for penitence—a penitentiary); the keeper became a *moral guider.* With the Industrial Revolution came the collapse of the solitude system of care, prayer, and work; the offender now simply became a *prisoner* and the keeper a *punisher.* From about the end of the Civil War, but at an accelerated pace after the turn of this century (in response to the influx of clinicians), rehabilitators in their need for work products (caseloads) recast the prisoner as a *patient,* and the keeper became *treater*. Following the erosion (but not yet the demise) of the medical model, the prisoner turned to the courts for status revision. In recent years, many groups in society have come to new levels of consciousness about their status—women, blacks, other minorities, students—and it is thus not surprising that the prisoner, who is increasingly a young, urban, minority male, would bring such consciousness-raising attitudes with him into prison.

In the last decade, clinicans and custodians declared a silent truce (although the rhetoric of conflict still flutters) because indeterminacy of sentence, a product of clinical thinking, remains a powerful custody weapon. Other linkages between them also exist which reduce to such common claims as: "You can't treat them unless you keep them," and "Treatment can only occur in orderliness." Both the treaters and keepers still insist upon great status deprivation for the convict as either a prisoner or patient. Assessing the keeper and treater, the convict could not see the promise of an improvement in his lot. The prisoner deemed it more useful to become a *plaintiff*. As a plaintiff he was able to find new definitions for himself; a victim of (correctional) political reprisals, and, as Justice Marshall said, an individual due "worth and dignity," a man having a "basic human desire." Prisoners, from the mid-1960s, unleashed a series of legal assaults on the unconstitutionality of aspects of their confinement which had the effect of reducing their sense of powerlessness thus raising their status.° At the same time his status was elevated by the courts, he saw, however meager, a transformation of power in his favor. Prison officials dug their heels in, sometimes assisted by embarrassed deputy attorneys general, and defended their old prerogatives inch by inch. When the prisoner turned from *patient* to *plaintiff*, the officials necessarily

---

°An ex-prisoner points this out: "It is not unusual, then, in a subculture created by the criminal law, wherein prisoners exist as creatures of the law, that they should use the law to try to reclaim their previously enjoyed status in society." (as cited in Turner, W. B., "Establishing the Rule of Law in Prisons," *Stanford Law Review*, Vol. 23, Feb. 1971, p. 480).

ndant. Unable to simply adjust to procedures
 constitutional extensions, prison officials defended themselves in odd ways. We will examine the legal assault in
greater detail in Chapter III.

Before turning to an analysis of the inmate's legal struggle with
his keepers, we need to understand more about the role of the
guard. Throughout correctional history, the keeper and kept
have had their roles redefined in belated responses to significant
events outside the prison. For example, Ohlin points out that the
use of the factory system brought the collapse of the Pennsylvania system of cell work and provided the atmosphere for
the ascendancy of the Auburn System based upon a rationalization of production—the prison factory.[133] Both the convict and
the guard were subsequently recast into new roles. The guard
has always been assigned the role of enforcing a daily regimen of
order and routine to fulfill presumably higher missions. Without
a deeper understanding of how he has emerged into his current
role we are unable to project ideas of orderly modernization. It
is a fact of prison life that the guard is the central manpower
issue around which all else revolves. The guard is the lynch pin
of operations and if, at present, he appears to be a stumbling
block, he is also the key to change.

FOOTNOTES

[1]Norman B. Johnston, "John Haviland," in Hermann Mannheim, ed., *Pioneers in Criminology*, London: Stevens and Sons Limited, 1960, p. 108.

[2]George Bernard Shaw, *The Crime Of Imprisonment*, New York: Philosophical Library, 1946, p. 13.

[3]Gerhard O.W. Mueller, "Imprisonment and its Alternatives," in *A Program for Prison Reform*, Annual Chief Justice Earl Warren Conference Sponsored by the Roscoe Pound-American Trial Lawyers Foundation, June 9-10, 1972, p. 39.

[4]Frederick Kuether, "Religion and the Chaplain," in Paul W. Tappan, ed., *Contemporary Correction*, New York: McGraw-Hill Book Co., Inc., 1951, p. 254.

[5]*Ibid.*, p. 255.

[6]William G. Nagel, *The New Red Barn: A Critical Look at the Modern American Prison*, New York: Walker and Co., 1973, p. 5.

[7]*Ibid.*, pp. 4-5.

[8]Sol Rubin, *The Law of Criminal Correction*, St. Paul, Minn.: West Publishing Co., 1973, p. 22.

[9]*Ibid.*, p. 23.

[10]Negley K. Teeters, *The Cradle of the Penitentiary: Walnut Street Jail at Philadelphia 1773-1835*, by the Pennsylvania Prison Society, 1955, p. 4.

[11]Charles L. Chute and Marjorie Bell, *Crime, Courts and Probation* (1956, pp. 18-19), as cited in *op. cit.*, n 8, Rubin, p. 20.

[12]*Op. cit.*, n 8, Rubin, p. 38.

[13]Thorsten Sellin, "The Philadelphia Gibbet Iron," *Journal of Criminal Law, Criminology and Police Science* 46, 1955, p. 16.

[14]Alice Morse Earle, *Curious Punishments of Bygone Days*, Rutland, Vermont: Charles E. Tuttle Co., 1972, p. 138.

[15]*Ibid.*, p. 141.

[16]*Ibid.*, pp. 144-145.

[17]*Ibid.*, Chapter 7.

[18]David Rothman, *The Discovery of the Asylum: Social Order and Disorder in the New Republic*, Boston: Little, Brown and Co., 1971, p. 45.

[19]*Ibid.*, p. 52.

[20]*Ibid.*, p. 53.

[21]*Op. cit.*, n 8, Rubin, p. 28.

[22]*Op. cit.*, n 18, Rothman, p. 57.

[23]Elio Monachesi, "Cesare Beccaria," in *op. cit.*, n 1, Mannheim, pp. 38, 48, 49.

[24]Harry Elmer Barnes as cited in *op. cit.*, n 6, Nagel, p. 7.

[25]*Op. cit.*, n 6, Nagel, p. 6.

[26]*Op. cit.*, n 8, Rubin, p. 28.

[27]*Ibid.*, p. 29.

[28]Wayne Morse, general editor, "The Attorney General's Survey of Release Procedures," in George C. Killinger and Paul F. Cromwell, Jr., eds., *Penology:*

The Evolution of Corrections in America, St. Paul, Minn.: West Publishing Co. 1973, p. 23.

²⁹James V. Bennett, "State Organization for Correctional Administrations," in *op. cit.,* n 4, Tappan, p. 70.

³⁰Thorsten Sellin, "The Origin of the 'Pennsylvania System of Prison Discipline,' " in *op. cit.,* n 28, Killinger and Cromwell, p. 13.

³¹*Op. cit.,* n 28, "Attorney General's Survey of Release Procedures," p. 24.

³²*Op. cit.,* n 30, Sellin, p. 19.

³³*Ibid.,* p. 20.

³⁴*Ibid.,* p. 21.

³⁵*Ibid.,* p. 20.

³⁶*Op. cit.,* n 28, "The Attorney General's Survey of Release Procedures," p 24.

³⁷*Ibid.,* p. 27.

³⁸*Ibid.,* p. 28.

³⁹*Ibid.,* p. 29.

⁴⁰*Ibid.,* p. 32.

⁴¹*Ibid.,* p. 33.

⁴²*Ibid.,* p. 36.

⁴³W. David Lewis, *From Newgate to Dannemora,* Ithaca, New York: Cornell University Press, 1965, p. 46.

⁴⁴*Ibid.,* p. 53.

⁴⁵David Rothman, "The Invention of the Penitentiary," *Criminal Law Bulletin* Vol. 8, September 1972, pp. 586, 585.

⁴⁶*Ibid.,* p. 95.

⁴⁷*Op. cit.,* n 43, Lewis, Chapter 4.

⁴⁸*Ibid.,* pp. 108-109.

⁴⁹*Op. cit.,* n 45, Rothman, p. 106.

⁵⁰*Op. cit.,* n 43, Lewis, pp. 93, 117-120.

⁵¹*Ibid.,* p. 147.

⁵²*Ibid.,* p. 151.

⁵³*Ibid.,* pp. 155-156.

⁵⁴*Op. cit.,* n 28, "The Attorney General's Survey of Release Procedures," p. 41.

⁵⁵Howard B. Gill, "A New Prison Discipline: Implementing the Declaration of Principles of 1870," in *op. cit.,* n 28, Killinger and Cromwell, p. 85.

⁵⁶*Op. cit.,* n 28, "The Attorney General's Survey of Release Procedures," pp. 38-39.

⁵⁷*Op. cit.,* n 43, Lewis, Chapter X.

⁵⁸*Op. cit.,* n 1, Johnston, p. 108.

⁵⁹Roy Lubove, *The Professional Altruist,* Cambridge, Mass.: Harvard University Press, 1964.

⁶⁰*Op. cit.,* n 55, Gill, pp. 80-83.

⁶¹Blake McKelvey as cited in Negley K. Teeters, "Prisoners in the United States: 1870-1970," in *op. cit.,* n 28, Killinger and Cromwell, p. 62.

⁶²*Transactions of the National Congress on Prison and Reformatory Discipline,* Albany, 1871. Reprinted by the American Correctional Association, Weed and Parsons, October, 1970, pp. 1-8.

[63] *Op. cit.,* n 55, Gill, p. 83.
[64] John Bartlow Martin, *Break Down the Walls,* New York: Ballantine Books, 1951, pp. 117-118.
[65] *Op. cit.,* n 28, "The Attorney General's Survey of Release Procedures," p. 48.
[66] *Op. cit.,* n 55, Gill, p. 85.
[67] *Op. cit.,* n 8, Rubin, p. 35.
[68] *Ibid.,* p. 36.
[69] *Ibid.,* p. 35.
[70] American Friends Service Committee, *Struggle for Justice,* New York: Hill and Wang, 1971, p. 27.
[71] *Op. cit.,* n 28, "The Attorney General's Survey of Release Procedures," p. 49.
[72] *Ibid.,* p. 46.
[73] James P. Campbell, et. al., *Law and Order Reconsidered,* Task Force on Law Enforcement, National Commission on Causes and Prevention of Violence, Washington, D.C.: Government Printing Office, 1969, p. 573.
[74] Blake McKelvey, *American Prisons,* as cited in Richard McGee, "State Organization for Correctional Administration," in *op. cit.,* n 4, Tappan, p. 76.
[75] *Op. cit.,* n 6, Nagel, p. 50.
[76] *Ibid.,* p. 41.
[77] Robert D. Barnes, "Prison Architecture and Function," in *op. cit.,* n 4, Tappan, p. 271.
[78] *Op. cit.,* n 6, Nagel, p. 48.
[79] *Op. cit.,* n 43, Lewis, p. 183.
[80] *Ibid.,* p. 260.
[81] *Op. cit.,* n 6, Nagel, p. 49.
[82] *Ibid.,* pp. 120, 122.
[83] *Ibid.,* p. 51.
[84] *Op. cit.,* n 74, McGee, p. 77.
[85] Frank T. Flynn, "Employment and Labor," in *op. cit.,* n 4, Tappan, p. 239.
[86] *Op. cit.,* n 28, "The Attorney General's Survey of Release Procedures," p. 50.
[87] Elmer Johnson, *Crime, Correction and Society,* Homewood, Ill.: The Dorsey Press, 1968, p. 289.
[88] *Op. cit.,* n 43, Lewis, pp. 180-194.
[89] *Ibid.,* pp. 190, 199.
[90] *Op. cit.,* n 28, "The Attorney General's Survey of Release Procedures," p. 40.
[91] *Ibid.,* p. 52.
[92] *Op. cit.,* n 85, Flynn, p. 240.
[93] *Ibid.,* p. 238.
[94] *Op. cit.,* n 28, "The Attorney General's Survey of Release Procedures," p. 46.
[95] *Op. cit.,* n 85, Flynn, p. 239.
[96] *Ibid.*
[97] *Ibid.,* p 243.
[98] *Ibid.*
[99] *Op. cit.,* n 43, Lewis, p. 158.

[100]*Ibid.*

[101]*Ibid.*, pp. 159, 188.

[102]*Op. cit.*, n 8, Rubin, pp. 311-312.

[103]Henrietta Addison, "Women's Institutions," in *op. cit.*, n 4, Tappan, p. 305.

[104]*Op. cit.*, n 8, Rubin, p. 311.

[105]*Op. cit.*, n 6, Nagel, p. 179.

[106]*Ibid.*, p 180.

[107]*Op. cit.*, n 13, Sellin, p. 15.

[108]*Ibid.*

[109]*Op. cit.*, n 55, Gill, p. 82.

[110]Kenneth L.M. Pray, "Social Work in the Prison Program," in *op. cit.*, n 4, Tappan, p. 204.

[111]*Ibid.*, p 207.

[112]*Ibid.*, p. 209.

[113]Ralph A. Brancale, "Psychiatric and Psychological Services," in *op. cit.*, n 4, Tappan, p. 191.

[114]Price Chenault, "Education," in *op. cit.*, n 4, Tappan, p. 225.

[115]*Op. cit.*, n 4, Kuether, pp. 256-257.

[116]Frank Loveland, "Classification in the Prison System," in *op. cit.*, n 4, Tappan, pp. 91-92.

[117]Charles McKendrick, "Custody and Discipline," in *op. cit.*, n 4, Tappan, pp. 159-160.

[118]Benjamin Kaysman, cited in Edwin Sutherland and Donald Cressey, *Criminology* (9th Edition), New York: J.B. Lippincott Co., 1974, p. 605.

[119]*Op. cit.*, n 117, McKendrick, p. 170.

[120]*Op. cit.*, n 70, AFSC, *Struggle for Justice*, p. 68.

[121]*Op. cit.*, n 73, Campbell, p. 575.

[122]*Op. cit.*, n 8, Rubin, p. 360.

[123]Gerhard O.W.Mueller, "Punishment, Correction and the Law," in H.S. Perdman and T.B. Allington, *The Task of Penology*, Lincoln, Neb.: University of Nebraska Press, 1969, p. 69.

[124]"Manual of Correctional Standards," American Correctional Association, 1966.

[125]H.H.A. Cooper, "Toward a Rational Doctrine of Rehabilitation," *Crime and Delinquency*, April, 1973, p. 239.

[126]*Op. cit.*, n 70, AFSC, *Struggle for Justice*, p. 73.

[127]Lloyd McCorkle, "Group Therapy," in *op. cit.*, n 4, Tappan, p. 216.

[128]Marvin E. Frankel, *Criminal Sentences*, New York: Hill and Wang, 1973, pp. 90-91.

[129]James V. Bennett, "Prisons of the Space Age," in Duane Denfeld, *Streetwise Criminology*, Cambridge, Mass.: Schenkman, 1974, p. 387.

[130]Joe Martinez, "Rehabilitation and Treatment," in Etheridge Knight, *Black Voices From Prison*, New York: Pathfinder Press, 1970, p. 63.

[131]NCCD *Newsletter*, January, 1970.

[132]Alexander Maconochie, as cited in *op. cit.*, n 8, Rubin, p. 620.

[133]Lloyd Ohlin, "Current Aspects of Penology: Correctional Strategies in Conflict," *American Philosophical Society*, Vol. 118, No. 3, June 1974.

2
Guarding in
Prisons

*"Until it [prison-guard reform] is accomplished,
nothing is accomplished. When this work is done,
everything will be done, for all the details of
a reformed prison discipline are wrapped up in
this supreme reform, as oak is in the acorn."*

Rev. James Woodworth,
  Secretary
California Prison Commission
1870

There is no dearth of literature on the inmate. Academicians, for the last generation, have been fascinated with the discovery of inmate types, cultures and, more recently, inmate political groups. Particular focus has centered on *sub rosa* inmate organizations, argot roles, the organization of life in total institutions, and inmate-staff conflicts resulting from. the peculiar social organization of a prison. There have been studies of the conflicting roles guards have to play and several on the treatment-versus-custody orientation issue. However, precious little is known about the guard himself—other than through questionnaires.[*] We do not even have a very good composite picture of the guard. The President's Crime Commission (1967), the Joint Correctional Manpower Commission (1969), and the National Advisory Commission on Criminal Justice Standards and Goals (1973) all recommended ways to improve management styles and skills and recruit better personnel, but none really probed with enough depth to understand and thereby know what to improve. All called for more better-trained and higher-paid guards, but none spoke to the basic question of how the guard sees himself, how he develops his view of the prison world in which he must contain and manage men against their will. There is a tacit assumption in the literature that guard improvement is a function of his infinite maleability, if only management could figure out the right mold. There are some problems with such a formulation.

Our hazy picture of the guard comes from sociologists and convicts. Convicts simply write more books than guards. Convicts also write more (and better) books than wardens. The latter, usually upon retirement, produce complacent, self-congratulatory collections of reminiscences. Only a few guards have written books after they have left the prison. Convicts' books are better because the selection process for becoming a convict draws upon a more representative group (that includes gifted writers) than guards under civil service and political procedures

---

[*]Leslie Wilkins once cautioned in a lecture that perhaps the least fruitful way to find out what a person is thinking or doing is to ask him.

of selection. Turnover is very high among guards in a prison, who do their "time" in eight-hour shifts; convicts are there full-time. Convicts, with a fairly uncomplicated mission—freedom and "working the system" until freedom comes—understand the prison better than do guards. This is not meant in denigration of the guard but rather as a beginning examination of his status.

Although the individual guard turnover is great (with the rate of 102% of new guards at Stateville, Illinois, in 1973), the role is a fixed one. The guard is a bearer of stability, fixity and the *status quo*. He is rewarded for prowess in uncovering situations that will upset routine and regularity. Upward mobility is a function of order. Evaluations made of the guard by superiors are heavily weighted in favor of doing the same thing repetitively well. He becomes a master of orderliness. His routine makes him a static entity. If he looks in one direction, he sees a few of his colleagues promoted, while if he looks toward the convict, he sees a very different phenomenon occurring.

Convicts are *expected* to change, to learn, to grow—morally, spiritually, academically, vocationally, emotionally and socially—or even if they regress, it is *expected*. It is no surprise to a guard to find an inmate acting badly; that is why the inmate is in prison. But the guard is *expected* to be a paragon of the honest controlled man. Guards are *supposed* to reflect (ultimately to a parole board) progressive *change* in convicts' behavior. If the guard is *static*, the convict is *dynamic*. The convict is *expected* to become something different, hopefully something better. Even where prisons are programmatically impoverished, guards do not fail to notice that convicts write prose, poetry, plays and occasionally saleable movie-scripts, and that it is possible in craft shops for convicts to produce paintings, leather works, sculpture and other works of art providing incomes that can run in multiples of a guard's wage. Nor is it unnoticed by guards that inmates are provided with vocational shops, staff, and expensive machinery and equipment for self-improvement. If, as has been repeatedly shown, parole preparation and release may be hazardous trips for the convict, these also represent *movement* from one status to another. The guard watches this from a *fixed* position. Guards watch convicts become certified mechanics, office machinery technicians, draftsmen, high school graduates, and even college graduates—all elusive goals for guards. Even if the training most convicts receive has little meaning in relation to recidivism, and this seems to be the case, the convicts are still recipients of much expensive attention. Convicts communicate this phenomenon to guards by making invidious comparisons between themselves and the guards, using their former status or their *anticipated* one as examples. Nor does society reward the occupation of guarding others honorifically or financially. Parents rarely if ever project guarding as a first choice profession for their children. There is little cultural pride attached to being a prison guard.

THE EVOLUTION OF THE GUARDS' ROLE

Guards can be better understood by our study of the organization of the prison and their expected work roles rather than by studying guard characteristics individual by individual.[1] We will trace how these expectations affected the guards and produced their contemporary view of their role. Warders, turnkeys or guards, as correctional officers and counselors were called in the old days, were hard to find. Lewis states: "Often the prison had to rely upon men who had been thrown out of work elsewhere and were willing to accept jobs at the penitentiary temporarily until they could find something better. In addition, staff positions were subject to political pressures."[2]

In 1823, an ex-convict, writing about his experience in Newgate, reveals that it was hard to get capable guards at $500 a year. This was especially true because the guard had to remain inside the stockade almost as constantly as the prisoner, being permitted to visit with his family or friends only once or twice a month.[3]

The guard had a clearer task in the early days. All he needed was a whip or a steel-tipped cane (later a rifle) to administer a lock-step, silent system of prisoner behavior management. His mission was unambiguous: "no escapes, order and silence." This sufficed until the mid to late nineteenth century when a slow erosion of the uncomplicated mission began. The only complication to that point was the convicts' desire for freedom, but that was expected and indeed formed the basis for the uncomplicated mission—an escape-proof order.

It was the Lynds-Cray-Wiltse mentality which set the historical dimensions of the guards' role. These men did not come to their ideas about prison governance (and hence the role of the keeper) accidentally. It was calculated. Nor did they shy away from implementation. Wiltse of Sing-Sing proclaimed: "The best prison is that which the inmates find worst."[4] Presumably, Wiltse's guard force was to make sure his prison was the worst. Lynds and Cray borrowed from the military to march (lock-step) inmates and inflict corporal punishment for the slightest infraction. In so doing, guards had to perform their jobs using a military model, complete with uniforms and weaponry. Enforcing silence upon inmates was never totally successful, but it had an effect upon guards who had to be constantly vigilant. Guards watched for facially expressive communications and patrolled cellblocks barefooted seeking violators of the no-talking rule. When violators were identified, wardens ordered flogging. Quite aside from the brutality of the use of the whip on convicts, guards were being debased first by having to crawl silently around ranges to report conversation and then by having to learn how to use a whip on violators. There was no training program for the use of the lash in early New York prisons but almost ". . . every officer in the prison, it seemed, had taken a hand in administering the stripes."[5] In Auburn, throughout the year of 1845, there was a flogging every two days for conversation-related offenses.[6]

In the beginning, guards were to consider their charges "wicked and depraved, capable of every atrocity, and ever plotting some means of violence." Menninger still refers to prison life as "a perpetual cold war which at times warms up. . . ."

Early newspaper accounts reported that "knives, in some form, are common with convicts, and edged tools in almost every shop are in their hands (1828)."[7] Constant frisks and searches had to be undertaken to reduce the number of homemade weapons available to convicts. Other forms of contraband also found their way into the prison and had to be watched for: beer, liquor, newspapers, letters, fresh fruit, etc. Guards were now given the impossible task of keeping the prison hermetically sealed. With the nexus of cash or other favors still binding the keeper and the kept, guards themselves early became involved in smuggling goods in short supply into the prison and therefore had to watch out for each other. Nor were early prison administrators content with the difficult task of merely ordering compliance of the convicts' public behavior. Masturbation was found by one investigating committee (1847) to be ". . . the besetting sin of all prisons. . . . Its existence is very marked at Auburn, and is doubtless one exciting cause of much of the insanity which has prevailed there."[8]

Except for the 1830-1850 period when the guard was simply told to be perversely vigilant, we find double-messages constantly given him by administrators. Thomas Eddy, the Quaker who was so instrumental in abolishing capital punishment for all but a few crimes at the end of the eighteenth century, is the man who warned of inmates "ever plotting some means of violence." At the same time, however, he also advised that no two inmates were alike and therefore, should not be treated alike, thereby further complicating the guards' role.[9] Following the New York (Sing-Sing) terror period, the guards watched a bewildering array of reformative programs and personnel enter the prison. Price Chenault said (1939):

> Chaplains and other religious enthusiasts were equally certain that they held the key to unlock the door to reformation. In turn have come the industrialist, the educator, the psychologist, the psychiatrist, and the case worker. . . . The claims of all these groups have been exaggerated; their expectations have presented a confused picture to the administrator.[10]

But it was not the administrator who was confused, it was the guard. The administrator brought these disciplines in at a time when the whole issue of whether to continue penitentiaries was in question. The reformative programs were to replace force in maintaining order. The pen was to substitute for the whip. The promise of early release for good conduct under the indeterminate sentence was now available. McKendrick, perhaps the most lucid custodian in correctional history makes this point (1951):

> In this sense, discipline is a central objective in the aims of the administrator and his rehabilitative staff. . . .
>
> Perhaps the most significant thing about prison discipline from a historical point of view is the tendency toward the mitigation of severe punishments as the evidences of reformative influences are increased in the prison community. Corporal punishments . . . have been abolished in many places. . . . *When prisoners know that a record of all infractions of rules will be submitted to the parole board considering their release, they recognize that strong evidences of failure to adjust within the prison community may be interpreted as sound reasons for withholding their release.*[11]

The guards also noticed that the reformative personnel worked 9 a.m. to 5 p.m. Monday through Friday, and were secure in their offices and chapels. Whenever the rhetoric of rehabilitation or reformation escalated, the guards' basic mission was further compromised. Again, McKendrick analyzes the problem:

> With each approach to the problem of correctional treatment, the job of the custodian becomes more complex. Each new service that enters the field requires the development of new attitudes, new thoughts, and often new duties for the custodial staff. It was a far simpler task to provide security when one resident chaplain and one physician were the only non-uniformed employees than it is today with the addition of teachers, physicians, psychiatrists, psychologists, representatives of various religious denominations,

Veterans, Alcoholics Anonymous representatives, all a part of the paraphernalia of reform. The liberalization of recreation, correspondence, and visiting privileges has complicated the picture.[12]

The guards were increasingly bewildered. Nobody had prepared them to speak to, much less to relate to, college educated professionals who often spoke a mysterious jargon. The guards withdrew to their familiar tasks. If the disparity of purpose involved in securing "the offender against escape at the same time that he is trained for responsibility and freedom" was not apparent to others, it was apparent to the guards. Tappan (1951) continues:[13]

Abstract ideal objectives are strenuously pursued—at the level of talk—but action betrays the gap when methods are employed that are quite inappropriate to the avowed ends. . . . At best, [the guard] . . . is often impelled by the principle of least effort to do the job routinely, with a minimum of mental exertion or of disturbance. In this he is frequently encouraged by his superiors and the public through their preference for a quietly moribund correctional system.[14]

CUSTODY VS. REHABILITATION

Accomplished by eminent scholars, the "Theoretical Studies in Social Organization of the Prisons" (1960) pointed out the folly of trying to maximize the aims of custody and treatment simultaneously under the same roof, behind the same wall.[15] Their statement was clearly a pessimistic view despite the disclaimer that they did not want others to see the work as a "criticism of the existing penal system, but rather as an analysis of its current operations and structure, which may contribute to the eventual improvement of our institutions."[16] No bright new vistas were proposed. The message left—at least for the guards—was extremely discouraging.

Studies which followed were in the same mold. They redis-covered dilemmas confronting prison administrators and sug-gested different patterns of management[17] or projected new theories for corrections based upon classification of types of prisoners. The basic problem of the prison's *raison d'etre*, to pro-vide custody, which was always crystal clear to the warden, was obscured by the researchers. Attempts to democratize admin-istrative styles or to integrate inmate culture with the guards' focal concerns related to securing custody were like two ships passing in the night. One influential researcher (1961), found that the guard was alienated because of the unilateral flow of in-formation (he being at the uninvolved bottom end of the hier-archy); that guards possessed only an "illusion" of unlimited authority; that autonomy of the official is a fiction; and that inmates, who might be classified as pro-, anti- and psuedo-social were (not suprisingly) more influenced by values built up over a lifetime than they were by their new-found participative pat-terns as prison inmates.[18] Another researcher (1968), found guards were co-operative, opportunistic or alienated, apparently not unlike the inmates.[19]

Guards, however, did not read this literature, nor did many of their superiors. They were listening to another, earlier drum beat, again from McKendrick (1951):

The prison is a totalitarian community. The prison is a com-munity in which the most significant values of the governed, the values of freedom, are limited in the interest of the state. . . .

Conflict between the agencies of reform and custodial forces exists, (when) . . . members of the professional staff fail to recognize the essentially totalitarian structure of the prison community. . . .

The pattern of custody is the oldest and first essential element of confinement. It is as much a part of the prison environment as the presence of inmates. All of the relation-ships in the prison community take place within the atmosphere of custody, and treatment processes cannot take place apart from it. . . .

For centuries, prisons have been constructed with a single objective, that of security. In a sense, each new prison was an experiment in construction. Whenever an escape occurred, some effort was made to strengthen the physical plant. A wall was constructed, more windows were barred, or perhaps a new position was created and a guard delegated to eliminate the weak point. The modern prison plant has developed as a result of earlier failures and, expensive as it may be, the modern walled prison is sufficiently secure to prevent escape, provided that neither the personnel nor the procedures of operation are in themselves defective.[20]

Ramsey Clark blamed the current (1971) plight of the guard on the prison environment itself.[21] This is not inconsistent with the view taken here that guards did indeed become the products of their moral and physical (work) environment. If we want to fully appreciate the position of the guard it is instructive to examine what the official and self-proclaimed professional leadership have said the purpose of the prison, hence the role of the guard, to be.

The American Correctional Association (1960) told custody officers the first responsibility of the prison is the "secure custody and control of prisoners." But this is not too helpful since the ACA in other places said that rehabilitation is the first purpose of the prison. The largest department of corrections in the nation informed its guards (1971):

Remember, CUSTODY is always first in order of importance. . . . Constant vigilance is the price of efficient custody.*. . . Never show the slightest uncertainty as to the course of your action. You must be a leader in the strongest

---

*McKendrick had said "eternal vigilance is the price of security," corrupting what Jefferson's "price of liberty" meant in the sense of citizen participation in government.

sense of the word; must know and show your authority. . . .
Do not fraternize with any inmate or group of inmates.** IT
COULD COST YOU YOUR JOB.[22]

Whatever else was being published in the journals about new
breakthroughs, or at best detentes between custody and treatment staffs, the guard in his confusion invariably focused on the
micro-world of the cell block.

Prisoners in maximum-security prisons have much time and
very little to do. They can afford to spend long hours in
patient watching to find any weakness in the behavior of
their custodians. They are quick to learn a guard's habits,
his interests, hobbies, likes, and dislikes. Every item of information thus acquired may be useful at some future time.
Some inmates watch carefully every time a door is unlocked
to see whether or not the key is left exposed. They are

** McKendrick was again more elegant quoting no less than Roberto Michels
for justification:
"Authority can neither arise nor be preserved without the establishment
and the maintenance of distance between those who command and those
who obey—all social relations whether they be those in the army and
navy, in the civil service, in the schools or even in the family circle, show
how necessary to authority is the maintenance of distance—if only by the
assumption of an imposing bearing."
(*Encyclopedia of the Social Sciences,* Vol. II, p. 320)

But there were other ways in which even the military model might have
been invoked, for example:
The discipline which makes the soldiers of a free country reliable in battle
is not to be gained by harsh or tyrannical treatment. On the contrary, such
treatment is far more likely to destroy than to make an army. It is possible
to impart instruction and to give commands in such manner and such a
tone of voice to inspire in the soldier no feeling but an intense desire to
obey, while the opposite manner and tone of voice cannot fail to excite
strong resentment and a desire to disobey. The one mode or the other of
dealing with the subordinates springs from a corresponding spirit in the
breast of the commander. He who feels the respect which is due to others
cannot fail to inspire in them regard for himself, while he who feels, and
hence manifests, disrespect toward others, especially his inferiors, cannot
fail to inspire hatred against himself."
(Major General John M. Schofield, speaking to the Cadets at West Point,
August 11, 1879.)

quick to note every change of assignment and the manner in which each employee carries out his job. . . .

Constant vigilance and alertness are essential preventives against escape from the housing units. Guards must react to unfamiliar sounds, strange odors, and the unusual behavior of any inmate. The guards' time is spent largely in the monotonous patrolling of galleries and in counting the inmate population.

Searching cells should never become a routine or carelessly performed task. Favorite hiding places for contraband are toilets and washbowls, brooms, floor coverings, bed legs, soap, ventilators, innocent-looking pieces of cardboard, and mattresses. . . .

The most important process in the administration of custody is the count. . . . When counts are made it should be determined that the prisoner is not only present but that he is alive and in suitable condition to fulfill his assignment.[23]

From some rehabilitators, the guard heard that things were getting better. (Loveland, 1951)

One of the major contributions of an effective classification program is better personnel and inmate morale. Aside from bringing all services and personnel together through a cooperative approach to institutional and individual problems, classification gives the custodial officer higher status and a more vital, interesting job. He is no longer just a guard. He has an important job to perform in the training and treatment program.[24]

But Menninger was probably closer to the truth when he observed that the prisoner was being "herded about by men half afraid and half contemptuous of him, toward whom all offenders early learn to present a steadfast attitude of hostility."[25]

Herman Schwartz, who since Attica has become one of the foremost correctional law scholar-activists, simply sees guards as frightened, hostile, rural types who are basically conservative.

He did hedge a bit, saying that the following picture might be overdrawn.

These people usually have no understanding or sympathy for these strange urban groups, with their unfamiliar and often 'immoral' lifestyles, with their demands and their resentments. Racial prejudice is often present, for the white backlash is particularly powerful among such rural types. . . .

Such frightened and hostile people are sentenced to prison as guards for 20-year or more terms—or as long as it takes to get a retirement pension—and are thrown into the most dangerous and frightening kind of encounters with these militant and resentful minorities. They are seen by the prisoners and often see themselves as policemen; they are often called that by the prisoners and their blue uniforms, para-military organization, billy clubs and the like reinforce that perception. In their unions' utterances and elsewhere, the guards often express a kinship and solidarity with law enforcement which is reciprocated: the Buffalo police force and its newspaper, for example, explicitly affirmed their solidarity with the Attica guards.[26]

George Jackson, in his famous "A Letter from Soledad Prison," picks up the themes of fear, unpredictability, and constant tension of the guard's world.

Since the guard controls the gate and may call on the organized violence of his and other government forces on up to the U.S. Airborne Army, it may seem odd for him to feel insecure. This is the case, however, in fact (and I speak here as objectively as is possible—I never underestimate the intelligence of the people), it is a matter of fact that the guard is less psychologically secure than the man he has trapped. He is more defensive, counter-active, 'hostile,' than his victim. Although he does control the greater violence he still feels that he can never relax. This is understandable when you consider that he knows how offending and disgusting his actions are. He knows that a man can die in seconds and although he does have help they are almost always too far away to save him from a determined attacker. He knows he is one of 40 men whose function is to suppress thousands and, although he can bring into play a superior arm, any one of the thousands streaming past him on normal errands could be armed with a crude but lethal knife, club, zip gun with silencer. Among the men he is commissioned to watch are probably hundreds of schizophrenic-reaction cases. He knows this and he is trying to remember them all or watch all directions. And he is also aware that he looks a great deal like all the rest of the guards, meaning he must also bear their guilt.[27]

PROFESSIONAL PRISON LITERATURE

In order to fully understand what the leaders of corrections intended, we surveyed their national publication known as the *Jail Association Journal* (from 1939-1940), then the *Prison World* (from 1941 to 1954) and since July 1954 as the *American Journal of Corrections*, the official organ of the American Correctional Association. We examined the journals in ten-year intervals beginning with the 1941-42 issues. These issues were chosen partly because momentous events° occurred in those years and we were interested in the profession's responses. Further, we were interested in recurring themes, stresses placed on certain aspects of practice and the development of new ideas.

In the early issues (1941-42), one could find a "guest" editorial by a sheriff; a parole board member; a governor; a president of the American Prison Association (predecessor to the ACA); a federal warden; commissioners of corrections from New York

---

°World War II; the increasing entry of rehabilitative services; the wave of prison riots in the early 1950s; the human rights explosion of the 1960s; the burgeoning of correctional case law; Attica and several lesser-known but major disturbances (Rafford, Florida; Pendelton, Indiana); the politicizationı of prisoner demands; the development of community-based corrections; and the reports of several National Commissions on Violence, on Crime, on Standards and Goals in Criminal Justice.

City and Alabama; Stanford Bates, head of the New York State Board of Parole; and Francis Biddle, the U.S. Attorney General. They respectively discussed running a sanitary jail; preparing convicts for parole; the high hopes for California's indeterminate sentence; the need to educate the public about corrections; the lack of good training programs for women; the impact of the war on prisons; military drills and the manufacturing of sand bags (anti-incendiary mats); and such themes as: prison is the last chance for convicts to change bad habits; parole should be used to maximize manpower in the war effort; the prisoners must help in the war industries or through induction in the army.

The editors also reserved a regular space called "Spotlighting—Our Editorial Comment" for more outspoken comment. Beginning in March 1941, the editors came out against whipping prisoners because it was inconsistent with the rehabilitative ideal. In July - August 1941, Morris Rudensky,° editor of *The Atlantian*, made his debut, noting that a humble prisoner could get an article published in the *Prison World* and praising the "new spirit" of cooperation between prison personnel and convicts. In the next issue Rudensky, deploring the murder of a warden, warned convicts that they could not "murder their way to freedom." In this same issue Dr. J.D. Wilson, an associate editor, lauds the contribution of psychiatry to penology, concluding:

Crazy and criminal both begin with the same letter so they have that much in common at least. And, on second thought, penologist and psychiatrist, also both commence with the same letter—which might be considered as another reason for thinking that it is just as much a crime to be crazy as it is crazy to be a criminal.

°Morris, better known as "Red," Rudensky was editor of the Federal Atlanta Penitentiary's inmate newspaper. A well-known writer, he wrote only intermittently since he was an even better-known escape artist. He was a chum of the Capones. Now in his late 70's he is a "security consultant" for a major Minnesota industrial firm and a few years ago published "The Gonif," (Yiddish for "the Thief"), an autobiography.

In 1947, the publication which was then *The Prison World* developed a "Corrections Officers Training Section" column under the editorship of Dr. Walter Wallace, Warden of Wallkill State Prison. In successive issues from 1947 to 1951, when it lapsed, the column was primarily concerned with "how-to-do-it." It begins with such custodial concerns as how to inspect a train or supervise a workgang "because we believe that good custody is basically essential to whatever else may be done in the correctional institution." A guard tells "How to Get Along with the Sergeant," averring that obedience is mandatory, "bite your tongue in face of an unwise order" and "familiarity with superiors breaks down morale." The next issues move on to "How to Search a Cell," "How to Search the Person of an Inmate," "The Prison Hospital" (with trade tips about assuring the inmate's ingestion of medicine through the use of flashlights after placing the medicine in the inmate's mouth yourself), also checking the bathrooms "where degenerates get together," "How to Handle Custody Problems in the Kitchen" (followed with a question which readers might think about: "Should inmates be permitted to talk while at meals?"), "How to Transport Prisoners," "How to Make Reports." In 1949, the column turned to "How to Promote the Institutions' Sanitation Program," "How the Custodial Officer May Assist the Chaplain," "How to Avoid Fraternizing with Inmates" (by maintaining an insurmountable wall between the inmate and all prison employees), "How to Organize an Institutional Staff to Function in Locating Hideouts Within a Maximum Security Prison," and "How to Patrol a Gallery at Night." In 1950, an issue was devoted to women's prisons and following a series of "how-to" questions, answers were found for the following issues: beautifying the institution, receiving new inmates, supervising a workgang, censoring mail, using a log-book, "how to keep prisoners' laundry straight," and how to deal with visitors. If guards didn't worry enough about routine day-to-day matters, a chief medical officer let them know that it was his:

> firm conviction that the great majority of delinquents present more than the mild psychoneurotic symptoms, and

that their psychoneuroses are of considerable importance in producing their delinquent behavior. . . . Two emotional processes prominent in psychoneurotics are anxiety and hostility. Our present means of detaining offenders certainly does not reduce these emotions but, instead, reinforces them. . . . The great majority of inmates are mentally, emotionally or socially 'sick'.

Having taken time out for a sprinkling of Freud, we return to the more pedestrian problems (still in 1950), "How to Avoid a Miscount" in which the editor states, "when an officer makes a wrong count, he ought to be regarded by his superiors to ascertain if he is feeble-minded, suffering from a certain nervous breakdown, in need of a literacy test, ill, drunk or taking dope." We also see articles on the guard as a counsellor needing to show inmates "sympathetic interest" and a column in using "Community Resources in Pre-release Programs" noting that it is not unusual to see a colored, a Mexican and a white man seated together trying to solve problems!

In 1951, after a wave of self-mutilations in southern state prisons, Dr. Rupert Koeninger (a psychologist) published, "What About Self-Mutilations?" describing the problem and most frequent types of mutilation—severing of the Achilles tendon and inducing infections through introducing lye into razor cuts. In May-June, 1951, a vitriolic attack is made by Louis Messolonghites upon the book, *My Six Convicts*. In the next issue, the guard is introduced to a new idea by Albert C. Wagner "Inmate Participation in Correctional Institutions" in which he calls for less censorship, honor groups, lowering security, respect for inmates, and inmate councils. By the May-June, 1952 issue, a wave of riots had swept the nation. The editorial calmed its readers proclaiming only "A relatively few prisoners in comparatively few prisons . . . participated, that there is a general unrest in the world and that the riots may have a constructive effect in awakening the public's interest in prisons." The November-December issue gave the annual conference report which contained nothing reflecting the historic riots earlier that Spring.

In 1954, the *Prison World* became the *American Journal of Corrections*, and later the "Training Section" column got a new editor, Walter Dunbar,* then associate warden of San Quentin. The first columns now turned to "How to Handle Prisoners' Mail," "Policies and Standards of Inmate Clothing," "Prison Discipline" and the "Components of Supervision." A few years later, the column told the guard that "the days of the illiterate, two-fisted type of prison guard were over." In his place, the new officer would receive training in the proper use of firearms, security equipment *and* good relationships with the public, fellow officers and the (unexplained) philosophy of rehabilitation, followed by a compulsory program in self-defense, firing on the range and the "Fundamentals of Revolver Shooting."

In 1960, with America beginning to experience the civil rights explosion, we return to the *Journal* to see what was occupying the minds of the leaders of corrections. Beginning in January, 1961, Sanger Powers, Director of the Wisconsin Department of Corrections and President of the ACA, wrote advocating a therapeutic atmosphere for juvenile corrections, described a new construction program in his state and emphasized the need for correctional curriculum in schools of social work. The achievements and challenges of Prison Industries (a dying institution) was extolled by James Curran of Maryland. James V. Bennett, Director of the Federal Bureau of Prisons, gave "A Penal Administrator's View of the Polygraph." Ralph Murdy of the Baltimore Criminal Justice Commission published his "Islam Incarcerated"—the only mention of racial issue in three years. Murdy, speaking of Black Muslims, concluded:

This organization, then, is led by a man capable of drawing a fanatical following. . . . While there is certainly a potential

---

*He subsequently became Director of the California Department of Corrections, and was heavily involved in Attica as Deputy Commissioner to Commissioner Oswald of New York State. At this writing he is Director of the New York State probation system.

danger [of Muslims taking matters into their own hands], this writer believes the continued close watchfulness of the FBI and local enforcement is sufficient to contain it.

The next two years' contributions concern particular types of therapies for types of inmates and an exposition of "success" stories from across the nation and abroad: "Psychological Needs of Women in a Correctional Institution," "The Aged Inmate," "The 'Difficult' Prisoner," and "Group Psychotherapy and the Criminal—An Introduction to Reality," which sweepingly finds "emotional infancy and the morbid fear of reality . . . fundamental characteristics of the criminal in this or any age." "Facts About Diabetic Inmates" and "Teaching Machines and Programmed Learning" found their way into Rikers Island in November, 1962, and in the same issue "Introductory Handicraft for the Segregated" was offered by the Hobby Craft Director of the Michigan Reformatory. These issues also took us to such exotic places as the "Tochigi Women's Prison, Japan," "Penology in Belgium and France," "Canada's Parole System," and "Penology in Sweden and Denmark." Also, we learned Sweden conducted a "Successful Fight Against Juvenile Delinquency." Closer to home "California Takes Men to the Mountains," "The Ohio Correctional Story," "Adventures in Rehabilitation" (by an architect), "Progress in New Mexico's Penal System," a "Decade of Changes in West Virginia," "The Georgia Penitentiary System" and "Adult Correction in Washington State." In the early 1960s, some academicians of note for the first time published articles in the *Journal*: Donald E. J. MacNamara on capital punishment; Alfred C. Schnur on research; Clarence Schrag on the malintegration of treatment and custody services in a prison. In addition, Peter O. Lejins became the ACA president.

A decade later in 1971, we find the main thrust into drugs, juvenile delinquency, reform in Washington and Florida, collective violence, the new ABA commitment to corrections, the prisoners' right to medical treatment, W. Clement Stone's "Positive Mental Attitude" programs, a report on the revision of the ACA's Correctional Standards and, in the issue following Attica, the

"Politicalization of Prisoners," about which the editor notes "the social separation of staff and inmates increases prisoner acceptance of anti-staff values." A final issue examined was January, 1974, in which it seems we were starting the cycle over; a sheriff writes of "Diverting Idle Hands, An Ideal Now Underway in Harris County Jail" (through art, band, religion and work programs.) Currently, most of the *Journal* is usually devoted to advertising, firearms, hardware, radio equipment and the latest security devices including Folger Adams' ubiquitous newest "fool proof" lock. By 1974 it was necessary to have an index for advertisers.

We have gone into this in such length because the ACA's publication is a reasonable index of leading thinking, and one can plausibly extrapolate what guards would be exposed to in their work environments by superiors who subscribed to the publication.*

THE AMERICAN CORRECTIONAL ASSOCIATION

The A.C.A. membership is currently about 10,000. The National Commission on Causes and Prevention of Violence (1965) estimated the total correctional work force at more than 121,000, with 80% of them custody-related personnel.[28] The A.C.A. believes that 80% of its membership (belonging to the $6.00 per year Regular Category) are mainly guards or other lower echelon practitioners, but its membership director could not identify custody staff as a separate entity. We can therefore estimate that of the 100,000 working guards less than 10% belong to A.C.A. (the figure for state prison personnel is probably less than 5%). We can liberally estimate the A.C.A. guard membership at 3-4,000. However, annual conference

---

*Another unexplored vehicle would be the annual conferences of A.C.A. The conference highlights are reported in the Journal but the full proceedings would shed more light on the subject under study. However, if we use the 1870 session as an index of representativeness or historical commitment to declarations, the later proceedings may be only of marginal historical value.

attendance and leadership positions are reserved for top echelon. A.C.A. estimates (conservatively) 60% of the annual conference participants to be top management and supervisory types. Line guards up through captains are infrequently found on national committees. However, in 1972 the association took great pains to make its 44-member national board reflect the diversity of correctional practice. The by-laws now assure the election of two line officers from both juvenile and adult correctional institutions and of four at-large members. Of these four, one must be black, one Spanish speaking and one Indian.

WARDENS' ASSOCIATION

There is only one other publication which has a specific albeit limited custody personnel audience. It is called "The Grapevine." Some six years old, it is the official organ of the American Association of Wardens and Superintendents. It is the field's best example of jingo press. Uncritical acclaim goes to wardens of all stripes, and critical scorn is poured on convicts, radical lawyers, reformers and the like. It very infrequently publishes any comment. It makes its points by reproducing articles and editorials from the daily press everywhere in the nation, judicial findings and letters to various editors. The 1973 editor of "The Grapevine," who presumably also writes the pithy commentaries, was G. Norton Jameson, Warden of the South Dakota State Prison. A few examples will convey the flavor of this xeroxed publication.

From southern Illinois, a guard's letter to the editor, in part, is reprinted (Vol. 5, No. 4):

Editor, the Southern Illinoisan:
I can tell by reading your editorials you are a Republican-orientated paper and also anti-establishment. It is disgusting to people like myself that work for a living. . . .

I also work at a prison. You don't like this either. You preach prison reform. You write about police brutality. . . .

I would like to know and am sure a lot of people who read your paper would too—have you ever worked behind the walls of a prison or have you ever ridden in a police car. Both jobs take a lot of abuse from do-gooders like you. . . .

You downgrade prison officials and guards. We are just people going to work, just like you. Not one prison guard put a man in prison and we can't get them out. We just do our job. . . .

I am writing this letter because I am fed up with this bull that you put about inmates being angels and guards being idiots.

I am sure more people would be interested in your paper if you did write both sides. You see I have worked at Menard for 10 years and am proud to be a part of the establishment.

I hope you put this in your paper.

Lennie Hill
Chester

Another issue contains a reprint of James J. Kilpatrick's attack on the National Advisory Commission on Criminal Justice Standards and Goals Report on Correctional Reform (*Washington Star,* no date). Finally, there is an editorial comment by Warden Jameson after a very long reprint of a U.S. District Court finding (erroneously refered to as a Supreme Court decision) in Southern Texas favorable to Director George Beto of the Texas Department of Corrections (in 1970).

I think you will agree that the foregoing decision is long overdue. But let's look further—this case indicates exceptional care in its preparation—my hat, and yours, should be off to Dr. Beto, his staff and the lawyers who so carefully presented the facts for their side. It should be kept in mind that the Supreme Court has only those facts that are presented in the trial court upon which to base a decision. If you let the inmates beat you to the punch and fail to present your case, you can expect little else from the high court than what you've been getting.

To their credit, most wardens with whom the author has contact disown "The Grapevine," are ashamed of it and rarely keep back issues for anyone to see—but it is the *official* publication of the Wardens' Association.

The Association has about 130 members out of a potential of nearly five times that number. The new president is Vernon Housewright of Vienna, Illinois, who has a dramatically different world-view of corrections than Jameson's. The Association, or at least its publication, is expected to break with its parochial past under its new leadership.

ADMINISTRATORS' ORGANIZATION

The Association of State Correctional Administrators (ASCA) is the adult prison system administrators' professional organization. It admits larger city (Chicago, New York, Philadelphia), federal, District of Columbia and Canadian penal executives into membership. There is also an "associate" category for retired well-known state, federal and armed service correctional administrators. Recently, and largely in response to Attica, the ASCA published "Unified Correctional Policies and Procedures." It is a relatively forward-looking document which federal judges increasingly consult in mediating disputes between the keeper and the kept. The ASCA membership turns over rapidly because top administrators are swept in and out of office following gubernatorial elections. It is not uncommon for 25% of the under 70 membership to turn over every two years. There is also turnover of a different type. In a limited personnel market, an administrator could represent one state in one year and another the following year. Ellis MacDougall represented South Carolina, Connecticut and Georgia before retirement. (This writer represented two states before political influence, but it has not yet put into action what it sometimes toys with—the hiring of an executive director and becoming a forceful national lobby for correctional change.)

ORGANIZED LABOR

Custody officer unions have yet to make their mark. Collective bargaining is a relatively new phenomenon for public workers and is even more novel for most guards. The field is divided between the American Federation of State, County and Municipal Employees (AFSME), the Teamsters Union, a variety of state employee associations and occasionally independent unions (which have generally become disaffected from the others). Being subject to a tight para-military style of work, uniforms and the unquestioning following of orders (even unreasonable ones while biting your tongue) does not prepare one well for union participation. Union programs, at the moment, are narrowly drawn to conditions of work, insurance, wages, seniority and job security. Getting a contract is first on their present agendas. Among custody workers, there is as yet no large-scale concern for correctional innovation. Even within AFSME, locals reflect widely different concerns throughout the nation. The National AFL-CIO (under its Community Service Division) sponsors a Labor-National Council on Crime and Delinquency (NCCD) Participation program which has a broad concern for criminal justice modernization. Under this program, organized labor is playing an increasingly important role in bringing about change. Unfettered from narrow AFSME ("local") concerns, the AFL-CIO-NCCD ("cosmopolitans") come at problems with broader concerns.

THE ETHNOGRAPHY OF GUARDING

One other line of study needs examination before we can make a statement about the emergent guard. There are very few ethnographic studies of the Guard. T. C. Esselstyn studied the off-duty behavior of a small sample of correction personnel in California (1966). Addressing the paucity of information about them he states: "It is as though everyone believed that the processes of social interaction and the emerging social systems do not occur among correctional workers, if they do, they have no significance to the correctional field."[29] Of the thirty-one respondents, which included some guards, county and federal probation workers, Esselstyn says: "Privately, they socialize frequently and spend much of the time in this rich setting for conversation, interaction and the weaving of social bonds."[30] He summarizes frequency of contracts as follows:

> He visits his co-workers; they visit him; and now and then, they go off for a big night together. These social contacts last anywhere from an hour to half a day or night or even more, and on average occupy from two to three hours in a typical week. This is not, then, momentary socializing.
>
> It occurs frequently, is wide-spread throughout the sample, and lasts a long while. When it happens, the conversations almost invariably turns to some phase of correction, often for as long as 20 per cent or more of any interval given over to informal social contact.[31]

In response to a question eliciting the origins of their "ideas about corrections," of the 31, 16 were mildly to greatly influenced by off-duty contact with fellow workers, 5 by clients, and 10 reported the mixed influences of journals, departmental directives or by off-duty contacts with correctional workers.[32] Some of the areas of greatest influence occurring during these contacts were in (1) morale, job satisfaction and sense of belonging; (2) exchange of views about their agencies; and (3) clarifying difficult or conflicting policy issues.[33] Esselstyn was very modest in his conclusions because of the methodological shortcomings of the study, but he did pose some long-range research projects: (1) a study of dropouts and their self-concept (dropouts from correctional jobs may have not developed the self-concept and growth which off-duty contacts seem to contribute to these who stay); and (2) a study of informal socialization patterns focusing on language (interaction is primarily through technical language which is a mix of "prison argot and jive, underworld and street-corner slang" and serves to fence out strangers while simultaneously speeding communication between in-group members and further strengthening bonds.) [34]

The most extensive and promising of ethnographic studies is *Prison Guard*, by James B. Jacobs and Harold G. Retsky.* Like Esselstyns' work, 31 guards at Joliet, Illinois were respondents to formal interviews. Jacobs and Retsky first document role incompatability:

> It is not surprising that contradictory organizational goals have caused considerable conflict in organizational microunits like the role of the guard. Under the role prescriptions dictated by the rehabilitative ideal, the guard is to relax and to act spontaneously. Inmates are to be understood, not blamed, and formal disciplinary mechanisms should be triggered as infrequently as possible. These are vague directives.
>
> . . . The rehabilitative ideal has no clear directives for the administration of a large scale people processing institution. In order to carry out primary tasks and to manage large numbers of men and materials bureaucratic organization and impersonal treatment are necessary. Furthermore, to distinguish between inmates on the basis of psychological needs leaves the non-professional open to charge of gross bias, discrimination and injustice. [35]

Guards caught in the crossfire of contradictory directives retreat to the good-old-days (iron discipline) of less complexity. Guards are not fearful of reprimands for failure to "meaningfully" communicate with convicts. However, laxness leading to an incident of violence or escape could likely cost him his job; hence he follows, not the Tappan course of "least effort" (guards are not lazy); rather, he follows the McKendrick course of

---

*Retsky, at this writing a correctional counsellor at Stateville Penitentiary Joliet, Illinois, is one of the few former guards to publish seriously Jacobs is on the faculty of Cornell University.

eternal vigilance. In the process, any pretense about rehabilitation fades.

Career development for the guard, Jacobs and Retsky find, is a peculiarly aimless one. Not unlike the early days of the nineteenth century (as Lewis earlier pointed out,) the prospective guard is usually coming off a period of unemployment elsewhere.

Well they had this piece in the paper, see I'm from Hamilton County; that's about 300 miles south of here. And they was wanting guards. I knew several fellows used to work here from down there at the time. The dust—the corn dust—I'm allergic to it and the lint offa cattle. So there's this piece to go to Vermont [an Illinois town] to take a civil service examination.

So I just drove up there that day and I took that civil service examination and in about 3 weeks, they called me up to the Menard Penitentiary.[36]

Despite a fairly good wage at Stateville, it had over 100% of new guard turnover in 1973. The guard's prestige is low. "Guards who we interviewed indicated that even friends do not know what to make of the common belief that prison guards are sadistic and brutal."[37] Like Esselstyn, they found guards withdrawing to themselves; but, unlike Esselstyn's California correctional personnel who did so under circumstances of high morale, Stateville guards clustered because of stigmatization. It was despair—not hope—which brought them together.

Being a prison guard is a dead end. To date no career ladders have been built to reward those guards who have shown particular promise on the job. The skills necessary for guarding are particularly limited to this occupation. While the guard may hope to be promoted through the ranks to sergeant, lieutenant and captain (and even to warden) these decisions are often made early in the guard's career. Without an outside sponsor or an immediate acceptance into the ruling clique the guard will have to wait many years for his promotion to sergeant, if indeed he is ever promoted at all.[38]

Further proof that the degradation of the prison routine negatively affects both the keeper and the kept is vividly portrayed in this study. Higher echelon guards assume that contraband smuggling is being conducted by lower echelon guards. Since the former hold power over the latter, they treat them as guards themselves are taught to treat convicts. Guards are "shaken down" or "inspected" on assignment to see that they are working and, as in the case of inmates, receive "tickets" for infractions. Peer level guards (and, not infrequently, convicts also) are encouraged to write reports on guards. Once these are written, as per convict treatment, guards appear before disciplinary tribunals, but, unlike some convicts, apparently without the prospect of due process safeguards.

I was disciplined once because I took a shoeshine in the barber shop and which only takes about 6 minutes. There was a sign in the shop which had fallen down forbidding this. But I did not see it. A captain spotted me and wrote me up, which was only his job and for which I hold no grudge, but I do feel he could have warned me that he was writing me up. I had no knowledge this had happened until I got a letter two weeks later telling me I had to go before the review board. They gave me three days off without pay. I think I was dealt with harshly. One man shouldn't take food from you.[39]

Jacobs and Retsky analyze the guard's work-world, the division of labor in a prison, the work areas, the cell block, the dependence they develop upon inmates, the security concerns of the tower and the gate (the two ways out), the upper echelon (sergeants, lieutenants and captains), and present a final section on "The Guard's World." It is a world of fear of the unanticipated. While the guard may not carry a weapon (except on the tower), inmates are commonly armed with homemade but lethal weapons.

Tension continually looms over the prison threatening to explode into assault or even riot. This is drilled into the recruit during his first training classes. The guard's manual stresses the need for vigilance and alertness lest the unexpected take one unaware. Rule after rule in this handbook deals with use of force, emergency measures and admonishments for protective and defensive actions. Not only is the new guard exposed to the word of mouth stories of fellow students and training officers, but at the prison he may immediately be exposed to situations which confirm his worst fears. 'When I arrived, I was almost immediately assigned to 'B' house which contained a gallery known as 3-gallery lock up. The inmates here had been under constant lock and key for almost a year. As a result of this they were acting like animals and their verbal abuse scared the shit out of me. I decided then and there to turn in my resignation but was talked out of it by my supervising officer.'[40]

Stereotypic images of inmates abound in the guard's world. The study discovers the upper echelon staff (in Goffman's terms, the "tradition bearers") using language to describe inmates which is reminiscent of that used by Eddy, Wiltse and Lynds over 150 years ago. The members of the upper echelon are the ideologists of the system. The younger guards still frequently identify with inmates. There may be obvious answers to account for the difference. In other professions one might see older workers become "case hardened" and, after much thankless effort, turn to frustration with a distrust of their unappreciative clientele. But it may also be, as the authors suggest, related to the fact that newer guards are from similar socio-economic (and most recently ethnic) backgrounds as the convict. Guards are increasingly chosen from high-reported crime areas, not from the less-reported white suburban areas: One of these newer guards said:

I often put myself in the inmate's position. If I were locked up and the door was locked up and my only contact with authorities would be the officer walking by, it would be frustrating if I couldn't get him to listen to the problems I have. There is nothing worse than being in need of something and not being able to supply it yourself and having the man who can supply it ignore you. This almost makes me explode inside.[41]

Both the treaters and the custodians end up juvenilizing the convict, from apparently different motivations. The keeper makes the inmate dependent through routines of counts, medicine, sick call, communication outside the cellhouse, etc. The treater already believes the convict to be a social, genetic or psychological problem, thereby withdrawing volition from the convict's makeup and in effect simultaneously removing his manhood. The positivist reaches this conclusion through concern for the wayward-individual-patient and the guard through what Jacobs and Retsky found to be efforts "calculated to reduce the inmate to a child."[42]

Interestingly, the closeness, and perhaps the danger in acting otherwise, reduces overt racism in guards—at least in the work situation.

. . .Guards do not openly indicate racist attitudes. Whatever prejudices may exist are kept to one's self. This is in sharp contrast to studies of the police which have found an abundance of openly stated racist comments. Even in informal discussions, we have not heard guards refer to Black inmates as 'niggers' or in other racist terms. We suspect that much of what has been explained as racist attitudes toward inmates in the literature stems from the organizationally sponsored conflict between guards and inmates.

In a prison like Stateville, where Blacks constitute 80% of the inmate population, racism may be a dead letter. There are too few whites to make white/black distinctions significant. The guards come to distinguish instead between the good and the bad inmates among the Blacks.[43]

REFLECTIONS OF A PSEUDO-GUARD

In 1974, Stanley Griffith, a member of the author's staff (Illinois Law Enforcement Commission) and an attorney, registered in Illinois' first Correctional Officer Training Academy class along with the upper echelon staffs of several of the state's prisons.[44] Having gained their confidence, he was accepted as "one of them" in the formal and informal "off-duty" sessions. Griffith found that the officers welcomed the opportunity for training but had special problems. They had been so long uninvolved and neglected that a considerable period of time was taken up in simply letting them talk about accumulated problems. Lack of involvement feeds on itself. It alienates, making feelings of isolation difficult to overcome even when a forum for involvement is finally provided. The officers lacking facile verbal and writing skills are first easily embarrassed, then made hostile by clerical and professional staff who communicate these shortcomings.

There seemed to be a noticeable decline in morale and spirit at breakfast. There was little, if any, breakfast conversation. When I returned to the lounge, I came into the midst of an agitated group of participants. Apparently one of the Academy secretaries had been overheard belittling the Academy participant evaluations which she has been assigned to type. The comment reflected on the poor writing ability of the participants. This was viewed with tremendous anger because throughout the earlier parts of the week Burns [a staff trainer] had bent over backwards to reassure everyone that participants could rely on his not revealing what was discussed to anyone. (E.g., when video-tapes of roleplaying had been used one officer was asked to apply the eraser to the tape.) Anonymity and confidence were ultimately important to free flowing participation. Words can barely describe the hurt, anger, embarrassment and sense of betrayal that pervaded the rest of the morning. However, since no trainer was around to intercept the problem, to reassure the participants, the mood continued into the classroom.[45]

The micro-world of the prison is the guard's world. He does not conceptualize it as well as the professional, but the professional, in his hasty anxiety to introduce program (and since he is not a part of that world), does not accurately conceptualize the problem facing the guard. The professional, encountering the guard's need for an orderly world, recasts the guard's hesitancy into resistance.

A part of the Academy training concerned itself with drug abuse in the prison. The Illinois Drug Abuse Program (IDAP) sent staff to teach the guards about drugs.

[An IDAP Trainer] then proclaimed that they were going to be coming around to visit the institutions to talk to correctional staff about a drug counseling program IDAP plans to run in the institution. He said this is where a real need exists and said that the reason for speaking to guards was to allay their suspicions about what it was they were doing with groups of inmates. At about that point one participant piped up: 'It ain't gonna work.' 'What do you mean.' [A Trainer asked.] . . . Well, the officer tried to explain that the institutions have so many programs which are underutilized already largely because staff is short, space is hard to come by, and because no one ever really plans out how new programs impinge on security, staff's problems of inmate transport, feeding, residence, work assignments and a dozen other little things that need to be adjusted to get an inmate to a program. . . . [The IDAP Trainers] replied—oblivious to what the officer had said—that the guard didn't understand inmates, that IDAP counselors could because [some of them] . . . were ex-offenders, and that by allowing IDAP counselors to work with inmates the guard's job would be easier because inmate tensions would be reduced. At that point the battle lines were drawn until the program drew to a close. . . The speakers preached and did not listen.

The information regarding drug abuse was useful and interesting, but the approach seemed overly alarmist and deficient in the area of actual, practical advice as to how to deal with the problem. It seemed as though this talk was aimed at suburbanites who needed to have their complacency and ignorance knocked out of them—they just had the wrong speech or the wrong audience. The speakers seemed to lay heavy emphasis on their superior ability to communicate, and yet they just couldn't seem to hear what the officers were trying to say about dropping another program into the prison without adequate coordination with the current requirements of the institution.[46]

Another area of guarding which assaults the guards' sense of integrity is the lack of clarity of working rules. The guard force merely looks like a military force, but discretion and accompanying confusion reign nearly supreme. It is hard for a guard to know what will be rewarded.

The group complained that there were no available standards and that officers were left on their own to decide the difference between major and minor infractions—the absence of disciplinary standards impedes consistent application. . . .

The participants complained of faulty communications. They frequently get word of events through inmates. The Stateville group commented favorably on the Warden's staff meetings, but at [another prison] . . . the officers complain they haven't seen a warden for six months.

The officers who routinely work the visitor's gates complained that there are inconsistent standards on visitors and that they are constantly being end-runned by counselors. This touched off a tirade against counselors. First of all, they never write tickets properly. Second, they get little or no orientation to the institution. Third, they have no appreciation of the considerations affecting security. Several officers suggested that all counselors should be broken in by six months' duty as a guard. Furthermore, counselors are never around when you really need them and can never be reached. . . .[47]

Griffith's findings support the contention that the confusion felt by the line worker is a built-in problem in prisons. It is not an Illinois problem. It emerges from a prison work environment which makes contradictory claims about its mission and permits several disciplines to independently "do their thing." Griffith also shows that the guards' focal concern cannot expand to encompass inmate treatment until their more ethnocentric ones are met: safety, accident insurance, legal liabilities, a grievance procedure, more training, involvement in implementing new programs (before they are ·started), rationalization of rank, job titles, work assignments and correlated pay grades, disability pay, retirement, etc.

Brodsky has suggested a vehicle for responding to the guards' need to be heard in the form of a "bill of rights." Not legal rights—rather organizational and interpersonal ones. Speaking to article I of his program he states:

> There are perspectives and experiences correctional officers have to contribute from their direct contact with the offenders. These perspectives represent important information sources upon which relevant decisions should be made.
>
> ... it is uncomfortable to be swept along in a process over which one has no control. ... Correctional officers should serve on boards, committees, and decision-making structures at all levels within penal institutions. ... Correctional officers should have a representative body who would meet with warden candidates and at the least would submit advisory recommendations ... a logical implication is that the same privilege should be allocated to inmates. Thus almost all boards and committees in prisons and all decision making—including warden selection—should have inmate participation and representation.[48]

His full "bill of rights," intended to help produce objectivity, pride, status and skill in the guard contains a self-explanatory six-point program.

1. A Piece of the Action.
2. Clearly Defined Roles and Loyalties.
3. Education and Training Relevant to Job Activities and Career Development.
4. Differential Assignments Related to Skills and Abilities.
5. Informed Behavioral Science Consultation on Managing People.
6. The Development of Professionalism.[49]

The fate of the keeper has always been linked to that of the kept. In colonial days, when the criminal-sinner was being detained and worked, the keeper was called upon to merely watch him. With the advent of the humanitarian reduction of death penalties, the elimination of mutilations, and the accompanying rhetoric of reformation, the guard began a long journey of role obfuscation. The humanitarians did not deliver humanity to convicts. Quite to the contrary, the convict was brutalized, and in this calculated schema the guard was brutalized by having to administer the program. Under the tutelage of the Lynds and Crays, and in the process of debasing the convict, the guard himself was debased. Putting a whip in a man's hand with an eye toward reformation was the first mistake. Lynds was not confused—he had no pretentions about reformation—but after he was swept out of office the guard was still holding the whip, cellular confinement was still the order of the day, and reformation remained the rhetoric.

The guard's role under the least complicated circumstances is unique, with no outside counterpart. Cressey has likened it to its closest model—the slave overseer.[50] Over the years many disciplines entered the prison to ply their trades, but they only complicated the role of the guard. Warden Casseles of Sing-Sing prison captured this plight well when he said (1971):

First psychiatry had the answer, then education was the answer, now it's environment—that made the prisoner the way he is? We're no longer trying to force a prisoner into a particular mold, so we have no criteria any more for running a prison. The only criterion is to keep it trouble free.

But maybe it's trouble free because the lid is on tight, who knows? You don't know when to join them or what side to take—and the nature of everything today is taking sides. The same thing that happened in Attica could happen to me. . . .[51]

Wherever prisons were built, men came to work at them but not usually as a first choice. The prison was close, sometimes the only industry around, and sometimes it was sought out by the unemployed. Workers came to it, donned a uniform and were alternately told that their role with prisoners was to keep, whip, counsel, treat, handle from a distance, get close, understand, but to shoot them if necessary. The leaders in the field did not serve the guards well; the literature was confusing, and, while administrators ordered, they did not involve guards. Guards were paid poorly, given low status and worked under hazardous conditions at hours out of tune with their culture. Politicians used them for votes, support, campaign funds and, opportunistically, to obtain more severe criminal sentences. And each time the guard agreed and took another step in the direction of the radical right, the net result was to heat up his own work environment with more desperate convicts in the cellhouse who were facing longer sentences with less hope. While reformers blamed guards for the miseries of the prison, professionals disdained them. Today's prison guard is the product of bewildering confusion. His education and ethos leave him poorly equipped to deal with his circumstance. He is disaffected, alienated and survives as a fossil in the anachronistic fortress prison. Winston Churchill said, with some relevance in this case, "We shape our buildings and then our buildings shape us." The guard has always been linked in a shared fate with the convict. They have both come from the same socio-economic group. They became victims of society's ambivalence in relation to crime and its treatment. In their mutual anger, the keeper and kept have only occasionally caught glimmers of their common nemesis—the caging of one set of human beings by another. Jackson once caught that glimmer.

> But the days and months that a guard has to spend on the ground (sometimes locked in a wing or cell-block with no gun guard) are what destroy anything at all that was good, healthy, or social about him before. Fear begets fear. And we come out with two groups of schizoids, one guarding the other. The spiral extends outward and up.[52]

VIENNA, ILLINOIS

It is nearly an 800 mile round trip for a Chicago visitor to see an inmate of the Vienna Correctional Facility close to the Illinois-Kentucky border. Opened in 1971, the new facility appears to be a suburban community at first sight. Cellblocks are neighborhoods, cells are rooms, the big yard is a town square, the chapel is a church, there are workshops and shopping areas, a barber, gymnasium, music facility, and a spacious school, library and gymnasium—each of these are separate detached facilities. The rooms all have locks, but the inmates (residents) have the keys. The academic program boasts 32 courses (day and night), but only 168 of the 300 students are convicts, the others are townspeople who come on campus as fellow students. Nearby Shawnee Community College furnishes the faculty. At least half of the convict population is black while only two families in the town are black. Vienna also represents the "rural types" Schwartz described as conservative, racist and back-lashers. The difference here is the condition of confinement and therefore the definition of the situation. Vienna has the full range of offenders from swindlers to murderers. But they are defined as safe, and are treated as aspiring humans. They respond, given the normal range of problems with 450 people in a congregate living situation, within the tolerable range of acceptability.

There are no cellblocks to break out of, no walls to climb or towers to shoot from. If a convict leaves, the countryside is no alarmed by what the *Chicago Daily News* recently described as "Killer Cons"; rather, they are "walk aways." In nine years, out of an aggregate of 2,500 men, 23 have left illegally. Vienna has been riot-free since it opened. The town and area are engaged with Vienna in an educational and economic symbiotic relationship. While Stateville, 350 miles to the north has a 102% new staff turnover rate, Vienna has a prospective staff waiting list of 1400 people!

The prisoners operate a multi-county radio-dispatched emergency ambulance service. It has already saved lives of area residents injured in accidents in remote locations of the vast rural expanse it services. In 1974, about 35 women prisoners moved to Vienna, making it one of the largest co-educational correctional facilities in the nation.

But it was not always that way. Under a previous administration in the early 1960s, Illinois had embarked upon a program to build a "minimum security" complex. The original design called for three-story four-winged facilities (nine of them), with central control furnished from a master bullet-proof unit in the middle of an X-shaped unit. The central unit was actually an internal fortress which could rake its four protruding wings with unobstructed fire power.[53] The author visited the only such unit built of the nine projected. It stands at the edge of Vienna's main facility. The leading Republican legislator in the area apologetically explained, pointing to the old facility, "well, that was billyclub Ragen's [former Corrections Director] idea of minimum custody." We didn't like it." What he apparently meant to convey was that the town felt safer with an actual minimum custody facility where there was very little danger of fire power being brought to bear on anyone. It is not at all clear from previous experiences with "urban-types," who are presumably more "sensitive" to ethnic differences, that they would tolerate such a minimal grade of custody in their neighborhoods.

If the facility has a humanizing effect on the convicts and "rural-type" citizens, it had an equally salubrious effect on guards. A study finding that both guards and convicts are humanized in this kind of work environment is the only spark of optimism one can locate in the history of guarding.[54] It corroborates the axiom that we come to believe and act in accord with the conditions under which we are socially structured.

108 / "... We Are the Living Proof ..."

FOOTNOTES

[1]D.R. Cressey, "Prison Organizations," in James March, ed., *Handbook of Organizations*, Chicago: Rand McNally, 1965, pp. 1023-1070.

[2]W. David Lewis, *From Newgate to Dannemora*, Ithaca, New York: Cornell University Press, 1965, p. 60.

[3]*Ibid.*, p. 38.

[4]*Ibid.*, p. 142.

[5]*Ibid*, p. 150.

[6]*Ibid.*, p. 133.

[7]*Ibid.*, p. 131.

[8]*Ibid.*

[9]*Ibid.*, p. 31.

[10]Price Chenault, "Education," in Paul W. Tappan, ed., *Contemporary Correction*, New York: McGraw-Hill Book Co., Inc., 1951, p. 254.

[11]Charles McKendrick, "Custody and Discipline," in *op. cit.*, n 10, Tappan, p. 167.

[12]*Ibid.*, pp. 162-163.

[13]*Op. cit.*, n 10, Tappan, p. 3.

[14]*Ibid.*, p. 4.

[15]*Theoretical Studies in Social Organization of the Prison*, SSRC, New York: Holt, Rinehard and Co., 1960.

[16]*Ibid.*, p. 4.

[17]Robert M. Carter, Daniel Glaser, and Leslie T. Wilkins, *Correctional Institutions*, New York: J.B. Lippincott Co., 1972.

[18]Clarence Schrag, "Some Foundations for a Theory of Corrections," in *op. cit.*, n 17, Carter, Glaser and Wilkins, pp. 149-172.

[19]Thomas P. Wilson, "Patterns of Management and Adaptations to Organizational Roles: A Study of Prison Inmates," in *op. cit.*, n 17, Carter, Glaser and Wilkins, pp. 248-262.

[20]*Op. cit.*, n 11, McKendrick, pp. 159-160.

[21]Ramsey Clark, "Prisons: Factories of Crime," in Burton M. Atkins and Henry R. Glick, eds., *Prisons, Protest, and Politics*, Englewood Cliffs, N.J.: Prentice-Hall, Inc., 1972, p. 18.

[22]Jessica Mitford, "Kind and Usual Punishment in California," in *op. cit.*, n 21, Atkins and Glick, p. 157.

[23]*Op. cit.*, n 11, McKendrick, pp. 161-166.

[24]Frank Loveland, "Classification in the Prison System," in *op. cit.*, n 10, Tappan, p. 102.

[25]Karl Menninger, "The Crime of Punishment," in *op. cit.*, n 21, Atkins and Glick, p. 49.

[26]Annual Chief Justice Earl Warren Conference sponsored by the Roscoe Pound-American Trial Lawyers Foundation, *A Program for Prison Reform*, June 9-10, 1972, p. 50.

[27]George Jackson, *The Village Voice*, September 10, 1970, as cited in Leonard Orland, *Justice, Punishment, and Treatment: The Correctional*

Process, New York: The Free Press, A division of the MacMillan Publishing Co., Inc., 1973, p. 131.

[28] *Op. cit.*, n 27, Orland, p. 139.

[29] T.C. Esselstyn, "The Social System of Correctional Workers," *Crime and Delinquency*, April, 1966, p. 117.

[30] *Ibid.*, pp. 118-119.

[31] *Ibid.*, p. 119.

[32] *Ibid.*

[33] *Ibid.*, p. 120.

[34] *Ibid.*, pp. 121-122.

[35] James B. Jacobs and Harold G. Retsky, "Prison Guard," *Urban Life and Culture*, Vol. 4, No. 1, April, 1975, pp. 7-8.

[36] *Ibid.*, p. 9.

[37] *Ibid.*, p. 10.

[38] *Ibid.*, pp. 10-11.

[39] *Ibid.*, p. 12.

[40] *Ibid.*, pp. 22-23.

[41] *Ibid.*, p. 23.

[42] *Ibid.*, p. 25.

[43] *Ibid.*, pp. 26-27.

[44] Stanley Griffith, "A Training Experience as a Pseudo-Guard," 1974 (unpublished, 50 pages plus appendices).

[45] *Ibid.*, p. 34.

[46] *Ibid.*, pp. 37-39.

[47] *Ibid.*, pp. 25-26.

[48] Stanley L. Brodsky, Ph.D., "A Bill of Rights for the Correctional Officer," *Federal Probation*, June 1974, p. 38.

[49] *Ibid.*, pp. 38-40.

[50] Edwin H. Sutherland and Donald R. Cressey, *Criminology* (9th Edition), Philadelphia: J.B. Lippincott Co., 1974, p. 515.

[51] Steven V. Roberts, "Prisons Feel a Mood of Protest," in *op. cit.*, n 21, Atkins and Glick, p. 104.

[52] *Op. cit.*, n 27, Jackson, pp. 131-132.

[53] William G. Nagel, *The New Red Barn: A Critical Look at the Modern American Prison*, New York: Walker and Co., 1973, p. 69.

[54] Arthur L. Paddock and James D. McMillin, "Final Report Vienna Staff Training Project," Southern Illinois University, Carbondale, dated June 30, 1972 (mimeo., 18 pages, plus 11 tables).

3
From
Patient to Plaintiff

There is a passion in the human heart stronger than the desire to be free from injustice and wrong, and that is the desire to inflict injustice and wrong upon others, and men resent more keenly an attempt to prevent them from oppressing other people than they do oppression from which they themselves suffer.

Lord Palmerston, 1859

In this chapter we will examine two parallel but related phenomena: (1) the research outcomes of experimental and demonstration rehabilitative services introduced into corrections during the last twenty years, and (2) the erosion of the court's traditional "hands-off" doctrine in relation to several different dimensions of prisoners' rights pleas. The two processes arise in different contexts but reflect propitious historical and political opportunities for expression. Later we will examine the processes using the analytic position that both phenomena represent attempts at self-empowerment by clinicians and prisoners respectively.

On the part of the clinicians, rehabilitation represents their attempt to establish their world-view, and thus their political power in the correctional kingdom. This was to be accomplished through a series of clinically-oriented program services. The program services, requiring the commitment of substantial manpower and financial resources, are here seen as the professionals' (social work, psychology, applied sociology, psychiatry, academic and vocational education) influence attempts to establish its pocket power in corrections. Later, as a result of the lack of results with "programs," that did not change the prisoners' status or alleviate the onerous conditions of his confinement, the convicts turned to the courts for relief. Moreover, the human rights explosion of the 1960s created an atmosphere in which both the activist public and the judiciary were amenable to the granting of that relief. But "relief" conveys only a part of the meaning. If such relief could indeed successfully ameliorate some of the burdensome conditions of confinement, it could also be considered, by both the keeper and the kept, as an attack upon the power of those responsible for the imposition and maintenance of those conditions. The smallest victory gives heart to the desperate and panics the manager. You must, in Warden Jameson's words, ". . . beat the inmates to the punch."

We will trace the course of the treatment adventure and its outcome, then analyze the rapidly developing correctional case law. We see the clinical programs as influence attempts *on* convicts by professionals, and view the legal assaults as influence attempts made *by* convicts to affect their low status. We will assess the impact of both, trying to illuminate some useful next steps in corrections.

PROGRAM SERVICES AND "THE INTERCHANGEABILITY OF PENAL MEASURES"

Surely it is ironic that although treatment ideology purports to look beyond the criminal's crime to the whole personality, and bases its claims to sweeping discretionary power on this rationale, it measures its success against the single factor of an absence of reconviction for a criminal act.

American Friends Service Committee Task Force

Using a panoply of interpersonal relations techniques revolving around the individual, the small group, the large group (cottage, cellblock or other institutional units), dozens of different programs have emerged in the last quarter of a century. As soon as proponents enthusiastically described their latest panacea in professional journals, it swept through the prisons. Some institutions simply divided their entire populations into small groups, promiscuously assigned staff to them, and declared that the convicts were now in group therapy. Many convicts quietly called these programs the biggest collective farce in prison history. As in so many other frontier programs, California led the nation.

Hundreds of new employees found their way into prisons, probation and parole demonstration projects. In 1967, the prospects and enthusiasm were still very high.

In several senses corrections today may stand at the threshhold of a new era, promising resolution of a significant number of the problems that have vexed it throughout its development. At the very least, it is developing the theory and practical groundwork for a new approach to rehabilitation of the most important group of offenders—those, predominantly young and lower-class, who are not committed to crime as a way of life and do not pose serious dangers to the community. It is beginning to accumulate evidence from carefully controlled experimentation that may help guide its efforts more scientifically. Its increasing focus on rehabilitation has, according to recent opinion polls, found widespread acceptance among members of the general public. And, sitting as it were at the crossroads of a dozen disciplines—among them law, sociology, social work, psychology, and psychiatry—dealing with problems of poverty, unemployment, education, and morality, corrections has also attracted the interest of increasing numbers of talented people.°

We will survey the results of the following treatment attempts: education, individual treatment, group treatment, community treatment, length of sentences, halfway houses and prevention programs.

I. EDUCATION

To date, no conclusive evidence has been presented in support of the commonly held belief that a rehabilitative institutional program of academic or vocational training is effective in reducing the rate of recidivism among offenders. For example, a New York prison study (1964) found that recidivism was unaffected by academic progress. An exception was found for the highest 7% of subjects (who also were possessors of high I.Q.'s and had previously excelled in free schools and in the institution's school)—not an unexpected outcome. [1]

Studies of vocational programs have generally reported

° The President's Commission on Law Enforcement and the Administration of Justice.

negative results as well. One such study of California male prisoners who received training in bakery or auto body-fender repair, when compared with a matched group receiving no program, showed, six months to a year later, that "trained parolees had significantly more major difficulties with the law than would have been predicted from their Base Expectancy scores, while a comparable group of *post hoc* matched untrained parolees had just about as much difficulty as might be expected."[2]

Negative results were also obtained from women prisoner vocational programs. Again in California, the experimental group, after training for five months to a year in a variety of skills, performed about the same on parole as the untrained group. Both groups had the same Base Expectancy score, similar records, and drug histories. After a year, the group had amassed the same recidivism rates.[3] A number of other studies have yielded similarly negative results, including Zivan's (1966) multifacet vocational guidance program at the Children's Village in Dobbs Ferry, New York;[4] Jacobson's (1965) social skill development program;[5] and Kettering's (1972) "exploration experiment" in vocational and academic education for women in a Milwaukee jail.[6] A promising study by Sullivan (1967), using academic education and special training in IBM equipment, showed a 66% failure rate for controls against a 48% rate for the trainees. But, in examining the data, Martinson states:

[It] appears that this difference emerged only between the controls and those who had successfully *completed* the training. When one compares the control group with all those who had been *enrolled* in the program, the difference disappears. Moreover, during this study the random assignment procedure between experimental and control groups seems to have broken down, so that towards the end, better risks had a greater chance of being assigned to the special program.[7]

Results with adult males are the most discouraging. Martinson surveyed six such programs from 1948-1965, concluding that they all fail for possibly the following reasons: the programs

1. have no relationship to life outside the institution;
2. teach skills which are obsolete on the job market;
3. are incapable of overcoming the deleterious effects of imprisonment; and
4. may have nothing to do with the parolee's proclivity for a life of crime.[8]

II. INDIVIDUAL TREATMENT

In the field of individual counseling for correctional inmates the results have generally, with one or two exceptions, been rather disappointing. Guttman's (1963) study of such a program for young males at the Nelles School (California) proved individual counseling to be ineffective in reducing the rate of recidivism.[9] In another study conducted by Guttman during the same year but at a different institution, it was found that individual psychotherapy was actually related to a somewhat higher rate of parole violation.[10] A lack of improvement in parole revocation and first suspension rates for California youthful offenders receiving psychiatric treatment was also found by Adams (1959, 1961).[11]

The Pilot Intensive Counseling Organization (PICO) in California tried to gauge the effects of individual psychotherapy conducted by clinical psychologists on imprisoned young adults. The young men were first classified according to "amenability to treatment" which was

ascertained through pooled clinical judgments. ... Although the most salient ingredient of amenability appeared to be the quality of anxiety, the typical amenable ward might be more fully described as 'bright, verbal and anxious.' In addition to these primary characteristics, the judgment of amenability was also influenced by evidence of 'awareness of problems,' 'insight,' 'desire to change,' and 'acceptance of treatment.'[12]

Four random groups were created: treated amenable (TA), treated non-amenable (TN), control amenable (CA), control non-amenable (CN). Thirty-three months after release, the TA group totaled far less time in custody than all the others. Although the other groups did not show marked discrepancies among themselves, the TN group did the most poorly. Inadequate arrest records and a vague set of reasons for violations, reduced whatever findings emerged to conjecture.[13] However, the TN's very poor performance suggests that it might be better *not* to treat convicts rather than risk using the "wrong" treatment.

In studying the outcomes of individual psychotherapy on delinquent teenage girls, Adams (1959, 1961) reported no significant effects. It was found, interestingly enough, that when therapy was conducted by a psychiatrist or psychologist, the rate of parole suspension was nearly two and one-half times greater than when a social worker was used![14]

California's Intensive Treatment Program was directed toward a prisoner gaining new insight into his problems. It was found, however, that this "psychodynamically" oriented program did not improve recidivism rates.[15] In fact, it was this specific study that led to California's reduced emphasis on individual counseling in its penal system and moved it instead to an increasing reliance on group methods.[16]

III. GROUP TREATMENT

Many variations of group treatment * have been instituted in prisons, but to date they have not produced either substantial findings or long-lasting positive effects. For the most part, results tend to be vague and inconclusive because of the lack of uniform

---

*Group counseling, group therapy, group psychotherapy, psychodrama, guided group interaction, positive peer culture, variants of Maxwell Jones' "therapeutic community," such as milieu treatment, community meetings, Lawrence Kohlberg's "just community," and variants on William Glaser's reality therapy, a series of group methods emerging from self-help groups: Alcoholics Anonymous, Synanon, Daytop, under the rubric of encounter groups.

criteria for judging the success or failure of these programs Kassenbaum, Ward, and Wilmer (1971) reported on a three-year followup study in California in which medium security prisoner were randomized into three T-groups and a C-group. Greenberg, in summarizing, states that none of the different group therapies could account for an ". . . effect on outcome for the prisoners as a whole, or for any distinguishable sub-group of prisoners."[17]

In another California study of group methods, randomization was again available for an "intensive living-group treatment' program. The first year's statistical significance in favor of the T-group eroded in the second year.[18]

In other programs, although positive results were obtained, it seems doubtful that the group counseling was solely responsible. For example, Truax (1966) found that girls participating in group psychotherapy were likely to spend less time incarcerated in the future.[19] It must be noted, however, that therapists were specially selected for their "empathy" and "non-possessive warmth." Thus, it could not be determined if the program's success was attributable to the group counseling provided or to the personalities of the staff members (Hawthorne Effect), or, in fact, to a combination of the two. As a result, group programs are difficult to assess. They seem to work well when new and when the therapists are "good people." But the different types of group programs (differing in size, frequency of sessions, age, sex, training of therapist, etc.) all combine to help keep the assessment results soft.[20]

No one has yet assessed the more plausible, to-be-expected, secondary gains from these programs such as reduced tensions as a result of emotional ventilation, reduced violence, less destruction of institutional property and generally a better behaved inmate population. The irony of such a finding would suggest that for all the clinical claims they reduce to better custody while not swelling considerably the pool of clinical redeemables.

IV. COMMUNITY TREATMENT

Norman A. Carlson, Director of the Federal Bureau of Prisons, recently stated, "The only thing we can say with certainty is that we still know comparatively little about how to deal effectively with offenders."[21] In light of the available data, it is embarrassingly obvious that we have not been able to devise effective methods of rehabilitating inmates inside the walls. Can we, however, apply these same treatment modalities in different settings (i.e., outside the walls)? Will they produce any more significant effects on offenders?

Massimo's (1963) study indicates that individual psychotherapy may be successful in the community setting.[22] Massimo's "pragmatic" psychotherapeutic approach included both insight therapy and vocational counseling. A decline in recidivism rates was due, at least in part, to the program's small size and its use of abundantly enthusiastic therapists.[23] Adamson (1965), evaluating another program employing individual therapy, found no significant difference in recidivism.[24] Similar findings were reported by the Schwitzgebels (1963, 1964). They found that through the various forms of therapy they employed improvements, at least in the attitudes if not in the arrest rates, of their boys were evident.[25]

Studies of group counseling in the community vary in their conclusions from mildly optimistic (Adams, 1965)[26] to quite pessimistic (O'Brien, 1961),[27] wherein group psychotherapy resulted in the experimental subjects performing worse than controls on a series of psychological tests.

A great deal of work has been done in an effort to determine whether the *means* of supervision and treatment of the offender who has been placed on probation or parole makes any significant difference. One such group of studies found, in comparing the use of probation with other sentences for offenders, that "probation may make an offender's future chances better than if he had been sent to prison. Or, at least, probation may not worsen those chances."[28] This finding has been supported in a study by the state of Michigan (1963) where "expansion in the use of probation actually improved recidivism rates"[29]—though the groups and systems studied were not matched for comparability.

Babst (1965) compared a group of adult male parolees with a similar group of offenders placed on probation and found that the first offense probationers committed fewer violations and "did no worse if they were recidivists."[30] Again, the problem of different standards of evaluating their respective changes arose between the probation and parole agencies. There was no way of knowing what would have happened if the men had been put right on parole, skipping the prison experience.[31] Summarizing a series of other similar studies Martinson concludes that:

> First-offender status, or age or type of offense was more important than the form of treatment in determining future recidivism. An offender with a 'favorable' prognosis will do better than one without, it seems, no matter how you distribute 'good' or 'bad,' 'enlightened' or 'regressive' treatments among them.[32]

Several studies have been made on the effect of the varying intensity of parole supervision on recidivism, mainly by the state of California parole agency. In one of the more elaborate ones, T-group members were placed in intensive 15-man caseload supervision for a time and then were placed on normal 90-man caseload assignments—recidivism, however, was unaffected. Increasing the T-caseload to 30 as well as the length of supervision did not improve results.[33] In Phase III, comparisons of parolees on full caseloads as opposed to parolees on caseloads 50% of the normal size (now 72 and 35-man caseloads) showed a slight improvement for the latter group after one year—but parole officer bias also played a role.[34] Variations of caseload numbers and studies of risk types failed to uncover significant leads to successfully guide future practice.[35]

It has been shown in both the United States and in England that a large proportion of those placed on probation now receive only nominal supervision and a minimum of "treatment" of any kind. Lohman's U. S. Federal Probation and Parole study (1967) failed to show a significant difference in the success rates of offenders who had been randomly assigned to "intensive," "ideal," "normal" and "minimium" supervision caseloads ranging from 25-man to 125-man caseloads.[36]

Studies in California (1963) tried reducing parole supervision sharply; "good risks" assigned to minimal supervision caseloads had the same failure rate as their counterparts on conventional caseloads.[37] Unsupervised parolees compared to ordinary caseload counterparts could not be differentiated from each other by success rates,[38] but "early discharge from parole is associated with somewhat lower rates of known criminal involvement."[39]

V. LENGTH OF SENTENCE

It has been found that for first offenders and recidivists of all age groups, fines and discharges are much more effective than either probation or imprisonment.[40] The length of sentence has received wide study: Narloch (1959),[41] Bernsten (1965)[42] and the State of California (1956)[43] all suggest that inmates going on parole earlier than scheduled or expected do no better or no worse than those inmates going on parole as scheduled. Hood and Sparks cite Johnson (1962),[44] Mueller (1965)[45] and Havel (1956),[46] all reporting similar findings in California. Davis (1964) also found no correlation between the frequency of probation use, in lieu of incarceration and the rates of revocation.[47] While recidivism rates do not seem to decline with early release or probation for a higher percentage of offenders, the rates do not increase when these measures are used. But there appears to be a danger of increasing the crime rate with a rise in the number of potentially repetitive offenders in the community.[48]

Weeks' (1958) study of the Highfields experiment in New Jersey lends further support to the theory that longer institutional sentences, even for a reformative purpose, are no more effective in preventing recidivism than shorter ones.[49]

"Weeks found that for youthful offenders sentences of three to four months in an open institution with a liberal regime and group counseling produced about the same results as a two year reformatory sentence."[50]

Glaser's (1964) data on the federal system, though uncontrolled for degree of risk within offender categories, showed a curvilinear relationship between shortness of sentence and rate of parole success. His findings reflected the unexpected high success rate of 73% for those who served less than one year. This rate declined to 65% for men serving up to two years and to 56% for those serving up to three years, but the rate rose to 60% for those serving more than three years.[51]

An important variable in the effect of sentence length on recidivism is the type of offender. Hammond (1963) found that shortening the sentence did not improve the recidivism rate for "hardcore recidivists."[52] Similar results were obtained by another British study,[53] by Bernsten's (1965) Danish study,[54] as well as others.

VI. HALFWAY HOUSES

The use of halfway house programs for released prisoners has been widely evaluated. The studies have not been optimistic. In Gary, Indiana, a halfway house for 18 to 25-year-old males provided jobs, residence, and counseling. Living in was completely voluntary and did not affect parole status. At the end of one year, the researchers' failure rate for residents was 5% *greater* than for nonresidents.[55] Other published evaluations of halfway houses in California demonstrate no measurable effect on recidivism outcomes.[56]

VII. PREVENTION

The Cambridge-Somerville Youth Project° was a ten-year study in delinquency and crime prevention, begun in the late

---

°We review this older experiment because of the recurrent and increasing attention being afforded some new "prediction" devices.

1930s. Six hundred and fifty boys under the age of 12 were selected, some of whom were *"believed destined"* to become delinquent. The subjects were grouped into controlled treatment groups each of 325, on the basis of about 100 factors (e.g., age, education, personality, intelligence, religion, etc.). This T-group was given help in educational problems, received special counseling, guidance, health and recreational services. The C-group received no services. This study was one of the first on this order of magnitude (1,900 potential cases were nominated) and enthusiasm. About a quarter of the group became officially delinquent as compared to 3% less than a quarter of the C-group. There were many other findings, but the key outcome of this elaborate experiment was the unfeasibility of identifying predelinquents.[57]

Another similar program divided hundreds of high school girls into a T-group receiving the latest (1965) array of therapeutic services to prevent them from becoming delinquent. The C-group, unserved, did better.[58] But we did learn that age alone seems to work with the young people eroding the delinquent's path to adult criminality.[59]

Walter C. Bailey (1966) carried out a survey of 100 reports of evaluation projects in treatment strategies of all sorts and concluded:

> Therefore, it seems quite clear that, on the basis of this sample of outcome reports with all of its limitations, evidence supporting the efficacy of correctional treatment is slight, inconsistent, and of questionable reliability.

> This negative conclusion regarding correctional treatment is in general agreement with those drawn from several reviews of the correctional outcome literature. For example, in 1952 Dalton reported his fairly pessimistic impression of the value of counseling techniques in probation work. In 1954, Kirby reviewed the literature on the effects of treating criminals and delinquents and concluded that 'most treatment programs are based on hope and perhaps informed speculation rather than on verified information.'

Two years later, Witmer* and Tufts reviewed the literature on the effectiveness of delinquency prevention programs and concluded that such programs had not been notably effective. . . .

But how can we account for the apparent fact that although the operational means and resources of correctional outcome research have substantially improved, there has been no apparent progress in the actual demonstration of the validity of various types of correctional treatment? There probably could be no one answer to this question which, at least for a period, must remain unanswered. However, one or more of the following explanations may be suggestive: (1) there is the possibility that reformative treatment is 'really' ineffectual either in its own right or as a consequence of the ambivalence of the 'crime and punishment' setting in which it takes place; (2) one may hazard that much of the correctional treatment currently practiced is not corrective and that little of the rehabilitation work being done should be dignified by their term *treatment;* (3) it may be that some types of correctional treatment are 'really' effective with some types of individuals under certain conditions, but so far we have been unable to operationally describe the independent variable (treatment), reliably identify in terms of treatment response the type of behavioral patterns being treated, adequately control the conditions under which such treatment takes place, or reliably delineate and measure relevant indices of the dependent variable; (4) perhaps much of the reformative treatment currently practiced is based upon the 'wrong' theories of delinquent and the criminal behavior.[60]

Nigel Walker sums up the dilemma of inconclusivity of treatment services in a pithy phrase suggesting what we have going on is "the interchangeability of penal measures." Some treatments apparently work differently for particular types of offenders. Along a continuum of "other things being equal" Walker lays out the probabilities as follows:

---

*Of the Cambridge-Somerville Youth Project.

1. females are less likely to recidivate after a sentence has been carried out;
2. older offenders are less likely to repeat after a sentence;
3. the more 'priors' an offender has the more he will be reconvicted;
4. the more time he has spent in prison the likelier he is to be reconvicted; and
5. reconviction rates are higher for certain type of crimes (burglary) than others (sexual offenders).[61]

Walker cautions, therefore, against what he sees as methodological shortcomings in most "success rate" studies. He summarizes the focal sequential results of the hundreds of investigations which have been reported.

(a) in general, *fines* are followed by fewer reconvictions than other measures;
(b) *heavy fines* are followed by fewer reconvictions than light fines;
(c) in general, next to fines, the measure followed by fewer reconvictions seemed to be *discharge* (absolute or conditional). The exceptions were the older 'first offenders' aged thirty or more who received a discharge; these tended to have an abnormally *high* reconviction rate;
(d) *imprisonment* was followed by more reconvictions than fines or discharges;
(e) but *imprisonment* compared better with other measures when applied to 'first offenders';
(f) *probation* was followed by more reconvictions than imprisonment;
(g) *probation* compared rather better with the other measures when it was applied not to 'first offenders' but to offenders with previous convictions (but was still the least often effective);
(h) for some reason, however, 'first offenders' convicted of house-breaking showed lower reconviction rates than

any other kind of probationer when placed on *probation*.[62]

Morris and Hawkins, in discussing Walker's interchangeability hypothesis, state that it may mean that imprisonment, which has produced

... the major penological problems of our time—over-crowding, shortages of adequate staff and equipment and all the social and economic cost of maintaining penal institutions—can be drastically reduced, without any increase in reconviction rates simply by sentencing fewer offenders to imprisonment.[63]

Leslie Wilkins stated in his report to the Council of Europe on *The Effectiveness of Punishment and Other Measures of Treatment*, "there is much that is unknown," yet at the same time, "much is known." In relation to policy-making for penal treatments, he proposes the following:

1. Humanitarian systems of treatment (e.g. probation) are no less effective in reducing the probability of recidivism than severe forms of punishment.

2. Money (if not souls) can be saved by revised treatment systems. The cheaper systems are more often than not also the more humanitarian.

3. Much money is wasted in many countries by the provision of unnecessary security precautions. The public pays very heavily for the marginal gains that may be provided by repressive custodial apparatus and systems.[64]

We now turn to an examination of the legal assaults on the penal system made by convicts in the last decade.

UP FROM "SLAVE OF THE STATE"

The emergence of the convict with the legal status of a "slave of the state°" also brought with it a dictum ". . . that a man who has violated a law is not entitled to as much of society's resources and consideration as the non-offender."[65]

The courts have traditionally kept a respectable distance from prisons with a "hands-off" posture, displaying a great reluctance to interfere with prison management. "Hands-off" is a doctrine—not a rule of law. Its policy implication is one of judicial abstention.[66]

> The rationale behind the doctrine is that prison officials should have a wide area of discretion in the administration of their institutions. It was felt that the court should not interfere in areas where it lacked the expertise that prison administrators possessed, that the operation of prisons was an administrative function, and that judicial interference might detract from penal goals. As the primary goal of incarceration has moved toward rehabilitation, judicial reluctance to intrude into areas of prison administration has eased. Initially courts would act only in rare and exceptional circumstances. Today the view is that 'under our constitutional system, the payment which society exacts for the transgression of the law does not include regulating the transgressor to arbitrary and capricious action.'[67]

The consequence of the "hands-off doctrine" had been to place the "prison officials in a position of virtual invulnerability and absolute power."[68]

We turn now to an examination of major substantive areas to see how prisoners have attacked this "absolute power." We will review the major cases under the following rubrics: challenges to

---

°"[The prisoner] has, as a consequence of his crime, not only forfeited his liberty, but all his personal rights except those which the law in its humanity accords to him. He is for the time being the slave of the state." *Ruffin v. the Commonwealth of Virginia*, (1871).

conditions of confinement, First Amendment religious rights, rights of access to the media, procedural due process and the rights of access to the courts.

I. CHALLENGES TO THE CONDITIONS OF CONFINEMENT

Definition

Conditions of confinement encompass all aspects of prison life, and the cases are correspondingly numerous. We present a sample. The most usual means of challenging prison conditions is in federal court in a 42 U.S.C. § 1983 suit for deprivation of a federally-protected right under color of state law.°

Usually, the constitutional basis for these suits is the Eighth Amendment's ban on cruel and unusual punishment, though the due process clause of the Fourteenth Amendment is sometimes invoked. Using these constitutional provisions, prisoners have challenged, *inter alia,* physical brutality, conditions in solitary confinement, punishment for improper reasons, failure of prison personnel to protect inmates from assault and other injuries, and failure to provide needed medical care.

These suits have been faciliated by legal developments which have broadened the scope of the Eighth Amendment. Once considered to apply only to physical tortures used in England and Colonial America, the Eighth Amendment was regarded as essentially a dead letter throughout the nineteenth century. But in 1910, the Supreme Court articulated a more flexible view of the amendment: "Time works changes, brings into existence new conditions and purposes. Therefore, a principle to be vital must be capable of wider application than the mischief which gave it birth." *Weems v. United States,* 217 U.S. 349, 373 (1910). And in *Trop v. Dulles,* 356 U.S. 86 (1958), the Court determined that a

---

°However, it has recently been held that federal habeas corpus is available to state prisoners to challenge the conditions of confinement, even where the remedy sought is not release. *Wilwording v. Swenson,* 404 U.S. 249 (1971).

punishment may violate the Eighth Amendment even though no physical mistreatment is involved. In his majority opinion, Chief Justice Warren said the Eighth Amendment "must draw its meaning from the evolving standards of decency that mark the progress of a maturing society. . . ." (At 101.)

Today, a punishment may be deemed cruel and unusual on several grounds. First, it may be so inhumane in itself as to "shock the conscience"; this conforms to the original meaning of the Eighth Amendment. Second, the punishment may violate the Eighth Amendment even though it is not cruel and unusual in itself, if it is disproportionate to the gravity of the offense for which it is imposed. Finally, a court may find a particular penal measure violative of the Eighth Amendment if it is more severe than necessary to achieve a legitimate penal goal.

1. Corporal punishment and physical brutality

The two major cases in the area of corporal punishment are *Talley v. Stephens*, 247 F. Supp. 683 (E.D. Ark. 1965) and *Jackson v. Bishop*, 404 F. 2d 571 (8th Cir. 1968). Both cases examined the constitutionality of whipping as punishment in the Arkansas prison system. By the time these cases were adjudicated, flogging as a means of disciplining prisoners had been outlawed by statute in most of the other states.

In *Talley v. Stephens, supra,* three Arkansas state prisoners brought a suit under § 1983 of the Civil Rights Act to enjoin, among other things, the use of the strap as punishment for rule infractions. The record in the case indicated that the offenses for which whipping could be imposed were not specified in prison regulations, nor were the number of blows which could be inflicted. As a result, both matters were left within the discretion of the administering officer. Predictably, abuses were frequent.

The plaintiffs contended that whipping was, *per se*, violative of the Eighth Amendment. The Court, with Judge Henley writing the majority opinion, was unwilling to go that far.

However, Judge Henley enjoined the whippings as they were then administered, ordering the State Penitentiary Board to promulgate safeguards, e.g., limitations on the number of blows to be administered and fair warning to the inmates of the offenses that may result in whipping.

Following the decision in *Talley v. Stephens*, the Board did draw up some standards for the administration of corporal punishment in Arkansas. They failed to prevent abuse and the constitutionality of whipping was challenged again in *Jackson v Bishop*, 404 F. 2d 571 (8th Cir. 1968).

In the majority opinion, Judge Blackmun, now Justice Blackmun of the Supreme Court, addressed the issue of the constitutionality of whipping, noting that prisoners do not forfeit their Eighth Amendment rights when they are incarcerated. Citing *Trop v. Dulles*, 356 U. S. 86 (1958), Judge Blackmun pointed out the flexible nature of the "cruel and unusual" concept. He wrote, "In determining whether a particular punishment violates the Eighth Amendment, notions of decency and civilized standards are relevant factors."

In reaching its decision, the Court considered the following factors: 1) that no conceivable safeguards could prevent abuse if whipping were permitted; 2) that existing safeguards were not followed; 3) that rules are easily circumvented; 4) that control of low-level personnel presents a difficult problem in this context; 5) that drawing the line between whipping and other forms of corporal punishment is very difficult once the former is permitted; 6) that corporal punishment frustrates correctional goals and engenders hatred among the inmates; and 7) that the use of the strap is opposed by public opinion. Considering all these factors, Judge Blackmun said: "... we have no difficulty in reaching the conclusion that the use of the strap in [the] penitentiaries of Arkansas in the 20th century, runs afoul of the Eighth Amendment. . . ." (At 579).

A more recent case, *Inmates of Attica Correctional Facility v Rockefeller*, 453 F. 2d 12 (2d Cir. 1971), challenged physical brutality in another context. Following the riot, the prisoners' complaints alleged that guards at the prison retaliated against the inmates with brutal and abusive treatment, including the beatings, forcing the inmates to run the gauntlet, and verbal abuse such as threats and racial slurs. These sorts of occurrences are common enough following prison riots as to be reasonably predictable.

Judge Mansfield's opinion for the majority reversed the District Court's denial of a preliminary and permanent injunction against such abuse. Where, as here, the physical force used went far beyond what was necessary to keep order, the guards' conduct amounted to a violation of the Eighth Amendment. And, Judge Mansfield concluded, since there was no adequate assurance in the record that inmates would be protected from future assaults, a permanent injunction was found to be the appropriate form of relief.

One of the major cases challenging treatment allegedly violative of the Eighth Amendment, *Holt v. Sarver*, 309 F. Supp. 362 (E.D. Ark. 1970), *aff'd* 442 F. 2d 304 (8th Cir. 1971), defies classification and therefore is included here. In this case, the Court considered the Arkansas penitentiary system and found that, in cumulative effect, the conditions existing therein constituted cruel and unusual punishment. In reaching its decision, the Court considered the extensive use of prisoners as guards, the lack of rehabilitation program, the open barracks system, and the conditions in solitary confinement. Judge Henley, in ordering injunctive relief, said:

> Apart from physical danger, confinement in the Penitentiary involves living under degrading and disgusting conditions. This Court has no patience with those who still say, even when they ought to know better, that to change those conditions will convert the prison into a country club. . . . Let there be no mistake in the matter; the obligation of the Respondents [correctional administrators] to eliminate existing unconstitutionalities does not depend upon what the Legislature may do or upon what the Governor may do. . . . (At 381.)

2. Solitary confinement

A large class of cases in which prisoners have invoked the Eighth Amendment to challenge prison conditions has concerned solitary confinement. None of these cases has declared solitary confinement to be cruel and unusual in itself (though this may be a future development), but they have prohibited some of its more inhumane applications.

In *Jordon v. Fitzharris*, 257 F. Supp. 674 (N.D. Cal. 1966), the Court considered the constitutionality of facilities for solitary confinement at Soledad Prison. The plaintiff had been confined in a "strip cell" which was never cleaned despite the convict-occupant's repeated vomiting. He was provided with no means of maintaining personal cleanliness, completely deprived of clothing for the first eight days of confinement, and given only a canvas mat on which to sleep. Granting an injunction preventing prison officials from confining the convict in this cell, the Court said:

> ... when, as it appears in the case at bar, the responsible prison authorities in the use of the strip cells have abandoned elemental concepts of decency by permitting conditions to prevail of a shocking and debased nature, then the courts must intervene—and intervene promptly—to restore the primal rules of a civilized community in accord with the mandate of the Constitution of the United States. (At 680).

Four years later, in *Landman v. Royster*, 333 F. Supp. 621 (E.D. Va. 1971), the following aspects of solitary confinement were enjoined: bread and water diet, use of chains and handcuffs as restraining devices, deprivation of clothing in unheated cells with open windows, putting more than one man in an isolation cell—unless justified by emergency conditions, and the use of tear gas against non-threatening inmates.

In *LaReau v. MacDougall*, 473 F. 2d 974 (2d Cir. 1972), an inmate at the Connecticut Correctional Institution brought a § 1983 suit seeking an injunction against certain conditions in

the prison's strip cells. The Court enjoined the practice of keeping the cell dark except for meals and writing as threatening to
the inmate's sanity and violative of the Eighth Amendment. It
also ruled the "Chinese toilet," i.e., a hole in the floor flushed
from the outside, to be too degrading to pass constitutional standards.

Sinclair v. Henderson, 435 F. 2d 125 (5th Cir. 1970), involved
a prisoner's challenge to conditions on Death Row. He alleged
that the inmates had only fifteen minutes per day to wash, shave,
and exercise; the toilets in the cells overflowed frequently; the
drinking water contained rust; the food was contaminated with
roaches and hair and served from filthy food carts on greasy
trays. Claiming that these conditions violated the Eighth
Amendment, the Fifth Circuit Court reversed the dismissal of
the complaint by the District Court, holding that it stated a
claim and remanding it for consideration on the merits.

There is a high degree of similarity in the approach the courts
used in these cases. They attack conditions in solitary
confinement on a hit-or-miss basis but refrain from declaring this
form of confinement unconstitutional. Logically, however, if a
court were satisfied that solitary confinement, even without the
degrading and brutal conditions and practices, threatened sanity
or was unnecessarily severe for the purpose it was designed to
serve, the court should have had no scruples about declaring it
unconstitutional *per se.*[69] But more to the point, it was not
declared unconstitutional, and "hands off" now meant cautious
warnings to the correctional administrator.

3. Punishment for improper reasons

Since a punishment may violate the Eighth Amendment if it is
excessively severe in proportion to the offense, it might be
logically argued that punishment imposed for no offense at all, or
for improper reasons, is also cruel and unusual. There are several
cases in which courts have declared punishment to be cruel and
unusual on this basis.

In *Sostre v. McGinnis,* 442 F. 2d 178 (2d Cir. 1971), the Second Circuit Court upheld the lower court's finding that the prisoner-plaintiff Sostre had been placed in solitary confinement to punish him for past legal successes and to prevent him from bringing a future suit. Imposition of punishment for political and religious beliefs, Judge Kaufman's opinion held, runs afoul of the Eighth Amendment. Similarly, the record in *Landman v. Royster, supra,* showed a pattern of punishment for legal activities such as bringing suit and consulting with an attorney. The District Court for the Eastern District of Virginia held that this was violative of the Eighth Amendment. Other cases with similar facts stand for the same proposition. *Corby v. Conboy,* 457 F. 2d 251 (2d Cir. 1972), and *Campbell v. Beto,* 460 F. 2d 765 (5th Cir. 1972), make the allegation that punishment was threatened or imposed for exercising legal rights states a cause of action under the Civil Rights Act. We can, therefore, see a pattern emerging. Visualizing a loss of control (power), correctional authorities in New York, Virginia and Texas segregated and otherwise punished prisoners who attempted to use legal means to change the conditions of their confinement.

4. Protection from assault and other injuries

In the tight confinement of the prison, physical attacks and sexual assaults by inmates against other inmates are frequent. In recent years, inmates have sought damages from the prison administration for these attacks.

A prisoner seeking redress for failure to protect him from attack may sue the individual responsible in a civil tort suit for negligence, may use the *Federal Tort Claims Act* if the officer responsible is employed by the federal government, or, in a proper case, may bring a § 1983 action. This analysis will concern itself chiefly with the latter remedy, but a few words should be said about the *Federal Tort Claims Act.*

The *Federal Tort Claims Act* allows citizens to sue the United States directly for the negligent acts of its employees in the scope of their employment. In *United States v. Muniz,* 374 U.S.

150 (1963), the Supreme Court held that the *Federal Tort Claims Act* was available to prisoners in suits against officials and guards. Thus, if a federal prisoner was assaulted by another inmate through the negligence of a guard, he could bring suit against the United States for money damages. Some states have analogous statutes covering negligent actions by state employees. The usefulness of the *Federal Tort Claims Act* is limited by two factors: first, it covers only negligent torts, and second, it excludes discretionary actions. Since, under existing prison regulations, so many decisions by prison officials are discretionary, this exception substantially curtails the utility of the Act in the prison context.

An alternative, prisoners have found, is an attack on the failure to protection from assault under § 1983 of the Civil Rights Act. Here, the prisoner may allege that failure to protect constitutes cruel and unusual punishment in violation of the Eighth Amendment, or that it amounts to deprivation of life, liberty, or property without due process of law in violation of the 14th Amendment. For the argument to prevail in either way, the plaintiff must prove more than mere negligence. He must demonstrate "egregious negligence" by prison officials, such as a pattern of attacks to which no protective response was made, or the knowing exposure of a prisoner to a dangerous inmate. The problems of proof here make it difficult for a prisoner to prevail on a constitutional claim. Finally, a § 1983 action is only available to state prisoners.

In *Curtis v. Everette,* No. 72-1935 (3d Cir., Dec. 17, 1973), the Third Circuit Court reversed the dismissal of a prisoner's § 1983 suit by the District Court. The Court, through Judge VanDusen, held that the officials knew of the dangerous nature of the attacker and failed to take protective measures, constituting a valid § 1983 claim under the 14th Amendment. (Judge McLaughlin, dissenting, said the officials' action was not under the color of state law and therefore not cognizable under the Civil Rights Act.)

In *Walker v. McCune*, 363 F. Supp. 254 (E.D. Va. 1973), a federal prisoner sued prison officials for failure to protect him from sexual assaults by fellow inmates. Since the officials here were not acting under color of state law, a §1983 suit was not available to the plaintiff. Instead, he sued under a theory articulated by the Supreme Court in *Bivens v. Six Unknown Named Agents of Federal Bureau of Narcotics*, 403 U.S. 388 (1971). *Bivens* held that violation of the Fourth Amendment by federal officials created a federal cause of action. Here, the plaintiff sought to apply that theory to a violation of the Eighth Amendment.

Judge Merhige's majority opinion denied relief. The record in the case failed to show either a pattern of attacks or a failure by prison officials to provide security for the plaintiff. On the contrary, the evidence showed that prison officials had responded to the attacks by transferring the plaintiff to safer surroundings each time. The specific facts are important to the outcome here. If the facts had revealed a pattern of neglect by the prison administration, the prisoner might have been awarded damages.

5. The denial of medical care

Prison medical facilities and personnel are frequently inadequate. When a prisoner brings suit for damages or injunctive relief because of failure to provide adequate medical treatment, he may either sue the prison doctor or other responsible officials in a state tort or bring a suit in federal court in a §1983 action under the Civil Rights Act. His chances of winning on the latter are slim, however, for he must show denial of treatment or mistreatment beyond what must be shown in a civil malpractice suit. In an addendum to *Ramsey v. Ciccone*, 310 F. Supp. 600 (M.D. Mo. 1970), Judge Becker outlined the kinds of inadequate medical treatment that must be shown to rise to the level of an Eighth Amendment violation. For instance, where a statutory duty to provide treatment exists, then an intentional denial constitutes a violation of the Eighth

Amendment. Similarly, gross negligence leading to injury is a claim cognizable under § 1983. On the other hand, simple negligence, even when it causes injury, was not found to be a constitutional violation and the prisoner had to seek relief in a state tort suit. Mere faulty judgment by a physician resulting in injury may not be made a constitutional claim.

An example of the egregious negligence that must be demonstrated to recover under § 1983 is *Martinez v. Mancusi*, 443 F. 2d 921 (2d Cir. 1970). In this case the plaintiff, an inmate of Attica Correctional Facility and a victim of infantile paralysis, had been taken to a hospital for a delicate operation. Shortly thereafter, the warden ordered him returned to Attica without a surgeon's discharge. The guards in charge of his return forced him to walk from the hospital, against the surgeon's orders. Upon return to Attica, he was kept in the prison hospital for one day, then returned to his cell with no facilities for medical care.

The District Court dismissed the complaint, but the Second Circuit Court reversed the dismissal, holding that the allegations here do state a cause of action under § 1983. The warden's failure to check with the surgeon before returning Martinez to prison, when he knew that the operation was delicate, and the prison doctor's failure to inquire of the surgeon about proper post-operative treatment amounted to *deliberate* indifference.

In *Tolbert v. Eyman*, 434 F. 2d 625 (9th Cir. 1970), the Ninth Circuit Court, in a *per curiam* opinion, reversed the District Court's decision of a § 1983 petition alleging inadequate medical care. The prisoner had an eye disease related to diabetes. Medicine for the disease sent by his wife and a druggist was repeatedly refused by the prison administration. As a result, the prisoner's condition worsened to the point of near blindness. The Court held that these facts constituted a *prima facie* case under § 1983.

Recovery in these cases is rare. A number of cases either dismiss the complaints or deny relief. In *Matthews v. Brown*, 362 F. Supp. 622 (E.D. Va. 1973), no negligence was shown in treatment received by a prisoner after an accident in the prison machine shop; in *Church v. Hegstrom*, 416 F. 2d 449 (2d Cir. 1969), no claim for relief was stated when there was no allegation that officials knew of the inmate's need for treatment; in *Ramsey v. Ciccone*, 310 F. Supp. 600 (M.D. Mo. 1970), no claim for federal relief was stated where the alleged mistreatment was not continuing or was unsupported by recognized medical opinion; in *Coppinger v. Townsend*, 398 F. 2d 392 (10th Cir. 1968), no claim was stated when alleged mistreatment was only a difference of opinion between the doctor and the inmate; in *Reynolds v. Swenson*, 313 F. Supp. 328 (W.D. Mo. 1970), no claim was stated where there was no allegation that needed treatment was knowingly withheld.

The cases demonstrate great reluctance to award relief for inadequate medical care. The reason for this may be a recognition of the inherently discretionary nature of medical judgments, as well as deference, perhaps excessive, to the expertise of the medical profession. Recoveries are possible, however, when extreme negligence or total disregard of medical needs is demonstrated. If the courts showed timidity in relation to some conditions of confinement, the tenacity of the "hands off" doctrine was more visible when the judiciary had the medical profession, rather than correctional officials, before the bar.

II. FIRST AMENDMENT RELIGIOUS RIGHTS

Definition

The religious rights of American citizens are grounded in the First Amendment to the U.S. Constitution: "Congress shall make no law respecting an establishment of religion, or prohibiting the free exercise thereof . . . ." Because freedom of religion is considered one of the fundamental or "preferred" freedoms, the federal courts have shown greater willingness to scrutinize prison practices allegedly burdening religious rights than they have in other areas of prison life. Federal courts have reiterated the importance of the First Amendment guarantee of freedom of religion and declared it a proper area for intervention. *Cruz v. Beto*, 405 U. S. 319 (1972); *Pierce v. LaVallee*, 293 F. 2d 233 (2d Cir. 1961); *Gittlemacker v. Prasse*, 428 F. 2d 1 (3rd Cir. 1970); *Brown v. Peyton*, 437 F. 2d 1228 (4th Cir. 1971).

This is not meant to imply that courts have denied correctional officials the ability to impose restrictions on religious expression. As in free society, a person's beliefs cannot be regulated, but reasonable restrictions on expression may be imposed if certain criteria are met. The test that the courts apply most frequently in evaluating the constitutionality of rules limiting the expression of religion is a two-fold one. First, the state must show a "compelling interest" in restricting the conduct. Second, the state's goal must be achieved by means which burden religious freedom as little as possible. *Brown v. Peyton, supra; Barnett v. Rodgers*, 410 F. 2d 995 (D. C. Cir. 1969); *Remmers v. Brewer*, 361 F. Supp. 537 (S. D. Iowa 1973), *aff'd* 494 F. 2d 1277 (8th Cir. 1974). If a given rule fails either of these tests, it will frequently be invalidated by the courts.

Defining religion for constitutional purposes is difficult. Technically, courts, in their wisdom, decline to examine the tenets of a religion and "validate" it as meriting constitutional protection; such an examination is not the business of a governmental body. But if no inquiries into the nature of an alleged religion were made, the opportunities for abuse are obvious, especially as might be expected in prison. Therefore, courts have made tentative inquiries into the nature of new sects before applying First Amendment guarantees. In *Theriault v. Carlson*, 339 F. Supp. 375 (N. D. Ga. 1972), for example, the District Court found that the prisoner-founded Church of the New Song had as one of its tenets a belief in a Supreme Being and other attributes of a religion, and therefore the state could not restrict its exercise without meeting constitutional criteria. (But later it did not go along with the wine, steak, etc. claimed by its adherents to be necessary for worship services.)

Similarly, courts distinguish between essential religious practices and those of more marginal importance, requiring less justification by the state for regulation of the latter. In *Rinehart v. Brewer*, 360 F. Supp. 105 (S.D. Iowa 1973), an inmate member of the Church of the New Song challenged the prison rules requiring shaving and periodic haircuts on the ground that his religion mandated the wearing of hair in a style conducive to "inner peace." The District Court upheld the regulations, declaring that, since no particular hair length was religiously required, the rules did not render practice of his religion impossible. In *Walker v. Blackwell*, 411 F. 2d 23 (5th Cir. 1969), the Black Muslim prisoners' request to listen to Elijah Muhammed's weekly radio program was denied, partly because they had not shown that it was essential to the practice of Islam.

1. Dietary laws

As with many other issues in the courts' treatment of prisoners' religious rights, the question of the obligation of the prison to provide for the religiously-mandated dietary requirements of its inmates arose in Black Muslim cases. The Islamic faith prohibits consumption of pork and sets aside the month of December (Ramadan) during which no food may be taken between sunrise and sunset. Challenges to prison practices which frustrate these requirements make up most of the dietary law cases.

In most of the cases, the courts assume that dietary practices impinging on religious rights are reviewable. One case, *Childs v. Pegelow*, 321 F. 2d 487 (4th Cir. 1963), held that arranging mealtimes is a matter of routine prison administration, so that a challenge to an official decision is nonjusticiable. However, other cases proceed by applying a "balancing" test, weighing the extent of the burden on religious freedom against the administrative burden of providing for the dietary requirements. Because of this mode of analysis, the result depends largely on the facts of the particular case or court.

In *Abernathy v. Cunningham*, 393 F. 2d 775 (4th Cir. 1968), the Black Muslims challenged the prison's failure to provide a pork-free noon meal. The court denied relief, finding that the petitioners could meet their nutritional needs by skipping the dishes containing pork. It is unclear what the outcome would be under different facts. Similarly, the court in *Walker v. Blackwell,* 411 F. 2d 23 (5th Cir. 1969), denied relief to Black Muslim petitioners seeking a nightly meal of coffee and pastry, both of a special type, during Ramadan. After applying the balancing test, the court concluded that the administrative burden and extra expense out-weighed the deprivation of the unbridled exercise of this religion practice.

In a similar case, *Barnett v. Rodgers,* 410 F. 2d 995 (D. C. Cir. 1969), the Court of Appeals for the District of Columbia Circuit put a heavier burden on the state, applying the two-fold "compelling state interest" and "least restrictive" means test. It remanded the lower court's denial of relief where the petitioners wanted one pork-free meal a day. The Court of Appeals noted that the state had made no showing of a compelling state interest in an extensive use of pork in the prisoners' diet, nor had it shown that such interest could be served by means less burdensome to petitioners' right of free exercise.

2. Religious literature and correspondence with a spiritual advisor

During the 1960s, Black Muslims in prison sought permission to receive religious literature like "Muhammed Speaks" and "Message to the Black Man in America." Because of their alleged black supremacist ideology, courts were at first inclined to support the prison officials' decision to ban them, either deferring to the administrator's discretion or finding on the merits that the publications posed a danger to prison security. Now the trend is toward allowing such literature, or at least requiring a careful scrutiny of the material to determine whether it can be provided under conditions mitigating its alleged potential disruptive effect. The Fourth Circuit Court, for example, ordered a reconsideration of whether or not "Muhammed Speaks" and "Message to the Black Man" constitute a danger to prison security in *Brown v. Peyton*, 437 F. 2d 1228 (4th Cir. 1971). after it had, three years earlier, decided to uphold a denial of the very same publications.

Other courts have also tended to carefully examine bans on religious literature, though it is not always clear which test they apply to determine the prison rule's constitutionality. In *Long v. Parker*, 390 F. 2d 816 (3d Cir. 1968), the court overturned the decision of the lower court, upholding a rule forbidding prisoners to subscribe to "Muhammed Speaks" because of the dangerous effect of its alleged racist content. Where religious literature is concerned, said Judge Forman for the court, the test must be whether it creates a "clear and present danger" of a breach in prison security. The court in *Walker v. Blackwell*, 411 F. 2d 23 (5th Cir. 1969), overturned a lower court holding on the merits, finding that the overall tone of "Muhammed Speaks" was not inflammatory, but encouraged blacks to improve themselves through work and study. However, in a Tenth Circuit Court case, *Hoggro v. Pontesso*, 456 F. 2d 917 (10th Cir. 1972), the court upheld the denial of Black Muslim religious publications on the basis of an earlier case in which, after a hearing, they were found to be inflammatory. Since we do not know the facts of the earlier case we cannot tell whether this case is distinguishable; conditions in the prison may have been, for example, unusually tense.

Related to the right to receive religious literature is the right to correspond with a spiritual advisor. Since this right also receives First Amendment protection, the state must show a compelling interest to constitutionally prohibit such correspondence. In *Walker v. Blackwell*, 411 F. 2d 23 (5th Cir. 1969), the lower court had upheld a rule prohibiting correspondence by Black Muslims with Elijah Muhammed. The Court of Appeals reversed the decision, ruling that the prison must allow inmates to write to Elijah Muhammed for the limited purpose of spiritual guidance. In a similar case, *Cooper v. Pate*,

382 F. 2d 518 (7th Cir. 1967), the Court of Appeals upheld the lower court's ruling that the prison could not constitutionally bar prisoners from writing to Elijah Muhammed for spiritual guidance unless the communication presents a "clear and present danger" to prison security. *Neal v. State of Georgia*, 469 F. 2d 446 (5th Cir. 1972), dealt with the same issue in a non-Black Muslim context. The Court of Appeals reversed and remanded the lower court dismissal of the petitioner's § 1983 complaint, in which he alleged that he had been denied correspondence with his spiritual advisor. Judge Wisdom said that the state must show either a compelling interest or the existence of a security or discipline problem to curtail First Amendment rights.

3. Provision of and access to religious facilities

The constitutional status of religious facilities in prison is a rather ambiguous one. The establishment clause of the First Amendment prohibits any state action tending toward an establishment of religion, yet state funds support chaplaincies and chapel facilities within prisons. It has been suggested that, since the state has deprived the prisoner of normal channels of religious expression by incarcerating him, failure to provide alternative religious facilities would be an act antagonistic to religion, also proscribed by the First Amendment's free exercise clause. *O'Malley v. Brierley*, 477 F. 2d 785 (3d Cir. 1973). However, Justice Rehnquist's dissent in *Cruz v. Beto*, 405 U.S. 319 (1972), suggests that the prison had no affirmative duty to provide religious services for anyone.

Whatever the ultimate resolution of a constitutional issue, the cases show clearly that, once religious facilities are provided at all, each sect has to have a reasonable opportunity to use them. Courts have shown a willingness to consider prisoner complaints that allege deprivation of religious facilities. For instance, in *Long v. Parker*, 390 F. 2d 816 (3d Cir. 1968), the Court of Appeals reversed and remanded for a hearing the lower court's dismissal of Black Muslim inmates' allegations of denial of chapel facilities, their holy book, religious medals, a minister, and dietary provisions.

Several courts have ruled that members of small sects must be allowed to hold worship services. The Seventh Circuit Court, though recognizing the potential disruptive effect of Black Muslim prayer meetings, held that prison administrations may not categorically ban such services without trying less drastic alternatives, *Cooper v. Pate*, 382 F. 2d 518 (7th Cir. 1967). And in *Theriault v. Carlson*, 339 F. Supp. 375 (N.D. Ga. 1972), the court said that, since the state had not shown the Church of the New Song poses a danger to prison security, the members must be allowed to meet.

Differences between inmates in provision of religious facilities have been upheld in cases where the courts felt that a valid reason for such different treatment existed. In *Sharp v. Sigler*, 408 F. 2d 966 (8th Cir. 1969), inmates with a record as security risks were confined in the maximum security unit and denied permission to attend religious services. Judge Blackmun's opinion stated that, since the denial was justified by security considerations and sacraments were provided in the maximum security unit (not unlike the way in which our founding fathers had arranged prison life in the Pennsylvania system), the petitioners were not entitled to relief.

A recent case, *O'Malley v. Brierley*, 477 F. 2d 785 (3d Cir. 1973), addresses the question of prisoners' right of access to religious leaders. Two priests, not the official Catholic chaplains of the prison, had the privilege of conducting services within the prison revoked because of alleged inflammatory activities. The priests and the prisoners challenged this revocation. The Third Circuit Court, through Judge Aldisert, held that the priests did not have First Amendment right to hold services within the prison. As to the inmates' case, however, Judge Aldisert said that the District Court must hold a hearing to determine whether the barring of the priests was a reasonable restriction, imposing the least burden on the prisoners' free exercise, consistent with security considerations.

III. MAIL AND ACCESS TO THE MEDIA RIGHTS OF PRISONERS

Definition

An often-noted characteristic of prison life is the inmates' sense of isolation from the world outside the walls. Their avenues of communication with people and events in the non-prison society are severely limited by incarceration. Historically, prisoners had not been permitted to correspond with family, friends, and legal counsel, ("buried from the world") and then grudgingly permitted to do so; albeit under carefully circumscribed conditions. In the past, prison officials have freely censored both incoming and outgoing mail, a practice which they contended was necessary to intercept contraband, weapons, plans of escape, and blueprints for future criminal activity, to say nothing of manuscripts, letters to newspaper editors, and criticisms of the prison officials themselves.

Recently, the necessity and constitutional validity of extensive censorship have been questioned by the courts. Written communication is protected under the free speech clause of the First Amendment, which means that it is a "preferred" freedom. Like freedom of religion, freedom of speech in the non-prison world may not be curtailed unless the state demonstrates both that a *compelling state interest* exists and that the interest is being served by the *means least restrictive* of individual liberty.

However, this constitutional standard has not always been applied to the mail rights of prisoners because the extent of their rights under the free speech clause of the First Amendment is unclear. There is general recognition that imprisonment necessitates *some* curtailment of these rights of expression, but *how much* curtailment is a matter of disagreement and is still evolving.

Right of access to the media is a vital one for prisoners in several respects. First, since the average citizen is unlikely to experience prison conditions first-hand, the public depends heavily on the news media for its information about the penal system. Prisoners depend on journalists too, to publicize their grievances and to increase pressure for reform. Second, it is important that prisoners have access to news publications. A characteristic of prison life is the sense of isolation and alienation it breeds among the inmates. A prisoner with a subscription to magazines and newspapers of significance to him may feel less cut-off from the outside world.

Here too, rights of communication with the press are "preferred" First Amendment freedoms, implicating both the free speech and free press clauses. Despite fairly numerous cases on the subject, the First Amendment rights of prisoners to communicate with the media remain unclear. Several cases analyze the issues in terms of the free addressee's right to receive correspondence, or the public interest in free and open debate, or the public's "right to know," rather than facing the questions of the *prisoner's* rights.

The access to media cases are divided into three subject areas; the right of access to the media, interviews with the press, and the right to receive publications. They follow the prisoner mail rights discussion.

1. Mail

The United States Supreme Court recently decided *Procunier v. Martinez,* —U.S.—, 40 L. Ed. 2d 224 (1974), a case challenging California's regulations for the censorship of general prisoner correspondence. The regulations applied to all non-legal correspondence, prohibited any material tending to "agitate, unduly complain, or magnify grievances." The regulations authorized prison officials to delete anything they considered to be "lewd, obscene, or defamatory; to contain foreign matter, or [to be] otherwise inappropriate." In addition, any material "expressing inflammatory political, racial, religious or other views or beliefs . . ." was declared to be contraband. In practice, these regulations allowed censoring officials to delete anything critical of the institution or its personnel. The District Court declared the regulations unconstitutional because they interfered with protected expression without adequate justification; further, the Court declared them void for vagueness.

The Supreme Court affirmed the District Court's decision, with Justice Powell writing the majority opinion. Noting the courts' traditional deference to the judgment of correctional personnel in this area, Powell nevertheless said: "[w]hen a prison regulation or practice offends a fundamental constitutional guarantee, federal courts will discharge their duty to protect constitutional rights. . . . The issue before us is the appropriate standard of review for prison regulations restricting freedom of speech." (At 40 L. Ed. 2d 236.) Mr. Justice Powell avoided reaching the issue of the prisoner's First Amendment rights in the mail area. Instead, he chose to decide the case on the narrower ground of the free addressee/sender's rights to unfettered communication. These regulations fairly invited prison officials and employees to apply their own personal judgments as standards for prisoner mail censorship. (At 40 L. Ed. 2d 241.) Further, when a letter is censored or rejected, the Court ruled that certain minimum procedural safeguards must be afforded the inmate: notification, an opportunity to protest, and referral of the matter to a non-censoring official.

Justice Marshall, though concurring in the result, did not agree with the majority's avoidance of the prisoner's First Amendment right to send and receive mail. He rejected the opinion's necessary implication that prison officials possess the general right to open and read all mail. Such wholesale reading of mail might well chill the inmate's free expression of ideas. A prisoner's free and open expression will surely be restrained by the knowledge that his every word may be read by his jailers and that his message could well find its way into a disciplinary file, be the object of ridicule or even lead to reprisals. (At 40 L. Ed. 2d 246.) Justice Marshall also found the state's justifications for reading all incoming and outgoing mail inadequate. The fears of transmission of contraband and escape plans were simply too speculative to permit all mail to be read. When prison authorities have reason to believe that an escape plot is being hatched by a particular inmate through his correspondence, they may well have an adequate basis to seize that inmate's letters; but there is no such justification for a blanket policy of reading all prison mail. (At 40 L. Ed. 2d 247.)

Finally, Justice Marshall disagreed with the state's contention that reading all mail was necessary to further rehabilitative goals. On the contrary, the inhibiting effect on communication of the knowledge that every word will be read by prison officials runs counter to true rehabilitation. "To suppress expression is to reject the basic human desire for recognition and affront the individual's worth and dignity." (At 40 L. Ed. 2d 248.)

2. Media.

The most important issues involved in the consideration of this topic are whether communication with the news media is to be permitted at all, and if so, whether and to what extent such correspondence may be censored.

In *Nolan v. Fitzpatrick*, 451 F. 2d 545 (1st Cir. 1971), the First Circuit Court considered a § 1983 challenge to a Walpole State Prison regulation that *absolutely* forbade letters to the press. Prison officials justified the ban by pointing to the inflammatory effect of communications critical of the prison administration—returning to the prison in the form of letters to the editor. The Court of Appeals, through Judge Coffin, ruled that this was not adequate to justify a total ban on prisoner-media letters. Judge Coffin, though speaking of the public interest in access to information about prison conditions, stated that the right to correspond must survive incarceration. Since First Amendment rights were involved, the state must not only have a legitimate goal, but must use the least restrictive means to further that goal. Judge Coffin's order required letters to be mailed to the media unless they contained contraband, a plan of escape, or a device to escape prison regulations. This, of course, was impossible to implement absent an elaborate censorship capability.

The District Court for Rhode Island's decision in *Palmigiano v. Travisono*, 317 F. Supp. 776 (D. C. R.I. 1970), favored a iberal approach to censorship of prisoners' mail. Petitioners were awaiting trial and sought a temporary restraining order preventing the prison officials from opening and censoring all their incoming and outgoing mail. Judge Pettine noted that the First Amendment includes the right to petition for redress of grievances as well as the right of a free press; both these rights were infringed by the blanket censorship. The state, ruled Judge Pettine, must show that uncensored correspondence presents a "clear and present danger" to prison security. It must further show that the danger is being contained by the least restrictive means possible. Judge Pettine granted the temporary restraining order, holding that outgoing mail may not be opened without a search warrant and incoming mail inspected only for contraband. The implications of this decision for confidential correspondence with the press are obvious.

In the federal prison system, confidential access to the media is assured via the "prisoners' mailbox," described in *Washington Post Company v. Kleindienst*, 494 F. 2d 994, 997 (D.C. Cir. 1974). Under this system, correspondence to media personnel is transmitted unopened. In other jurisdictions, however, censorship of prisoner mail to the media is governed by their own rules and court decisions, subject to the limitations of *Procunier v. Martinez*.

3. Interviews with the press

In two companion cases decided the last week of the 1973 term, the Supreme Court dealt a severe blow to the access of prisoners to news personnel. Both cases concerned regulations forbidding press interviews with specific inmates, and both sustained the prison's regulations.

Saxbe v. Washington Post Company, —U.S.—, 41 L. Ed. 2d 514 (1974), concerned a challenge to Federal Bureau of Prisons directive 1220.1A, which forbids individual press interviews with specific prisoners. The suit was brought on the ground that petitioners, in this case news reporters, had been denied their First Amendment right to gather news. Justice Stewart wrote the Court's opinion, which upheld the constitutionality of the Bureau's regulation. Avoiding the First Amendment issues, Justice Stewart reasoned that, since the general public has no right to interview specific inmates, and the press has no constitutional right to special privileges, the regulation was found not to discriminate against the press and was therefore held constitutional. The Bureau's justifications, found persuasive by the Court, were that individual interviews would *enhance the status* and the disruptive influence *of certain inmates* within the prison (the "big wheel" phenomenon) further jeopardizing the Bureau's policy of "equal treatment" for all inmates, (although elsewhere the rhetoric is "individualized treatment.")

Justice Powell dissented on the ground that the total ban on interviews, covering minimum, medium, and maximum security institutions, was too broad and an infringement of First Amendment rights. The rights Justice Powell referred to are not the prisoners' rights (appropriate in this case because the petitioners were not prisoners), or even the reporters' rights, but the *public's rights* to receive information.

The companion case, *Pell v. Procunier*, —U.S.—, 41 L. Ed. 2d 495 (1974), involved a challenge to a nearly identical California regulation on inmate interviews. The crucial difference here was that both prisoners and news personnel challenged the regulation, forcing the Court to give some consideration to the *prisoners' rights* in this matter. Again, the regulation was upheld, and again Justice Stewart wrote the opinion. Though mentioning the point that the regulation did not discriminate against the press, he stressed other factors at this time. As to the prisoners' claim that they had been denied the right to free speech, the Court rejected the notion that prisoners have the right to speak with a willing interviewer. The Court noted that, since mail censorship was less stringent after *Martinez* and California's visitation policy was liberal, adequate alternative channels of communication with the press and public existed. The Court further found that the regulation was justified by security considerations.

Both Mr. Justice Powell and Mr. Justice Douglas filed dissenting opinions. Justice Powell rested his dissent on the same arguments advanced in his *Washington Post* dissent, but agreed with the majority that prisoners have no constitutionally-protected right to speak to reporters. Mr. Justice Douglas, however, contended that prisoners' First Amendment rights are among the most crucial freedoms that follow them into prison. Any infringement of First Amendment rights must be justified by a compelling state interest and very narrowly drawn. The regulation considered here, they said, was definitely too broad under this standard.

These cases go further in limiting prisoner interviews than at least one lower court decision upholding the federal restriction. In *Seattle-Tacoma Newspaper Guild, Local No. 82, of American Newspaper Guild v. Parker*, 480 F. 2d 1062 (9th Cir. 1973), the Ninth Circuit upheld Federal Bureau of Prisons regulations 1220.1A as applied to a maximum security institution. Judge Wright's opinion, however, limited the holding to maximum security institutions, leaving open the question whether the total ban on interviews was constitutional as applied to medium and minimum security facilities. The *Washington Post* decision upheld the validity of the regulation without regard to the custody nature of the facility.

4. Access to publications

Since First Amendment freedoms are involved, courts have been willing to scrutinize with care prison regulations that deny inmates access to news publications. As with infringement of religious rights, the state must show a compelling interest in defense of its regulations limiting access. Sometimes, the court requires the state to demonstrate that the publication creates a clear and present danger to prison security.

Where regulations on receiving publications are arbitrarily applied or inherently discriminatory, the courts have ruled on the basis of the equal protection clause of the 14th Amendment. Courts have been particularly solicitous if they suspect racial discrimination.

In *Fortune Society v. McGinnis*, 319 F. Supp. 901 (S.D.N.Y. 1970), the Fortune Society, a prisoner aid and reform group, and a group of state prisoners brought a class action seeking a cease and desist order against the Commissioner of Corrections of New York State and the Superintendent of a prison for preventing inmates from receiving the *Fortune Society Newsletter.*

Judge Weinfeld, in granting a preliminary injunction, found that the prison administration had presented no justification for banning the newsletter, other than a statement to the Fortune Society that its publication misrepresented the prison system. Even if true, he said, this would not be sufficient to ban the newsletter, for the First Amendment requires a showing of a *compelling* state interest. Here, the state must demonstrate that the material it seeks to exclude creates a "clear and present danger" to prison security.

Jackson v. Godwin, 400 F. 2d 529 (5th Cir. 1968), is another case in which exclusion of publications was overturned by the court. It was decided on equal protection grounds. Florida state prisoners brought a § 1983 action alleging denial of access to black-oriented, "non-subversive" publications, while white prisoners were permitted white-oriented material. The regulations permitted the inmate to subscribe only to his hometown newspaper and to magazines on a restrictive list. The Court of Appeals, through Judge Tuttle, first said that the court has "a duty to protect the prisoner from unlawful and onerous treatment of a nature that, of itself, adds punitive measures to those legally meted out by the court." (At 532.) Noting that constitutional rights attach to all persons, the court found that the rules in question had been arbitrarily applied and were racially discriminatory, in effect, even when applied equitably. The "hometown rule" had not been fully enforced since white prisoners were afforded easy access to white-oriented newspapers not published in their hometowns. In addition, non-inflammatory black-oriented publications like *Sepia* and *Ebony* were regularly excluded from the approved list as "unhealthy" (a medical model term borrowed by custody officials, herein referring not to physical health but rather to political unhealthiness as they viewed it.) Considering the 50% black composition of the prison population, the court hinted that conscious discrimination might be at work. Further, the "hometown rule" was inherently discriminatory because few black inmates were likely to be from a town that published a black-oriented newspaper. Judge Tuttle therefore ordered that all black inmates might not have their health impaired by permitting them to subscribe to one black newspaper and that at least one black-oriented magazine be placed on the list of approved publications.

IV. DUE PROCESS IN PRISON

Definition

The late Supreme Court Justice Felix Frankfurter once stated: "The history of liberty has largely been the history of observance of procedural safeguards." *McNabb v. United States,* 318 U.S. 332, 347 (1943). In recognition of the truth of Frankfurter's observation, a large number of cases brought by prisoners have challenged the lack of procedural safeguards in the prison context. As interpreted by the courts, the due process clause of the Fourteenth Amendment requires procedural safeguards when an individual is threatened with "grievous loss" by state action. *Goldberg v. Kelly,* 397 U.S. 254 (1970). In the prison context, courts have ruled that "grievous loss" may be incurred, and thus due process must be provided, in disciplinary hearings, classifications and transfer of prisoners, determinations of parole eligibility, revocation of probation and parole, and sentencing when it is deferred until a subsequent probation revocation hearing. Courts differ on how much process is due in each of these areas, though the Supreme Court has spoken to several of them and settled the debate at least for the present.

The cases discussed in the following sections are intra-prison disciplinary hearings, classifications and transfer of prisoners, and parole and probation proceedings.

1. Intra-prison disciplinary hearings

During the last week of its 1973 term, the United States Supreme Court handed down its decision in *Wolff v. McDonnell*, —U.S.—, 41 L. Éd. 2d 935 (1974). The case concerned a challenge by prisoners to Nebraska's prison disciplinary procedures, in which they sought the restoration of good time taken from them at disciplinary hearings they alleged were constitutionally defective. According to those procedures, an inmate accused of major misconduct received a hearing before the prison Adjustment Committee based on a "conduct report." The accused inmate was permitted to respond orally to the charges. He did not have the right to call his own witnesses, to cross-examine adverse witnesses, to have assistance in the preparation of his defense, or to receive a written statement of the grounds for decision. The Court of Appeals for the Eighth Circuit, at 483 F. 2d 1059 (8th Cir. 1973), remanded the case to the District Court, with directions that it formulate guidelines for in-prison due process based on *Morrissey v. Brewer*, 408 U.S. 471 (1971). *Morrissey* set out minimum due process requirements for parole revocation hearings, mandating written advance notice of charges, disclosure of adverse evidence, the opportunity to present witnesses and cross-examine adverse witnesses, an impartial hearing body, and a written statement of the grounds for decision. The State appealed, and the Supreme Court granted certiorari.

The Court, speaking through Justice White, affirmed the Eighth Circuit decision, in part, and reversed it, in part. White concluded that the full spectrum of *Morrissey* safeguards need not be afforded in prison discipline hearings. He reasoned that in-prison hearings differ from parole revocation hearings in two respects. First, the withdrawal of good time imposed as punishment in the former is less of a "grievous loss" than the loss of conditional liberty that may flow from the latter. Second, the volatility of the prison environment creates a state interest in controlled proceedings not present in parole revocation hearings.

Following this analysis, the Court decided that the right to cross-examine adverse witnesses would be a potential source of danger, unrest, and retaliation within the prison. The presence of counsel, either retained or appointed, would also, in the Court's view, engender tensions by altering the nature of the proceedings in more adversary directions. Though noting that the right to present evidence and call witnesses is ordinarily basic to a fair hearing, the Court declined to order it in all cases, leaving the matter in the discretion of the prison officials. The Court did, however, order the Nebraska system to provide two procedures not granted heretofore. One is written notice of the charges at least 24 hours in advance of the Adjustment Committee hearing, and the other is a written statement of the decision containing the evidence upon which it was based.

Justice Douglas and Justice Marshall dissented. Justice Douglas objected to the Court's decision to leave the prisoner's right to call his own witnesses and cross-examine adverse ones within the unreviewable discretion of the prison administration. These are constitutional rights, Justice Douglas contended, and as such "should not yield to the so-called expertise of prison officials more than is necessary."

Justice Marshall analyzed the issues more extensively. He noted that, without an enforceable right to call witnesses and present evidence, the accused inmate is effectively deprived of the means to defend himself. In those circumstances, the hearing could be little more than a swearing contest in which the inmate is doomed to lose. Justice Marshall disagreed strongly with the majority's conclusion on the cross-examination issue. Viewing cross-examination as an essential component of a fair hearing, he contended that the need to keep the identity of witnesses confidential would exist in only a small proportion of cases. Citing the experience of states which allowed cross-examination, Marshall found the majority's fears of disruption unsubstantiated. Finally, he expressed the view that an inmate in a serious disciplinary case should be constitutionally entitled to the assistance of a counsel substitute—fellow inmate, staff member, or law student—in the preparation of his defense.

The majority opinion recognized the rapidly changing nature of the law in the correctional field. By holding that "at this stage of development of these procedures" the inmate would not require counsel, either retained or appointed. The Court seemed to suggest that it might reconsider this aspect of the decision, and perhaps others as well, at some future date.

When a rule infraction by a prisoner is also a crime for which the state may prosecute him, the accused faces a dilemma. If he exercises his right to remain silent, he deprives himself of an important means of defense—the only means where the hearing rules do not provide him with the right to call his own witnesses or cross-examine adverse ones. If he speaks, then anything he says may be used against him in a subsequent criminal trial. Several courts have grappled with this problem, and predictably their solutions differ.

Clutchette v. Procunier, 328 F. Supp. 767 (N.D. Cal. 1971), involved a challenge to disciplinary procedures at San Quentin. Those procedures provided only for the accused's right to orally defend himself; they did not provide for disclosure of evidence against him, the presence or cross-examination of his accusers, or the right to call witnesses on his own behalf. Where the rule infraction was also a crime, the accused was given the *Miranda* warnings (the right to remain silent, to consult with an attorney, and a caution that anything said may be used against him in a court of law); but where, as here, speaking out was his only means of defense, he was given the choice of forfeiting this defense or having anything he said used against him in subsequent criminal proceedings. The right to consult an attorney was a hollow one, since the prison interpreted it to mean that a lawyer must be provided only in questioning before the District Attorney and not in the prison hearing. But Judge Zirpoli held that, in these circumstances, the accused must be afforded counsel to assist him in protecting his rights. Though he must still choose whether to speak or remain silent, he at least would have competent legal advice in making his decision. In addition, Judge Zirpoli ruled that, where an alleged rule infraction could also be prosecuted as a crime, the accused must be permitted to present witnesses on his behalf and cross-examine adverse witnesses.

The First Circuit Court considered the same problem in *Palmigiano v. Baxter*, 487 F. 2d 1280 (1st Cir. 1973). Here a state prisoner, accused of a disciplinary infraction, received a hearing during which he was not represented by counsel. Remaining silent, he was sentenced to thirty days in segregation on the basis of a report by an observing official. He claimed that his rights under the Fifth and Fourteenth Amendments were abridged by the prison officials' failure to inform him that any statements he made could not be used against him in subsequent criminal proceedings.

Discussing the general need for fairness within the prison system, Judge Coffin said: ". . . the orderly care with which decisions are made by the prison authority is intimately related to the level of respect with which prisoners regard that authority. There is nothing more corrosive to the fabric of a public institution such as a prison than a feeling among those whom it contains that they are being treated unfairly." (At 1283). On the specific issues in the case, he first concluded that an unqualified right to remain silent without prejudicial effect would seriously impede the fact-finding process. As an alternative, he proposed a grant of "use immunity" to any accused inmate facing criminal prosecution for the same offense. Under use immunity, any statements made by the prisoner at the disciplinary hearing, or derived therefrom, could not be used against him in subsequent criminal proceedings. Having granted this protection, the Court declined to follow *Clutchette* and mandate the appointment of counsel, declaring that this would involve considerable state expense and tend to prolong the proceedings, but privately retained counsel must be permitted. Another District Court case, *Fowler v. Vincent*, 366 F. Supp. 1224 (S.D.N.Y.. 1973), reached the same conclusion.

2. Classification and transfer

Classification and transfer of prisoners are two areas in-

158 / "... We Are the Living Proof ..."

creasingly recognized by the courts as involving important rights.
An inmate's security classification (minimum, medium, or maximum) largely determines the conditions of his confinement, his
freedom of movement in prison, and many of the privileges he
may enjoy. A change in classification resulting in more severe
conditions of confinement, therefore, can be a "grievous loss"
requiring due process safeguards.

Transfer from one institution to another involves similar
considerations. When an inmate is transferred, he is usually
placed in segregation at the new institution pending classification. He may be ineligible for educational or rehabilitative programs at the transfer facility, and his work in programs at the old
facility is interrupted. The fact of transfer appearing on his
record can influence his success in obtaining parole,* since it is
often interpreted by officials as denoting a "troublemaker." All
these factors contribute to make transfer a "grievous loss" to the
prisoner, which should be attended with due process safeguards.

There is also general agreement in the cases that some sort of
hearing must be granted before a prisoner is reclassified. Because reclassification may result in more severe conditions of
confinement or transfer, there is the *potential* for "grievous loss"
and *some* due process must be provided. Even where the reclassification is based on a rule infraction that the inmate admitted before the Adjustment Committee, a reclassification
hearing must be held. *Cousins v. Oliver*, 369 F. Supp. 553 (E.D.
Va. 1974).

Though the need for a hearing of some sort is conceded,
courts diverge somewhat on the safeguards they prescribe. A
1973 decision in the District Court for the Eastern District of

---

*Transferring troublesome inmates between prisons is an old practice. John
Bartlow Martin (1954) refers to it in Illinois and other states *(Break Down the
Walls*, p. 221). Transfers between corrections and mental health institutions i
described by old hands as bus therapy. When a *prisoner* acted "crazy," he wa:
sent from prison to a mental hospital. Once there if the *patient* acted "crim
inal," he was bussed back to prison. The bus trip was thereby deemed to be
the therapy, as it relieved the drudgery of both institutions.

Virginia saw significance in what it perceived to be the non-punitive (rehabilitative) nature of reclassification; this, it concluded, justifies *fewer* procedural safeguards. *Almanza v. Oliver,* 368 F. Supp. 981 (E.D. Va. 1973). A year later, the same court, more realistically, stated that the key to analysis is the *effect on the inmate,* whether the proceeding is labelled punitive or non-punitive. Where the effect is punitive, due process applies, *Cousins v. Oliver, supra.*

The cases generally require fewer safeguards for reclassification hearings than for prison disciplinary proceedings. Several courts agree that the essentials of due process in the reclassification context are advance notice of the charges and an opportunity to controvert them. *King v. Higgins,* 370 F. Supp. 1023 (D. Mass. 1974); *Almanza v. Oliver,* 368 F. Supp. 981 (E.D. Va. 1973); *Benfield v. Bounds,* 363 F. Supp. 160 (E.D. N.C. 1973). According to *Almanza v. Oliver, supra.,* an inmate may be temporarily reclassified without a hearing if there is *probable cause* that he has committed another crime, but only during the pendency of the charges. If the prison administration wishes to continue his new classification beyond that, they must conduct a hearing with advance notice of the charges and provide the inmate with an opportunity to answer them.

As with classification, there is a general recognition by the courts that the transfer of an inmate (at least out of state), requires due process protection. In *Gomes v. Travisono,* 490 F. 2d 1209 (1st Cir. 1973), Rhode Island state prisoners transferred to an out-of-state facility without notice, reasons, or a hearing brought a class action under § 1983. The First Circuit Court, speaking through Judge Coffin, said: ". . . we work from the premise that once the application of due process requirements is justified by the loss or disadvantage stemming from the institution's action, the state must afford minimally those processes which are of little or no burden." (At 1217.)

The Court held that, absent an emergency, minimum requirements of due process before transfer are prior notice, reasons for transfer, a hearing and the opportunity to controvert· the charges. In an emergency, an inmate could be transferred without a hearing, but a hearing must be granted as soon as possible after transfer. The Court declined to mandate prior investigation of the charges, assistance of a lay advocate, a decision based on substantial evidence, or administrative review. This decision is limited to interstate transfers.

There is wide divergence among the cases on the procedures that must be followed in transfer hearings. *Aikens v. Lash,* 371 F. Supp. 482 (N.D. Ind. 1974), prescribed extensive procedural safeguards. However, it should be noted that the "grievous loss" considered by the Court in determining what process is due is the thirty-day minimum segregation imposed on disciplinary transfers, not the transfer itself. The petitioners in the case had been subjects of disciplinary transfer without a prior hearing. District Judge Grant held that, where transfer results in automatic segregation, the inmate must be provided with adequate notice two days in advance of the hearing, an impartial decision maker, the right to speak on his own behalf, the right to call favorable witnesses and to cross-examine adverse witnesses unless the hearing officer determines otherwise, the assistance of a lay inmate advocate, and administrative review of the decision. In an emergency situation, a hearing which meets these requirements must be held within five days of the transfer.

Other cases proceed on the assumption that the transfer itself represents a "grievous loss" to the inmate apart from conditions of confinement imposed in the receiving institution. The cases are not uniform, however, in their determinations of what safeguards are constitutionally required. Conceding that a transfer from an Oregon prison to Leavenworth 2,000 miles away is a "grievous loss" to an inmate, the Court, in *Capitan v. Cupp,* 356 F. Supp. 302 (D.C. Ore. 1972), said only that a hearing must be provided either before or a reasonable time after transfer, but failed to specify how the hearing should be conducted. *Croom v. Manson,* 367 F. Supp. 586 (D.C. Conn. 1973), went further in describing what a constitutionally sound transfer hearing should contain.

In *Hoitt v. Vitek*, 361 F. Supp. 1238 (D.C. N.H. 1973), the District Court for New Hampshire laid down a comprehensive set of procedural guidelines for transfer. The case arose when, during a prison-wide lockup, nine inmates were transferred to the Lewisburg Federal Penitentiary in Pennsylvania without notice or hearing. For non-emergency transfers, the Court ordered that the inmate be provided with three days' advance written notice, a lay advocate, an impartial tribunal with at least one non-prison official, the right to present testimony and confront and cross-examine witnesses, a record of the proceedings, written findings with a copy provided to the prisoner, a verdict based on substantial evidence, and provision for administrative review. If the transfer were made under emergency conditions, a prior hearing was not required, but if permanent transfer was contemplated, the inmate had to be returned to New Hampshire for a hearing immediately after the emergency. To minimize the negative effects on parole and ongoing criminal trials, the inmate had to be returned to New Hampshire for parole hearings and criminal proceedings.

As the preceding cases show, the courts have not yet reached a consensus on the procedural rights due an inmate who is reclassified or transferred. Many of the cases are recent and on the District Court level. For the present, it is only significant that the courts recognize that a prisoner may possibly have grievous consequences in change of classification and transfer and agree that some procedural safeguards are constitutionally required, even if they diverge on the dimensions of such safeguards.

3. Parole and probation proceedings

The Parole Commission and Reorganization Act, 18 U.S.C. § 4201 et seq, effective May 14, 1976, has now codified the due process safeguards earlier dictated by the courts for parole proceedings.

In *Johnson v. Heggie*, 562 F. Supp. 851 (D.C. Col. 1973), the District Court considered a § 1983 class action by state prisoners to compel the State Board of Parole to furnish reasons for denial. Though the adoption of rules requiring such notification rendered the case moot, the Court had this to say:

> In particular, due process attaches when an administrative body has discretionary power over an individual's liberty. . . . Contrary to defendants' position, the Court finds that an inmate has a substantial interest in knowing the reason or reasons from the Board for denial of parole. . . . An inmate has a right to know why his parole was denied so that, *inter alia,* he can attempt to correct his misdoings in a proper and successful manner. Further, the administrative processes must conform to some orderly and fair scheme, however informal. (At 857.)

On the Court of Appeals level, the Second and Third Circuits have dealt with this issue. In *Fischer v. Cahill,* 474 F. 2d 991 (3d Cir. 1973), the Third Circuit upheld the right of New Jersey prisoners to a statement of reasons for the denial of parole. And the recently-decided *United States ex rel. Thomas Johnson v. Chairman of New York State Department of Correctional Services,* No. 72-2581 (2d Cir. June 13, 1974), addressed the due process considerations extensively. Judge Mansfield analyzed the issues in terms of *Morrissey v. Brewer,* which

> . . . rejected the concept that due process might be denied in parole proceedings on the ground that parole was a 'privilege' rather than a 'right' [citation omitted]. Parole was thenceforth to be treated as a 'conditional liberty,' representing an 'interest' entitled to due process protection. A prisoner's interest in prospective parole, or 'conditional entitlement,' must be treated in like fashion. . . . [Therefore, an inmate who is denied parole must be furnished with written reasons for the Board's action.]

The due process rights of a probationer or parolee threatened with revocation have been fairly well established by a trio of Supreme Court Cases: *Mempa v. Rhay,* 389 U.S. 129 (1967), *Morrissey v. Brewer,* 408 U.S. 471 (1971), and *Gagnon v. Scarpelli,* 411 U.S. 778 (1973).

In *Mempa v. Rhay*, the petitioner was convicted of "joy-riding" and placed on probation, with his sentencing deferred. Subsequently, he was given a hearing at which his probation was revoked, and he was sentenced to ten years in the penitentiary. At the hearing, he was not given the chance to speak on his own behalf or present evidence, nor was he represented by counsel. After denial of his petition for a writ of habeas corpus by the Washington Supreme Court, the Supreme Court of the United States granted certiorari.

The Court, in an opinion by Justice Marshall, held that "appointment of counsel for an indigent is required at every stage of a criminal proceeding where substantial rights of a criminal accused may be affected." (At 134). Since Mempa's hearing combined probation revocation with sentencing, the Court found such a hearing to be *part of a criminal proceeding,* and therefore the guarantee of counsel applied. The determination that the hearing was part of a criminal proceeding is crucial, since there is general agreement in the courts that the procedural safeguards attaching during a criminal proceeding are more extensive than those due in other types of hearings.

The difference may be observed in two other cases dealing with the rights of parolees and probationers. In *Morrissey v. Brewer*, the Supreme Court addressed the question whether the 14th Amendment requires a hearing before parole revocation. Chief Justice Burger's opinion held that it does. Chief Justice Burger first determined whether due process must be afforded at all. Following the *Goldberg v. Kelly* analysis, he found that the deprivation of the conditional liberty of the parolee was indeed a "grievous loss" requiring some procedural safeguards.

The opinion went on to discuss the extent of the constitutionally-mandated safeguards. Since parole revocation is *not* part of a criminal proceeding, Burger said, the full panoply of rights due a criminal defendant do not automatically apply. Concluding that the proceeding should be "effective but informal," the opinion held that due process requires a preliminary hearing to determine probable cause at the place where the arrest or violation took place and a revocation hearing. At the hearings, the parolee was to have the following safeguards: written notice of the charges, disclosure of adverse evidence, the opportunity to speak and present witnesses, the right to cross-examine adverse witnesses unless the hearing officer thinks it inadvisable, an impartial hearing body, and a written statement of the grounds for decision. The opinion did not reach the issue of whether counsel should be allowed or provided.

Gagnon v. Scarpelli applied the *Morrissey* safeguards to probation revocation. Justice Powell, writing for the majority, also considered extensively whether counsel should be appointed in probation revocation proceedings. The presence of counsel would, in the Court's view, alter the nature of the parole and probation proceeding in a more adversary direction, and would almost certainly prolong it. According to Powell's analysis, counsel should be appointed when an accused parole or probation violator presents a colorable claim that he did not commit the alleged violation, or, if he did, that there were mitigating circumstances; further, the issues should be of a sufficient complexity that would make it difficult for the accused to adequately defend himself.

Following these decisions, federal law now provides for appointment of counsel in parole revocation hearings, and representation of inmates by "a representative who qualifies under rules . . . [of] the Commission" at parole determination proceedings. (18 U.S.C. § 4208, 4214, eff. 5-14-76.) These new laws are clearly indicative of the legislative response possible when patterned judicial intervention occurs.

V. PRISONERS' RIGHTS OF ACCESS TO THE COURT

Definition

Recognizing that rights are meaningless without a way to vindicate them, the courts protected prisoners' access to the courts relatively early. The basic case is *Ex parte Hull,* 312 U.S. 546 (1941), in which the Supreme Court invalidated a regulation requiring inspection of inmate-drawn legal papers by the parole board's legal investigator. The Court said that ". . . the state and its officers may not abridge or impair petitioner's right to apply to a federal court for a writ of habeas corpus." While the courts may have shown ambivalence and hesitancy toward prisoners' access to attorneys, religious advisors, newspaper reporters, visitors, etc., no such uncertainty exists when it comes to protecting the prisoners' right of access to the courts themselves!

With the basic right of access to the courts established, individual decisions elaborated the meaning of the right in specific circumstances. In addition to access to the courts, cases deal with the related areas of access to other legal services and access to legal materials (law libraries, for example).

1. *Access to the courts*

Because most prisoners are indigent, they must prepare and file their own petitions for post-conviction relief, be they habeas corpus or § 1983 actions.[70] Because of the limited education and resources available to these prisoners, their so-called *pro se* (whereby they represent themselves) complaints may often be confusing and difficult for the courts to interpret. But if dismissed by the courts because of legal insufficiency, legitimate grievances may never be heard. The Supreme Court recognized this in *Haines v. Kerner et al.,* 404 U.S. 519 (1972). The Court favored liberal interpretation of *pro se* prisoner complaints, holding that such complaints should be held to "less stringent standards than formal pleadings drafted by lawyers." (At 520)

A related concern is the ability to consult other inmates (called "jailhouse lawyers") for assistance in legal work. In the absence of other legal aid programs, these inmates, who have picked up some considerable knowledge of the law, are the only means prisoners have to obtain legal help. The Supreme Court addressed this issue in *Johnson v. Avery,* 393 U.S. 483 (1969). The Court, speaking through Justice Fortas, held that the state could not constitutionally prevent inmates from consulting "jail-house lawyers" unless it provided an adequate alternative means of legal assistance. Fortas' opinion stated that any other ruling would unconstitutionally burden the prisoners' right of access to the courts:

> There can be no doubt that Tennessee could not constitutionally adopt and enforce a rule forbidding illiterate or poorly educated prisoners to file habeas corpus petitions. Here Tennessee has adopted a rule which, in the absence of any other source of assistance for such prisoners, effectively does just that. (At 487.)

Other cases have removed obstacles to the bringing of suits by prisoners that could render the right of access to the courts meaningless in practical terms. *Almond v. Kent,* 459 F. 2d 200 (4th Cir. 1972), dealt with a Virginia statute providing that a committee be appointed to represent felons in suits by or against felons. The Fourth Circuit held that prisoners may bring suits under § 1983 on their own behalf regardless of the statute. When prison officials hampered prisoners' access to the courts indirectly by imposing or threatening to impose punishment for exercising legal rights, the courts have intervened to stop it.°

Smartt v. Avery, 370 F. 2d 788 (6th Cir. 1967), dealt with a parole board regulation that automatically delayed for one year the parole hearing of any inmate who filed an unsuccessful habeas corpus petition. The Sixth Circuit Court invalidated this regulation as imposing an unjustified burden on the constitutional right of access to the courts. Though parole is not constitutionally mandated, the court said that the state has authorized it by statute and may not use its deprivation to discourage inmates from actively asserting their rights.

°In *Corby v. Conboy,* 457 F. 2d 251 (2d Cir. 1972) and *Campbell v. Beto,* 460 F. 2d 765 (5th Cir. 1972), the Second and Fifth Circuit Courts respectively held that a cause of action under § 1983 was present when punishment or threat of punishment was imposed for legal activities.

Since prisoners so rarely can afford to retain counsel, they may try to contact various legal aid services for assistance. The First Circuit Court held in *Nolan v. Scafati*, 430 F. 2d 548 (1st Cir. 1970), that the right of access to the courts carries with it a corollary right to seek legal assistance. Therefore, the claim of the petitioner, an inmate at Walpole State Prison, that the prison officials refused to mail a letter to the Civil Liberties Union of Massachusetts stated a cause of action.

2. Access to legal materials

Because of prisoners' reliance on themselves in preparing legal complaints, the guarantee of access to the courts would be hollow indeed without the provision of facilities for legal research.

A 1961 Ninth Circuit case, *Hatfield v. Bailleaux*, 290 F. 2d 632 (9th Cir. 1961), upheld state prison restrictions on the times and places for legal research by prisoners. The restrictions required the prisoners to make appointments to use the library, provided for confiscation of legal documents outside designated areas, and forbade prisoners in isolation to write to courts and attorneys.

A key case in the field of prisoners' rights to legal materials is *Gilmore v. Lynch*, 319 F. Supp. 105 (N.D. Cal. 1970), *aff'd sub. nom., Younger v. Gilmore*, 404 U.S. 15 (1971). State prisoners challenged prison rules on access to law books as well as the restricted list of legal materials in prison law libraries of California. The *per curiam* opinion rejected the prison's contention that, since prison law libraries are a privilege, the state may regulate them any way it wishes, saying that even a privilege may not be granted or withheld arbitrarily. The court enjoined the enforcement of the restrictions on the titles in prison law libraries, noting that prisoners must have access to all the aid necessary to obtain a fair hearing and finding the state's justifications of economy and standardization inadequate.

These cases reveal that courts do protect the inmate's access to legal redress. Yet they do not require prisons to provide both adequate legal materials *and* a legal assistance program. The cases further recognize the legitimacy of reasonable prison regulations on the time, place, and manner of the inmate's legal activities, as long as those restrictions do not actually interfere with the inmate's access to the courts.

SUMMARY

For a free-wheeling *keeper* or *treater* to suddenly become a *defendant* is status-costly. Inside the walls his discretion reigned supreme, but it looked odd when it had to be explained in a courtroom. The prisoner as plaintiff enjoys the status of "equality" before the bench. The judge, however, was not likely to listen as sympathetically to a latter-day Elam Lynds in the person of James Park, Associate Warden of San Quentin (1971), explaining how he "knew" he had his culprit.

> That's simple; we know who did it from the other inmates. . . . If several reliable inmates point to this guy, or refuse to clear him, we know he's guilty. We don't have the type of case we could take to court: it would be too dangerous for our inmate-informers to have to testify. You middle-class due-processors don't understand; it's an administrative matter, not judicial.[71]

In another strange notion of due process in New York, deputy warden Perry DeLong, after taking 100 days of good-time from an inmate, explains the process of forfeiture in this excerpt:

Q. At the disciplinary hearings, are inmates entitled to call witness in their behalf?
A. No.
Q. Are they entitled to cross examine guards?
A. They are not.
Q. What record is made of the proceeding at a disciplinary hearing?
A. As you see here, on the disciplinary report, the punishment is noted. This disciplinary hearing is not a judicial hearing, it corresponds to, I believe, a *potter familus* [sic]. I could be wrong on the *potter familus*.

Q. *Potter familus?*

A. It is probably known as the authority figure, as meting out what is family punishment, or family discipline. This is not a judicial thing in the sense of a court of record, and there is no provision for it as a court of record, and this is an internal disciplinary thing, very much as a father and mother in the home say, 'Johnny, you have done so and so, and you are forbidden to do it, and therefore you will stay in your room.'*

With the unlimited ability to defend themselves, correctional administrators dug in on even minor issues. In *Conklin v. Wainwright*, 424 F. 2d 516 (5th Cir. 1970), the court decided against the prisoner who wanted more than ten sheets of paper a day for preparing a legal argument. Presumably, if the allotment was less than ten sheets, the case may have been decided in the plaintiff's favor!

Moving along the continuum of pariah-penitent-prisoner-patient-plaintiff, we see increasing activity on the part of the offender. Being a pariah merely entailed leaving the community, having a punishment performed upon the body, or execution—one-time summary acts. Becoming a penitent began to involve the offender in a moral venture. It was minimal and sedentary, but it did require a response. Being a prisoner, in the common-sense meaning of the term, began to require active and even more rigorous responses—marching, working, obedience to routine. The patient status (as with the penitent) engaged the convict on an inner level. In addition to the normal burdens incumbent upon occupants of prison cells, the convict now could, by a display of insight, climb a clinical ladder to improve his status. If the treaters looked at the treated through a prism of determinism the prisoner, in peering back, was refracting free will. Heeding their admonishment to change, he simply chose another path to change. The course turned out to be a legal one

---

*Deposition of Perry J. DeLong, Jan. 10, 1969, at 39-41 *Visconti v. LaVallee*, No. 68 Civil 403 (N.D.N.Y., filed Nov. 1968). (As cited in Turner, *Stanford Law Review* Vol. 23 p. 500).

in which the prisoner wished to be seen as a competent (political) being. Correctional administrators were not ready to accept it. Sol Rubin describes the foot-dragging by the correctional establishment:

> . . . Aside from what they do or do not do in regard to sentencing, the rights of prisoners, and the rights of probationers and parolees, court decisions have had an impact on the correctional process that is clearly discernible in the reactions of correctional administration. Administrative responses to court decisions may be classified into three self-explanatory categories—the positive response, the provocative response, and the defensive response. From all that I can discover, there is little in administrative behavior that is positive and somewhat more that is provocative; the great bulk of administrative behavior is defensive. By that I mean administrators sit tight on those they are dealing with until they are forced by a court decision or a legislature to change their pattern. And even then, they resist compliance.[72]

The net result of the correctional case law development to date seems to be the construction of an uncertain "shield against authority, or zone of inviolability" for convicts. More specifically it has simply condemned conditions of

> lengthy solitary confinement, dark cells where no light burns, . . . no bed or mattress, bad or no food, being kept nude, being kept in cells which are full of filth and excrement, cells otherwise unhygienic, as well as the use of physical force . . . [requiring] some kind of notice or statement of the case against them, and some kind of opportunity to respond.[73]

Why did we have to undergo torturous and lengthy litigation to be forced to acceed to such amelioratives? Why were they not simply administratively ordered! Perhaps in the last analysis it was administrative resistance to the prisoner's micro-world concerns which generated counter-resistance in the form of litigation. The irony of this chapter of correctional history lies in the fact that the unlawful, in bringing the agents of law to court, received more lawful treatment. The offender demonstrated that he was quite volitional. Indeed the idea of the offender-as-responsible opened a frightening Pandora's Box.

FOOTNOTES

[1]New York State, Division of Parole, Department of Correction, "Parole Adjustment and Prior Educational Achievement of Male Adolescent Offenders, June 1957 - June 1961," September 1964, as cited in Robert Martinson, "What Works?—Questions and Answers about Prison Reform," *The Public Interest*, No. 35, National Affairs, Inc., 1974, p. 25.

[2]California Department of Corrections Research Division, *Annual Research Review*, Sacramento, 1962, p. 39, as cited in David F. Greenberg, "Much Ado about Little: the Correctional Effects of Corrections," *Final Report of the Committee for the Study of Incarceration*, June 1974, p. 23.

[3]Carol Spencer and John Berecochea, "Vocational Training at the California Institute for Women: An Evaluation," *Research Report No. 41*, Department of Corrections Research Division, Sacramento, 1971, as cited in op. cit., n 2, Greenberg, p. 24.

[4]Morton Zivan, "Youth in Trouble: A Vocational Approach," Final Report of a Research and Demonstration Project, May 31, 1961 - August 31, 1966, Dobbs Ferry, New York, Children's Village, 1966, as cited in op. cit., n 1, Martinson, p. 26.

[5]Frank Jacobson and Eugene McGee, "Englewood Project: Re-Education: A Radical Correction of Incarcerated Delinquents," Englewood, Colorado, 1965, as cited in op. cit., n 1, Martinson, p. 26.

[6]Marvin Kettering, *Rehabilitation of Women in the Milwaukee County Jail: An Exploration Experiment*, Ph.D. Dissertation, University of Michigan, 1972, as cited in op. cit., n 2, Greenberg, p. 25.

[7]Clyde E. Sullivan and Wallace Mandell, *Restoration of Youth Through Training*, Wakoff Research Center, New York, 1967, as cited in op. cit., n 1, Martinson, p. 27.

[8]*Op. cit.*, n 1, Martinson, p. 28.

[9]Evelyn S. Guttman, "Effects of Short-Term Psychiatric Treatment on Boys in Two California Youth Authority Institutions," *Research Report No. 36*, California Youth Authority, Sacramento, 1963, as cited in op. cit., n 1, Martinson, p. 29.

[10]*Op. cit.*, n 1, Martinson, p. 29.

[11]Stuart Adams, "Assessment of the Psychiatric Treatment Program: Second Interim Report," *Research Report No. 15*, California Youth Authority, December, 1959, and "Assessment of the Psychiatric Treatment Program, Phase I: Third-Interim Report," *Research Report No. 21*, California Youth Authority, January 1961, as cited in op. cit., n 1, Martinson, p. 29.

[12]Stuart Adams, "The P.I.C.O. Project," in Norman Johnston, Leonard Savitz and Marvin E. Wolfgang, *The Sociology of Punishment and Correction*, New York: John Wiley and Sons, 1970, as cited in op. cit., n 2, Greenberg, p.28.

[13]*Ibid.*

[14]Stuart Adams, "Effectiveness of the Youth Authority Special Treatment Program: First Interim Report," *Research Report No. 5*, California Youth Authority, Sacramento, 1959.

[15]Stuart Adams, "Assessment of the Psychiatric Treatment Program, Phase I: Third Interim Report," *Research Report No. 21*, California Youth Authority, Sacramento, 1961, as cited in *op. cit.*, n 2, Greenberg, p. 28.

[16]California Department of Corrections, "Intensive Treatment Program: Second Annual Report," Prepared by Harold B. Bradley and Jack D. Williams, Sacramento, California, December 1958, as cited in *op. cit.*, n 1, Martinson, p. 30.

[17]Gene Kassebaum, David Ward and Daniel Wilner, *Prison Treatment and Parole Survival*, New York: John Wiley and Sons, 1971, as cited in *op. cit.*, n 2, Greenberg, p. 25.

[18]The one-year follow-up is reported in James Robison and Marinette Kevorkian, "Intensive Treatment Project, Phase II, Parole Outcome: Interim Report," *Research Report No. 27*, California Department of Corrections Research Division, Sacramento, 1967; the two-year follow-up by James Robison and Richard Bass is reported in the *1970 Annual Research Review* of the California Department of Corrections, p. 19, as cited in *op. cit.*, n 2, Greenberg, p. 25.

[19]Charles B. Truax, Donald C. Wargo and Leon D. Silber, "Effects of Group Psychotherapy with High Adequate Empathy and Nonpossessive Warmth upon Female Institutionalized Delinquents," *Journal of Abnormal Psychology*, Vol. LXXI, No. 4, 1966, pp. 267-274, as cited in *op. cit.*, n 1, Martinson, p. 32.

[20]*Op. cit.*, n 1, Martinson, p. 32.

[21]*Corrections Digest*, Volume 5, No. 9, May 1, 1974, p. 1.

[22]Joseph L. Massimo and Milton F. Shore, "The Effectiveness of a Comprehensive Vocationally Oriented Psychotherapeutic Program for Adolescent Delinquent Boys," *American Journal of Orthopsychiatry*, Vol. XXXIII, No. 4, 1963, pp. 634-642, as cited in *op. cit.*, n 1, Martinson, p. 40.

[23]*Op. cit.*, n 1, Martinson, p. 40.

[24]Le May Adamson and Warren H. Dunham, "Clinical Treatment of Male Delinquents. A Case Study in Effort and Result," *American Sociological Review*, Vol. XXI, No. 3, 1956, pp. 312-320, as cited in *op. cit.*, n 1, Martinson, p. 40.

[25]Robert and Ralph Schwitzgebel, "Therapeutic Research: A Procedure for the Reduction of Adolescent Crime." Paper presented at meetings of the American Psychological Association, Philadelphia, August 1963; and Robert Schwitzgebel and D. A. Kolb, "Inducing Behavior Change in Adolescent Delinquents," *Behavior Research Therapy*, Vol. I, 1964, pp. 297-304, as cited in *op. cit.*, n 1, Martinson, p. 40.

[26]Stuart Adams, Roger E. Rice and Borden Olive, "A Cost Analysis of the Effectiveness of the Group Guidance Program," *Research Memorandum 65-3*, Los Angeles County Probation Department, January 1965, as cited in *op. cit.*, n 1, Martinson, p. 40.

[27]William J. O'Brien, "Personality Assessment as a Measure of Change Resulting from Group Psychotherapy with Male Juvenile Delinquents," *The Institute for the Study of Crime and Delinquency* and the California Youth Authority, December 1961, as cited in *op. cit.*, n 1, Martinson, p. 40.

[28]Le Mar T. Empey, "The Provo Experiment: A Brief Review," Los Angeles, Youth Studies Center, University of Southern California, 1966, as cited in *op. cit.*, n 1. Martinson, p. 41.

[29] *Op. cit.*, n 1, Martinson, p. 41.

[30] Dean V. Babst and John W. Mannering, "Probation Versus Imprisonment for Similar Types of Offenders: A Comparison by Subsequent Violations," *Journal of Research in Crime and Delinquency,* Vol. II, No. 2, 1965, pp. 60-71, as cited in *op. cit.,* n 1, Martinson, p. 41.

[31] *Op. cit.,* n 1, Martinson, p. 41.

[32] *Ibid.*

[33] Stuart Adams, "Some Findings from Correctional Caseload Research," 31(4) *Federal Probation* 48, December, 1967, as cited in *op. cit.,* n 2, Greenberg, p. 40.

[34] James O. Robison and Gerald Smith, "The Effectiveness of Correctional Programs," *Crime and Delinquency* 67, January, 1971, as cited in *op. cit.,* n 2, Greenberg.

[35] Joan Havel, "Special Intensive Parole Unit, Phase Four, The Parole Outcome Study," *Research Report No. 13,* California Department of Corrections, Sacramento, 1965, as cited in *op. cit.,* n 2, Greenberg, pp. 40-42.

[36] J.D. Lohman, A. Wahl and R.M. Carter, *The San Francisco Project, Research Report No. 11: The Intensive Supervision Caseload,* Berkeley, California, School of Criminology, University of California, 1967, as cited in Roger Hood and Richard Sparks, *Key Issues in Criminology,* New York: McGraw-Hill Book Co., 1970, p. 189.

[37] *Annual Research Review 1962,* California Department of Corrections, Sacramento, 1963, p. 73, as cited in *op. cit.,* n 2, Greenberg, p. 41.

[38] *California Prisoners 1968, Summary Statistics of Felon Prisoners and Parolees,* California Department of Corrections Research Division, Sacramento, p. 121, 125; P.F.C. Mueller, "Advanced Releases to Parole," *Research Report No. 20,* California Department of Corrections Research Division, Sacramento, 1965, as cited in *op. cit.,* n 2, Greenberg, p. 41.

[39] Dorothy R. Jaman, Lawrence A. Bennett, and John E. Berecochea, "Early Discharge from Parole: Policy, Practice and Outcome," *Research Report No. 51,* California Department of Corrections Research Division, Sacramento, 1974, as cited in *op. cit.,* n 2, Greenberg, pp. 41-42.

[40] *The Sentence of the Court. A Handbook for Sentencers,* London: H.M.S.O., 1969, as cited in *op. cit.,* n 36, Hood and Sparks, p. 188.

[41] R. P. Narloch, Stuart Adams, and Kendall J. Jenkins, "Characteristics and Parole Performance of California Youth Authority Early Releases," *Research Report No. 7,* California Youth Authority, June 1959, as cited in *op. cit.,* n 1, Martinson, p. 36.

[42] Karen Bernsten and Karl O. Christiansen, "A Resocialization Experiment with Short-Term Offenders," *Scandinavian Studies in Criminology,* Vol. I, 1965, pp. 35-54, as cited in *op. cit.,* n 1, Martinson, p. 36.

[43] California Adult Authority, Division of Adult Parolees, "Special Intensive Parole Unit, Phase I: Fifteen Man Caseload Study," Prepared by Walter I. Stone, Sacramento, California, November, 1956, as cited in *op. cit.,* n 1, Martinson, p. 36.

[44] B. M. Johnson, "An Analysis of Parole Performances and of Judgments of Supervision in the Parole Research Project," *Research Report No. 32,* California Youth and Adult Correction Agency, Sacramento, California, 1962, as cited in *op. cit.,* n 36, Hood and Sparks, p. 190.

[45]P. F. C. Mueller, "Advanced Release to Parole," *Research Report No. 20*, Research Division, California Department of Corrections, Sacramento, California, 1965, as cited in *op. cit.*, n 36, Hood and Sparks, p. 190.

[46]*Op. cit.*, n 36, Hood and Sparks, p. 190.

[47]G. F. Davis, "A Study of Adult Probation Violation Rates by Means of the Cohort Approach," *Journal of Criminal Law, Criminology and Police Science*, Vol. 55, 1964, p. 70, as cited in *op. cit.*, n 36, Hood and Sparks, p. 187.

[48]*Op. cit.*, n 36, Hood and Sparks, p. 189.

[49]H. A. Weeks, "Youthful Offenders at Highfields, Ann Arbor, Michigan," University of Michigan Press, 1958, as cited in *op. cit.*, n 36, Hood and Sparks, p. 190.

[50]*Op. cit.*, n 36, Hood and Sparks, p. 190.

[51]Daniel Glaser, *The Effectiveness of a Prison and Parole System*, New York: Bobbs-Merrill, 1964, as cited in *op. cit.*, n 1, Martinson, p. 37.

[52]W. H. Hammond and E. Chayen, *Persistent Criminals: A Home Office Research Unit Report*, London: H.M.S.O., 1963, as cited in *op. cit.*, n 1, Martinson, p. 37.

[53]Great Britain, Home Office, *The Sentence of the Court: A Handbook for Courts on the Treatment of Offenders*, London: H.M.S.O., 1964, as cited in *op. cit.*, n 1, Martinson, p. 37.

[54]Bernsten and Christiansen, as cited in *op. cit.*, n 1, Martinson, p. 37.

[55]Robert Vasoli and Frank Fahey, "Halfway Houses for Reformatory Releases," *Crime and Delinquency* (16:292), as cited in *op. cit.*, n 2, Greenberg, p. 45.

[56]Gilbert Geis, *The East Los Angeles Halfway House for Narcotic Addicts*, Institute for Crime and Delinquency 1966; John E. Berecochea and George E. Sing, "The Effectiveness of a Halfway House for Civilly Committed Narcotics Addicts," *Report No. 42*, California Department of Corrections, Sacramento, 1971, as cited in *op. cit.*, n 2, Greenberg, p. 46.

[57]Edwin Powers and Helen L. Witmer, *An Experiment in the Prevention of Delinquency — The Cambridge-Somerville Youth Study*, New York: Columbia University Press, 1951, as cited in Sutherland and Cressey, *Criminology* (9th Edition), New York: J.B. Lippincott Co., 1974, pp. 630-631.

[58]Henry J. Meyer, Edgar F. Borgatta, Wyatt C. Jones, *Girls at Vocational High: An Experiment in Social Work Intervention*, Russell Sage Foundation, 1965.

[59]Sheldon and Eleanor Glueck, *Five Hundred Criminal Careers*, New York: Knopf, 1930; *Later Criminal Careers*, New York: Commonwealth Fund, 1937.

[60]Walter C. Bailey, "Correctional Outcomes: An Evaluation of 100 Reports," *Journal of Criminal Law, Criminology and Police Science*, Vol. 57, No. 2, pp. 153-157.

[61]Nigel Walker, *"The Interchangeability of Criminal Sanctions,"* as cited in Leonard Orland, *Justice, Punishment, Treatment: The Correctional Process*, New York: The Free Press, A Division of the MacMillan Publishing Co., Inc., 1973, pp.5-6.

[62]*Ibid.*, p. 6.

[63]Norval Morris and Gordon Hawkins, *The Honest Politician's Guide to Crime Control*, Chicago: The University of Chicago Press, 1969, p. 119.

[64]Leslie Wilkins, "A Survey of the Field from the Standpoint of Facts and Figures," *Effectiveness of Punishment and Other Measures of Treatment,* Council of Europe Report, 1967.

[65]"Beyond the Ken of the Courts: A Critique of Judicial Refusal to Review the Complaints of Convicts," *Yale Law Journal,* Vol. 72, pp. 506-517.

[66]Phillip J. Hirschkop and Michael A. Milleman, "The Unconstitutionality of Prison Life," *Virginia Law Review,* Vol 55, June 1969, p. 812.

[67]*Landman v. Peyton,* 370 F. 2d 135, 141 (4th Cir. 1966).

[68]*Op. cit.,* n 66, Hirschkop and Milleman, p. 813.

[69]"The Constitutional Status of Solitary Confinement," *Cornell Law Review,* Vol. 57, 1972, p. 476.

[70]Jacob and Sharma, "Justice After Trial: Prisoners' Need for Legal Services in the Criminal-Correctional Process," *Kansas Law Review,* Vol. 18, 1970, p. 494.

[71]Jessica Mitford, "Kind and Usual Punishment in California," in Burton M. Atkins and Henry R. Glick, eds., *Prison, Protests and Politics,* Englewood Cliffs, N.J.: Prentice-Hall, Inc., 1972, p. 159.

[72]Sol Rubin, "The Impact of Court Decisions on the Correctional Process," *Crime and Delinquency,* Vol. 20, No. 2, p. 133.

[73]Annual Chief Justice Earl Warren Conference sponsored by the Roscoe Pound-American Trial Lawyers Foundation, *A Program for Prison Reform,* June 9-10, 1972, pp. 51, 52.

4
Pursuing Justice

From a 1676 letter on behalf of King Louis XIV of France to the Paris Parlement:

Since His Majesty urgently needs more men to strengthen his rowing team crews ... to be delivered at the end of the following month, His Majesty commands me to tell you that He wishes you to take the necessary steps in his name in order to have the criminals judged quickly.

From the response of the court:

You have frequently done me the honor of writing to me in connection, with the supply of prisoners for the galleys and of transmitting to me the express orders of His Majesty relating to the use of such prisoners in execution of his glorious projects. You will be gratified to learn that this Court has twenty prisoners who will be chained together this morning and sent off.

(From Georg Ruche and Otto Kirchheimer, *Punishment and Social Structure*, 1939, p. 55, as cited in Joan Fried and William Fried, *The Uses of the American Prison*, 1974).

The lid has not yet come off Pandora's Box, but the offender is hesitantly peering over its edge. He looks a bit different now than in the past. He is still alive, despite those who persist in calling for the death penalty. He may walk in a group and infrequently marches, but when marching his head is erect. There are few enthusiasts left in prison: the preachers and teachers and treaters have not produced a pay-off to equal their rhetoric. The prisoner-as-plaintiff now looks increasingly to the courts, and the courts continue to draw narrow issues around prisoner complaints until large stacks are amassed. The Supreme Court then levels them one at a time [see Chapter III]. Not much may be expected in the way of enduring correctional change through the drama of litigation when the central actors are reluctant judges and resistant prison administrators. In any case ". . . prison reform cannot be made acceptable just by ensuring rights or the comfort of the inmates."[1]

On the dim horizon one sees a group of the newest enthusiasts clamoring for their place in the torturously convoluted history of prisons. They are generically known as "behavior modifiers." Though not new, their language is not well-known because they are just now emerging from animal laboratories and the back wards of hospitals in ·search of defectives. Their therapeutic arsenal is equipped with positive and negative reinforcements, pills, chemicals, electrodes and neurosurgical instruments. With corrections experiencing an "end of ideology" and its weary leadership floating in a vacuum, this new wave of enthusiasm based upon behavior manipulation may become attractive to them. What follows is an alternative less enthusiastic perhaps, but certainly less manipulative.

"Corrections is much too important an issue to be left in the hands of wardens," Clemenceau might have said. Unfortunately, this is a fair picture of current American correctional practice, which is still insulated and isolated. It remains uninformed by a theory of human behavior; hence it may be found to be using several simultaneously. It remains uninformed by a theory of the purpose of the criminal law; hence it passively watches itself become an explosive warehouse in response to legislative whim and caprice. Correctional objectives, such as they are, have developed aimlessly, Tappan observed (1951):

> . . . In different periods of social evolution certain ones have emerged out of society's particular climate of values and have been more highly prized than others. Yet each, as it has been crystallized in law, custom, and correctional practice, has impressed a persisting influence upon subsequent policy. Moreover, each objective has become encrusted with layers of rationalization to justify and perpetuate the established treatment methods. The ultimate consequence is a melange of purposes, some deeply bedded in the channels of history . . . it is not unusual to find correction exerting, in turn, vindictive, deterrent, and rehabilitative measures in relation to the same offender.[2]

As a result of aimlessness and public neglect, the prison never acquired a specific correctional purpose; it inherited vestiges of the Puritan Ethic and added to it middle-class values of mobility through work and education. Packer (1968) called this a "leap of faith."

> We can use our prisons to educate the illiterate, to teach men a useful trade, and to accomplish similar benevolent purposes. The plain disheartening fact is that we have very little reason to suppose that there is a general connection between these measures and the prevention of future criminal behavior. What is involved primarily is a leap of faith, by which we suppose that people who have certain social advantages will be less likely to commit certain kinds of crimes. It is hard to make a good argument for restraining a man of his liberty on the assumption that this connection will be operative in his case. It is harder still if he already possesses the advantages that we assume will make people less likely to offend.[3]

We will propose a limited set of objectives for prisons devolved from a series of propositions concerning our view of man and law in the context of justice. Meaningful prison objectives cannot be successfully divorced from a conception of human behavior and the criminal law.

Much of criminologic theory development has taken us down a primrose path searching for a "unified theory" of criminality. It has been in the tradition of early demonology, albeit seeking more "scientific" unifying themes such as physique, mental aberrations, glandular dysfunction, genetic disabilities, atavistic behavior, social ecology, cyclic variation in the economy or weather and associational patterns. Theories have tried ". . . to explain criminal behavior itself, but they do not concern themselves with why certain acts are defined as crimes;" sometimes oblivious to the interconnectedness of ". . . the acts [themselves] defined in the law as crimes and the forces that impel some people to commit these acts."[4] In either case, the notion of responsibility is frequently downgraded. Corrections, if not criminology, must come to terms with this problem. We can no longer await the refinement of theories before acting to modernize the field. Theorists, unlike convicts, are not quite so desperate but, like them, have plenty of time. Correctional administrators are not at such leisure.

We are not sure whether the sentence of imprisonment or any other penal sanction really deters (generally or specifically), but we are in agreement with Norval Morris and Gordon Hawkins when they observed that this endless debate seems to have deteriorated since the days of Beccaria: ". . . Discussions of this ancient antinomy which have consumed gallons of jurisprudential ink turn out on examination to resemble nothing so much as boxing matches between blind-folded contestants."[5] However, we do have a substantial guide for future correctional action from the work of Walker and Wilkins (cited in Chapter III).

We propose the following proposition, based upon a perspective suggested by Stephen Schafer, upon which the model of justice in corrections can be operationalized:

1. Criminal law is the "command of the sovereign."*
2. The threat of punishment is necessary to implement the law.
3. The powerful manipulate the chief motivators of human behavior—fear and hope—through rewards and punishments to retain power.
4. Socialization (the manipulation of fear and hope through rewards and punishments) of individuals, however imperfect, occurs in response to the commands and expectations of the ruling social-political power.
5. Criminal law protects the dominant prescribed morality (a system of rules said to be in the common and best interest of all) reflecting the enforcement aspect "of the failure of socialization."**
6. In the absence of an absolute system of justice or a "natural law," no accurate etiological theory of crime is possible nor is the definition of crime stable.

7. Although free will may not exist perfectly, the criminal law is largely based upon its presumed vitality and forms the only foundation for penal sanctions.
8. A prison sentence represents a punishment sanctioned by a legislature and meted out through the official legal system within a process of justice against a person adjudged responsible for his behavior. Although the purpose of such a punishment may be deterrence, it is

---

*And, as Schafer reminds, this "may be a gloomy truth whether the origin of the law is traditional or revolutionary." (Stephen Schafer, *The Political Criminal*, p. 47).

**Schafer states: "Morality is not the product of law; the law exists to enforce morality," and ". . . criminal law is a kind of back up instrument in the socialization process, and it comes into operation whenever the state of any moral issue so warrants." (Stephen Schafer, *The Political Criminal*, pp. 84, 104).

specifically the deprivation of liberty for a fixed period of time.*

9. The entire process of the criminal law must be played out in a milieu of justice. Justice-as-fairness represents the superordinate goal of all agencies of the criminal law.

10. When corrections becomes mired in the dismal swamp of preaching, exhorting, and treating ("resocialization") it becomes dysfunctional as an agency of justice. Correctional agencies should engage prisoners as the law otherwise dictates—as responsible, volitional and aspiring human beings.

11. Justice-as-fairness is not a *program*; it is a *process* that insists the prisons (and all agencies of the criminal law) perform their assigned tasks with non-law-abiders lawfully. No more should be expected, no less should be tolerated by correctional administrators.

12. William Pitt said: "where the law ends tyranny begins"; so does the exercise of discretion. Discretion "may mean either beneficence or tyranny, either justice or injustice, either reasonableness or arbitrariness."[6] Discretion cannot be eliminated, but the justice perspective seeks to narrow, control, and make it reviewable.[7]

Having stated the propositions, we now use them as a springboard for examining their rational implementation in correctional institutions. Of the major areas in correctional administration that most vitally affect the operation of prisons, three will be discussed: sentencing and parole boards (taken together), and prison administration. We are interested in how the prison stay is determined, organized and, for most prisoners, ended. Following this analysis we will propose some alternatives. But in preface

---

*"... if punishment is to be considered as aim of imprisonment, it must be what the Germans termed 'Zweckstrafe,' or punishment for a purpose, rather than 'Vergeltungsstrafe,' or punishment as retribution." (A.C.A. "Manual of Correctional Standards," as cited in Killinger and Cromwell, *Penology*, p. 76).

some thoughts on justice are offered so that whatever bias the reader may have previously overlooked may once again be refocused.

ON JUSTICE—A PERSPECTIVE

Philosopher John Rawls identifies justice as: ". . . the first virtue of social institutions, as truth is of systems of thought, . . . a theory however elegant and economical must be rejected or revised if it is untrue; likewise laws and institutions no matter how efficient and well-arranged must be reformed or abolished if they are unjust."[8] In order to develop an operational model of justice in corrections we must move from the philosopher's chair to the cellblock. Speaking about the student of ethics, Hans Reichenback suggested: ". . . [he] should not go to the philosopher, he should go where the moral issues are fought out."[9] A concept of justice is useful to the scholar, but it contains an urgency in practice. Great ideas are played out by average men, not, as Edmond Cahn reminds us, by the legally constructed "reasonable man" who is usually too dull to get into trouble with officials.[10]

The human rights explosion of the 1960s—a postponed extension of unfinished American agendas of 1776 and 1861—is belatedly finding its way over the prison walls. In this process, correctional administrators are not the only ones being shaken up among the professions. Young doctors and medical students as well as young lawyers and law students have in the last decade challenged the long-accepted entrepreneurial styles of their seniors. It was not until the 1960s that internal dissension forced these professions to seriously consider new ways of treating and representing the poor in need of their services. In other professions, internal revolts also brought style changes: social workers became advocates for their "clients" who in turn, at least rhetorically, become "constituents." Wide-spread rebellions in education, involving dissatisfied parents and students, gave birth to thousands of "alternative schools." Educators in the public school system scurried to compete by bringing ideas out of the backroom that lay dormant for years. We need not here recount the insurrections that hit higher education nationally. Rump groups appeared at the annual conclaves of many professional organizations in both the social and physical sciences. Youth, minorities, women, and the aged rebelled. Long-quiet groups also reacted in uncustomary militant styles: the Department of Justice was picketed by the newly-formed Italian Defamation League; and police, who were otherwise angered at the suggestion of amnesty for thousands of draft evaders, students and prison rioters, now demanded it for themselves after returning from illegal strikes, slowdowns and "blue flu" epidemics.

Corrections, however, had only a few sputtering responses to this national upsurge—mostly reactive. The correctional counterpart to this quiet and sometimes not-so-quiet revolution came mainly from prisoners inside the walls and reform groups outside the walls. The "revolution" has yet to deeply penetrate the profession. Prison officials, as in the past, with some notable exceptions, participated in innovation through rhetoric. Guards became officers and officers became counselors, but they remained in uniform and at the bottom of a poorly paid occupational heap. The "hole" became a quiet room, a meditation room, a time-out room—but, in most cases, it was still the hole. There was a fitful start for community-based corrections, deinstitutionalization, decriminalization, and decentralization. The death penalty was, in the inimitable style of the judicial mind, declared to be cruel and inhumane—sometimes. As 1974 came to an end, several states reenacted constitutional death sentences—presumably uncruel and humane laws if they pass the Eighth Amendment test. Since 1968, when we redeclared the "war on crime," the prison population and crime have been inching upward. The Commander-in-Chief and his crime war's general staff of Agnew, Mitchell and Kleindienst went into a forced retirement of sorts. They scored only one Pyrrhic victory in a Saturday Night Massacre resulting mainly in Bostonian casualties. Like the first Boston Massacre, the victims became heroes and the perpetrators villains. However, a momentous event occurred in the late 1960s that provided an opportunity for correctional leadership to demonstrate its morality—and it did.

Tom Murton of Arkansas uncovered, or rather made public, the calculated use of electrical torture in that state's prison; and then he dug up, from shallow graves, the decapitated remains of three convicts. The response was immediate: a grand jury met planning to indict Murton for exhuming human bodies, and Murton was fired by the late Governor Winthrop Rockefeller (his brother Nelson would three years later also be inscribed in correctional history at Attica). A colleague writing in a national journal felt that: ".... Actually the governor apparently was not disputing the fact that many inmates had died suspicious deaths in the past years; he simply recognized that nothing could be gained by digging up bones except to embarrass and antagonize the legislature. The important job was not to exhume the past, but to build the future."[11] An extraordinary view: an agent of justice urging participation in a cover-up of multiple homicide! A President has since fallen (although pardoned) for less. Would the same action follow upon discovery of the decapitated bodies of three guards? A few years later at the A.C.A. annual conference in Miami, 101 years after the Cincinnati Declaration, the A.C.A. refused to pass a resolution requesting Arkansas to investigate the 200 missing and possibly dead prisoners while concurrently condemning the unnecessary force used against inmates that often results in death. Chairing the resolutions committee was Walter Dunbar, who in a month would be a party to the use of such force at Attica, this time resulting in the death of guards as well. Dunbar stated that the A.C.A. has for a century been in favor of humane treatment but that this was a police matter—the resolution was defeated.*

---

*In recent months Germany experienced a similar problem, but the responsible officials' action was quite different.

   ... An extraordinary prison scandal in West Germany, involving murder, torture, bribery and corruption, shows no sign of abating after three weeks of revelations. ... The details which have emerged so far

JUSTICE IN THE CONSUMER PERSPECTIVE

We used the Murton-Arkansas-A.C.A. event to illustrate the meaning of the justice approach necessary to free corrections from its rhetoric of godliness and practice of devilishness.

We are not interested in "utopian diagrams about abstract justice . . . justice will mean . . . the active process of remedying or preventing what would arouse the 'sense of injustice',"[12] as Edmond Cahn wrote. He captured well the gut-level feeling that might have been aroused at Miami in relation to Arkansas:

> When we see or hear or read about this sort of conduct we feel that sympathetic reaction of outrage, resentment, and anger and those affections of the viscera and adrenal secretions that prepare human beings to resist attack, for our physiology has equipped us to regard an *act of injustice* to another as a personal aggression against ourselves . . . whenever officials misuse their power, or oppress the innocent and unoffending, they provoke our sense of injustice.[13]

But it is more than a "sense of injustice" that calls up empathetic reactions.

----

do not make good reading. The prisoner who died, Hans-Peter Vast, aged 25, was found dead in his cell on December 27. He had choked to death on his own vomit after being savagely beaten up and kicked by warders. . . . The miasma of brutality and corruption which has so far emerged appears to be only the tip of the iceberg. The authorities have now ordered all the files on allegations of ill-treatment of prisoners or unnatural death in custody, closed since 1970, to be reopened and investigated.

The State Attorney's office has been told to pay special attention to all current and new investigations into allegations of ill-treatment in all the state's prisons. . . .

At a press conference today, the first he has given since the scandal erupted at the beginning of this month, Dr. Traugott Bender, the state's Minister of Justice, made it clear that there was more to come. He broke off his summer holiday to deal with the affair.

It was 'not to be excluded' that further irregularities would come to light. They would be fully investigated. . . .

(From Dan van der Vat, Bonn, Aug. 27, 1974.)

The correctional model of justice we arrive at is an adaptation of Cahn's "consumer perspective." It focuses the official processor of justice on the consumer—on the people caught in the machinery of the agencies of justice: the offender, the guard, the victim, the witness and the taxpayer. Tappan (1951) had long ago brought this to our attention when he called for the protection of the innocent against injustice: "Three groups require some special consideration. In order of their numbers, they are the taxpayer who bears the cost, the actual or potential victim of the criminal who is most directly injured, and the innocent suspect who may be unjustly convicted and punished."[14] In relation to the "War on Poverty," Cahn's son Edgar and his wife Jean called this approach the "civilian perspective" rather than the "military perspective."[15] Jonathan Caspar, in relation to the criminal justice system, identifies it as the "consumer's perspective."[16] Similarly, it is what Philip Selznick refers to when he speaks of the imprisoned in need of "justice as therapy."[17] It is a concern for the micro-world of the participants in action, not in abstraction.*

The "consumer perspective," or "justice perspective" as we shall now refer to it, can be distinguished from the "imperial" or "official perspective" (Cahn, 1963):

> The official perspective has a typical rhetoric which, when expertly manipulated, can seem very persuasive. . . . Some of the familiar phrases are: the public interest in getting things finally settled; the duty to abide by established principles and precedents; the necessity of showing respect for expert judgment and administrative convenience; the dominant need for certainty in the law; the obligation to

---

*There is a parallel stream of thought encompassed in Lawrence Kohlberg's *Just Community* (two volumes, Harvard University School of Education), but in the last analysis it turns out to be a form of group therapy using morality as its rationale rather than the psyche. At times the two are indistinguishable. Niantic Women's Prison in Connecticut is the current setting for Kohlberg's correctional demonstration project.

preserve the law's predictability so that men will know how to order their affairs; the danger of opening the floodgates of litigation; the danger of opening the gates of penitentiaries; the danger of inviting collusion, fraud, and perjury; the deference due to other organs of government; the absurdity of heeding mere speculations; the necessity of leaving certain wrongs, however grievous they may be, to the province of morals; the paramount need to maintain strict procedural regularity; and (by way of solace to a man on his way to the electric chair) the undeniable right to petition for executive clemency.[18]

The justice perspective involves a shift of focus from the processor to the consumer.

... but among the various consumers and their diverse interests, it offers no simplistic formula, no *a priori* preference, no lazy hierarchy of values. Some consumers need bread; others need Shakespeare; others need their rightful place in the national society—what they all need is processors of law who will consider the people's needs more significant' than administrative convenience. . . .

In the consumer perspective, there is something repulsive about the complacent grin with which we are assured that not many judges have been caught taking bribes, that the third degree is not so common as it used to be, and that not many prosecutors suppress evidence favorable to the defense or, if they do, it is seldom proved. [Or that uncovering convicts' corpses embarrasses legislators and thereby retards correctional reform.]

How can one expect to solace them by promising that some day the law will awake to needs like theirs? Unless a litigant happens to be an Olympian philosopher or a legal historian, he probably desires justice here and now. . . . What he cannot understand is inertia and smug indifference.[19]

Corrections has long been cut off from ties with the general field of public administration. Speaking of the courts, but with equal validity in corrections, Judge Marvin Frankel states: "One need not be a revolutionist or an enemy of the judiciary to predict that untrained, untested, unsupervised men armed with great power will perpetuate abuse."[20] Low visibility and high discretion eventually corrupts. An unhealthy wall of absolute power has kept correctional administrators shut off from the mainstream of the history of ideas, the spirit of open political conflict (other than those of parochial localisms), their constituencies, and general involvement in the public arena. Wardens have long resisted public accountability (Kadish, 1962):

> . . . [t]he common demand twenty-five years ago for freedom of the administrator to get on with his job free of the harassment of legal imperatives is the same demand made today by those who administer the new penology. A beginning in the correctional area awaits a general recognition that the correctional agency is not *sui generis,* but another administrative agency which requires its own administrative law if it is to make its maximum contributions harmoniously with the values of the general social order in which it functions.[21]

The usual correctional response has been that large dosages of discretion are necessary if correctional administrators are expected to treat (rehabilitate) criminals. But we have also been warned by Justice Brandeis: "Experience should teach us to be most on our guard to protect liberty when the Government's purposes are beneficent."[22] George Bernard Shaw, speaking of the ruthlessness of the pure heart, said: "Malice and fear are narrow things, and carry with them a thousand inhibitions and terrors and scruples. A heart and brain purified of them gain an enormous freedom . . . presumably to do anything in the name of benevolence."[23]

> There is growing recognition that correctional agencies exercise a very significant form of governmental power, even more important to the lives of individuals than most governmental agencies . . . there is also need to [administer]

> ... in ways that are just and that inspire in the offender, as far as possible, and in the community a confidence in the justice of the correctional process. ... But the most important question is whether corrections should actively be concerned with the fairness of its processes beyond conforming to legal standards and participating in the creation of new ones. Legislative and judicial standards for the conduct of administrative agencies are necessarily minimum standards. ... Reliance must be placed upon the administrative agency itself to achieve that goal.[24] (Dawson, 1969.)

It is evident that correctional administrators have for too long operated with practical immunity in the backwashes of administrative law. They have been unmindful that the processes of justice more strictly observed by the visible police and courts in relation to rights due the accused before and through adjudication must not stop when the convicted person is sentenced.[25] The justice perspective demands accountability from all processors, even the "pure of heart." *Properly understood, the justice perspective is not so much concerned with administration of justice as it is with the justice of administration.*[26]

Using the justice perspective, we now examine sentencing, parole and life in the prison.

ON SENTENCING AND PAROLE GRANTING

Judge Marvin Frankel wrote a book entitled *Criminal Sentences* (1973), and after reading it one can very clearly understand the double entendre intended. It might have been entitled *The Crime of Sentencing* or, more charitably, *The Lawlessness of Sentencing.* It was not, nor is this analysis intended, as an attack upon judges; but rather on a sentencing system which is anomic. With few guidelines and many judges we are effectively, in the area of sentencing, a government of men, not laws.[27]

Experience, and wisdom flowing out of that experience,

long ago led to the belief that agents of government should not be vested with power and discretion to define and punish as criminal past conduct which had not been clearly defined as a crime in advance. To this end, at least in part, written laws came into being, marking the boundaries of conduct for which public agents could thereafter impose punishment upon people. In contrast, bad governments either wrote no general rules of conduct at all, leaving that highly important task to the unbridled discretion of government agents at the moment of trial, or sometimes, history tells us, wrote their laws in an unknown tongue so that people could not understand them or else placed their written laws at such inaccessible spots that people could not read them. *Ginzburg v. United States*, 383 U.S. 463, 477 (1966).[28]

It is of vital interest to administrators of correctional agencies that the people committed to them, because of the usual bitterness they have upon arrival, must also have the feeling that the judicial process immediately undergone was fair, just, and that the sentence received was offense-related and appropriate.[29] This is largely not the case at present.

SENTENCING PATTERNS

The nation has several different adult sentencing schemes: (1) a system of both maximum (MA) and minimum (MI) terms fixed by the court (each offense has its own upper and lower limits set by law); (2) both MA and MI (within legal limits) fixed by court with MI not to exceed a portion of the MA; (3) MA (within limits set by law) fixed by court and the MI fixed by law; (4) MA fixed by law and MI by court; (5) MA and MI fixed by law for each offense; (6) MA fixed by law but no MI in law, rather the MI is fixed by the parole board; (7) MA fixed by court, no MI; and (8) MI is fixed by law and MA by the parole authority.[30]

In addition to this national crazy-quilt sentencing system, sentence disparities occur within the same jurisdiction. It is too facile to permit the disparities to be explained as individualized justice being meted out by different judges.° Absent sentencing criteria, the individual judge's attitude surfaces as the controlling force. Like others, judges have strong attitudes about sex, mugging, narcotics and other crimes. The difference in the case of judges is that their attitudes, translated into largely unbridled discretion, produce the longest prison terms in the western world. Blacks are treated more severely°° by prison sentences than their white counterparts for similar crimes.[31] But race is not the only problem, as James Bennett has observed:

> In one of our institutions a middle-aged credit union treasurer is serving 117 days for embezzling $24,000 in order to cover his gambling debts. On the other hand, another middle-aged embezzler with a fine family is serving 20 years, with 5 years probation to follow. At the same institution is a war veteran, a 39-year-old attorney who has never been in trouble before, serving 11 years for illegally importing parrots into this country. Another who is destined for the same institution is a middle-aged tax accountant who on tax fraud charges received 31 years and 31 days in consecutive sentences. In stark contrast, at the same institution last year an unstable young man served out his 98-day sentence for armed bank robbery.[32]

Indeterminate sentences, said to be a treatment tool, have produced more severe prison terms.[33]

> 70 per cent of definite sentence prisoners actually serve two years or less; whereas only 57 per cent of the indeterminate sentence prisoners actually serve two years or less. . . .

°Richard McGee calls our attention to the fact that the "hanging judge" and "softheaded judge" (disparities within a jurisdiction) are largely the same product of rulelessness sentencing systems. ("A New Look at Sentencing-Part II," *Federal Probation*, September 1974.)

°°Blacks, in the Federal system in 1969 and 1970 were averaging 88.5 months compared to whites at 75.1 months. *Federal Bureau of Prison Statistical Report*, 1969 and 1970 (table A-3A).

Clearly, therefore, in practice the indeterminate sentence system serves to keep a substantially greater proportion of men in prison for longer terms than the definite sentence system.[34] (Rubin, 1973)

The sentencing procedure itself, which presumably represents the apex of the adjudication process (up to this point justice was largely procedural), where the sovereign now "restores the balance" by meting out justice, is largely lawless. Legislatively prescribed procedures are practically non-existent. Regardless of what the judge finally selects as a sentence, the process itself, with rare exception, is inscrutable. We do not know because we do not require an explication of sentence selection norms. "We do not allow each judge to make up the law for himself on other questions. We should not allow it with respect to sentencing," said Judge Frankel.[35] Continuing, he points out:

In deciding where to fix any particular sentence, he will presumably consider a host of factors in the case: the relative seriousness of the particular offense—the degree of danger threatened, cruelty, premeditation; the prior record of the defendant; situational factors—health, family disturbance, drug use; the defendant's work history, skills, potential; etc. In the existing mode . . . the judge is under no pressure—and is without guidelines—toward systematic, exhaustive, detailed appraisal of such things one by one. He probably does not list them even for himself.[36]

Even if some judges do list these factors when imposing sentences, the process is still ambiguous since we have not developed a uniform procedure mandating all judges to do so.* Moreover, even when judges are thoughtful, the information they have before them upon which to base a consideration is frequently inadequate, of a bland generalized nature and this criti-

---

*In 1974, the Alaska Supreme Court, by rule, directed the sentencing judge to list and explain one or more reasons for the sentence imposed. The Supreme Court listed the following as properly representing reasons for incarceration: punishment, incapacitation, rehabilitation, and upholding of community mores.

cism "... is not mitigated by the appending of diagnostic charts and summaries that are sometimes legible, and less often intelligible, to the sentencing judge."[37] Finally, whatever the sentencing process is, it is not adversary and is rarely reviewable.

One might think that with such unbridled and unassailable power the judge's sentence would indeed be carried out to the letter. That may have been true at an earlier time, but it is no longer the case.

> The correlation between courtroom pronouncement and actual outcome has virtually disappeared. The history of penal policy during this interval is in no small measure one of erosion of judicial power and the evolution of a highly complex process of administrative punishment-fixing that directly involves prosecutors, parole boards and the disciplinary committees. ... From this functional perspective, judges are doing less and less of the real decision-making, their role being merely one step in a process in which law enforcement, prosecutors, probation officers, parole boards, parole agents or correctional staff may play major roles.[38] (Caleb Foote, 1972)

At the front end of the criminal justice system, the district attorney, using his bargaining power, makes key decisions concerning the severity of the sentence. And at the other end of the system, the parole board determines the actual length of the sentence.* The prisoner, "... kept in the dark about how to behave," in order to minimize his sentence, finds his life cast in a "pattern of cryptic taciturnity."[39]

Parole boards, without a legal mandate to sentence, continue to play a larger role than judges in sentencing. Caleb Foote (1972) comments on parole board decision making:

---

* "When you think about it, parole boards really have more to say about how long a person's liberty must be taken away from him than the courts do." (Maurice Sigler, Chairman of the U.S. Parole Board, *The Courts and Corrections,* Speech 8/17/73, Kirksville, Mo.)

The same basic criteria are usually employed whether the arena is a courtroom or some prison parole hearing room, e.g.: (1) a determination of how much time is right for the kind of crime at issue, with the decision-maker's own sense of values and expectations usually (but not always) heavily influenced by the pressures of his environment and what he perceives to be the norms of his colleagues; (2) classification within that crime category of the offender's particular act as mitigated, average or aggravated; (3) his past criminal record (slight, average or aggravated); (4) the extent of his repentence, his attitude towards available 'treatment', and the official prognosis of his reformability; or (5) the anticipated public (usually meaning law enforcement) reaction to a proposed disposition.[40]

Parole boards, without benefit of legislation, have inherited much of the sentencing power normally associated with the judiciary.[41]

Parole board decisions are also unreviewable and are not hammered out in an adversary clash; rather they are five to fifteen minute sessions with members frequently using a combination of whim, caprice, and arbitrariness. Speaking of the Federal Parole Board, Kenneth Culp Davis (1973) states:

Board members never deliberate together. They do not write memoranda discussing pros and cons. They think separately. They vote separately. No board member knows the reasons for his colleagues' votes . . . in 1964 a pamphlet entitled 'Functions of the United States Board of Parole,' . . . explained: Voting is done on an individual basis by each member and the Board does not sit as a group for this purpose. Each member studies the prisoner's file and places his name on the official order form to signify whether he wishes to grant or deny parole. The reasoning and thought which led to his vote are not made a part of the order, and it is therefore impossible to state precisely why a particular prisoner was or was not granted parole. . . . If a board member is in such a hurry to get to his golf game that he votes in sixteen cases without looking inside the files, no one under the board's system can ever know the difference, even

198 / "... We Are the Living Proof ..."

though the personal liberty of sixteen men may be at stake. How could a board member have less incentive to avoid prejudice or undue haste than by a system in which his decision can never be reviewed and in which no one, not even his colleagues, can ever know why he voted as he did? Even complete irrationality of a vote can never be discovered.[42]

And as if to say "amen," Maurice Sigler, following *Morressey v. Brewer*, 408 U.S. 471 (1971), said in a speech (1973): ". . . perhaps it should have been foreseen that eventually parole actions would have to be governed by considerations of due process."*[43]

Compared to the open courtroom, the parole board hearing is secret. Only recently have reasons for denial been given to convicts in a systematic manner, but decisions, short of a finding of abuse of discretion, are not successfully appealed.[44]

We find vague the rhetoric of the imperial or official perspective guiding judges and parole boards in their decisions. The justice perspective challenges the lack of clarity and degree of certainty of such expressions as: "the sound exercise of judicial discretion," "the consideration of the crime and the criminal," "the gravity of the deed," "the guilt of perpetrator."[45] They are, Caleb Foote points out, no more than slogans; none are law.[46] In the quest for fairness using the justice perspective, we seek a justification *in law* for the decisions of those who exercise wide discretion. "The largely unbridled power of judges and prison officials stir questions under the clauses promising that life and liberty will not be denied except by 'due process of law.'"[47] Justice Stewart once described some sentencing practices as discriminatory, wanton and freakish.[48]

---

*Following this and other court decisions, the Parole Commission and Reorganization Act now provides due process safeguards in parole proceedings (see Chapter 3, herein, at p. 161 et seq). Other notable provisions of this Act are: access to documents upon which parole decisions are based, notification of reasons for denial of parole, appeal of all parole decisions, and the opening of regional offices to expedite parole matters. The Act also changes the name of the U.S. Parole Board to the U.S. Parole Commission. See 18 U.S.C. § 4201 et seq, (1976).

We have made this brief excursion into the realm of ruleless sentencing and parole granting not for the purpose of extensive analysis, but rather to better understand the prisoner as he enters and tries to legally leave the prison.° Prison life is largely a product of the anomie of sentencing and paroling. Like both, it too is effectively ruleless. How could it be otherwise with 95% of its prisoners unable to calculate when they will be released or even what is demanded of them for release candidacy by parole authorities? These two processes, uncontrollable by prison officials, have crucial impact on life inside the walls, to which we now turn.

A RESTATEMENT OF THE PURPOSE OF PRISON

At one level the problem with prisons is that they have never bitten off a digestable chunk. A narrowing of the rhetoric and purpose is necessary. A prisoner who enters with feelings of despair after having received a sentence he feels improper but unreviewable, now has to settle down to life in a cage. First he must turn his attention to protecting his internal integrity from a sequence of largely lawless events—prison life. This would be a herculean task for most. But he also learns that still another lawless (in the sense of ruleless) process needs to be under-taken—his preparation for parole. As a stranger in a zoo-like world, he begins to seek out others who can significantly speed his process of release. But who can make such judgments in a prison? What appears to be a rational, even tightly-drawn mili-tary-like prison staff organization, is, upon closer examination, chaotic.°° Again the question turns on discretion.

Theoretically, the staff of the prison regularly furnishes the

---

°See Appendix IV. The sham of "clinical" parole decisions is obvious in California, where release dates have been set for a large number of inmates only in order to lower 1977 budget projections, and where prison population has fluctuated according to the political aspirations of Governor Reagan (*down* 7000 in 1966-72 for political "economy," and *up* 4500 in 1972-74 in his "get tough" preparation for a presidential bid).

°°"Seen from outside, the criminal justice and correctional system presents

parole board information assessing the prisoner's clinical progress, its pace or its absence. Of the myriad events that take place, how can discriminating information be sensibly selected, collected, distilled and reported to the board? After the board "studies" the convict's behavior in prison, it must make a decision concerning his future community behavior—no small task.[**] Unaided by rules, reviewable findings or precedents, the board usually makes its decision using a melange of whim, time served, caprice, the amount of "noise" created by law enforcement agencies, arbitrariness, and authoritative testaments from clinical and other staff concerning the convict's reformative progress (which very few board members are trained to understand even if one concedes relevancy). It is in this process that prison staff decision-making fades into unbridled, low visibility discretion. If

---

the appearance of a virtually omnipotent conspiracy for the organization of human misery. But once having won his way in, the outsider—now a participant—discovers a shocking fact. Except for the universal penchant of bureaucrats to cover their own trails, there is no conspiracy. Indeed, there is hardly any 'organization.' What appeared at a distance to be a monolithic system turn out to be no system at all—but rather a concatenation of several interest groups, frequently operating at cross purposes or, worse, without reference to each other at all. In the chaos thus propagated, accident, apathy, non-account ability and sheer inertia are fully capable of producing fortuitously what the most efficient, concerted malice might have achieved by design: the almost total debasement of human aspiration." (Richard R. Korn, "The Prisoners of Affirmation: Correctional Administrators as Penal Reformers," in *Prisoner Rights,* by Michele Hermann and Marilyn Haft (editors), 1973, p. 441).

[**]The *Attica Commission Report, 1972* found:

While the board acts favorably in most cases, it engenders hostility because of the inconsistency of its rationale. Some inmates who have had good behavior records in prison are "hit" [denied parole], while others with many infractions are granted parole. Some inmates with a long record of prior offenses may receive parole, while others, including first offenders, may be denied it. Nobody gives the inmate an explanation for these apparently inconsistent decisions or describes in anything more than meaningless generalities the criteria used by the board in arriving at its decisions. Institutional parole officers give inmates pointers on what might subsequently impress the board, such as enrolling in Bible classes. But inmates who follow this advice carefully often find they are hit nevertheless. As a result, inmates are left to speculate among themselves as to the reasons for the board's decisions. Corruption and chance are among the favorite inmate speculations.

⁂

at first blush discretion looks like power, in prison it also produces an arena in which indecisiveness, favoritism, racism, suppression and lawlessness are acted out daily. The system calls
forth such responses from staff and convicts because it gives no
direction, has no accountable mission, and, in the absence of
accountability, claims much more than it can produce.

We have to conceive of the period of incarceration and its
place in criminal justice in a new way. Consider the problem
facing Thomas Edison when he was pondering a new technology
for developing artificial light.* The imagery he labored under at
the time was "candle power" and how to increase its potency.
Staring at the candle and acting upon that model, he would have
simply produced larger and larger candles. Edison needed and
produced a flight in imagination to arrive to the electric light
bulb. In corrections we are still toying with the candle. The following suggestions are based upon a two-pronged strategy:
(1) the immediate and short range, and (2) the middle range. No
long range is offered because of the critical urgency to move
rapidly; "progress" in corrections is usually counted in decades.
The distinguishing characteristic between the two strategies is
that the short range requires no legislation or new appropriations
while the middle range requires both.

Far from instilling confidence in the Parole Board's sense of justice, the
existing procedure merely confirms to inmates, including those receiving
favorable decisions, that the system is indeed capricious and demeaning.
(pp. 97, 98)

Hans Mattick, describing the parole process, states: [paraphrased] "It has
transformed American prisons into great centers of drama with convicts playing the role of actors and parole boards as drama critics awarding prizes called
freedom."

*See Richard Korn's elaboration of the theory of social gradualism: "One of
the abiding doctrines of evolutionary social theory is that radical change is
illusory and therefore fruitless to attempt. . . . If [this] were true, one could
have confidently predicted that gradual improvement in the sailing ship would
have eventually produced the steamboat, that progressive refinement of the
gas lamp would have resulted in electric light. . . . The doctrine of evolutionary gradualism . . . still remains persuasive to many who rely on it for major
improvements in the social realm." (Richard R. Korn, "A Review," in *Crime
and Delinquency,* NCCD Journal, October, 1970, p. 446.)

IMMEDIATE AND SHORT RANGE

We need to conceptualize imprisonment differently and narrow our rhetorical claims. A penal sanction should *only* mean a temporary deprivation of liberty. It is the legal cost for the violation of some laws. *The prison is responsible for executing the sentence, not for rehabilitating the convict.*

> In seeking to make criminal justice more redemptive and less punitive, we may have asked too much of institutions that can barely hold their own, let alone develop the competence to be curers of souls. A retreat from rosy hopes may well be inevitable, if only because rehabilitation entails supervision, and ineffective rehabilitation coupled with open-ended control has little to commend it.[49] (Selznick, 1968)

The sentence must be seen as a part of the continuum of justice—it must be experienced justly, reasonably and constitutionally. It is in the contest of justice that a mission arises for the prison and its staff. The mission is *fairness*. Until sentencing and parole problems can be resolved, discretion must be harnessed by as much voluntary administrative explication of norms as is necessary to produce a sense of fairness for both the keeper and the kept.

The prison sentence should merely represent a deprivation of liberty. *All the rights accorded free citizens consistent with mass living and the execution of a sentence restricting the freedom of movement should follow a prisoner into prison.* The prisoner is volitional and may therefore choose programs for his own benefit. The state cannot with any degree of confidence hire one person to rehabilitate another unless the latter senses an inadequacy in himself that he wishes to modify through services he himself seeks. This should be evident from historical experience.

C. Wright Mills saw professional pathologists as possessed of an ". . . occupationally trained incapacity to rise above [a] series of 'cases'."[50] A proposal by David Greenberg[51] for corrections to use a voucher system for the delivery of services elicited a response reminiscent of Mills' critique. In this case the pathologist is unable to visualize an offender apart from his therapist.

> My objection to the Greenberg article is its subtle concept that offenders can do a better job *alone* in the gearing of services to needs and that correctional agents would be dysfunctional in this task. *Progress in corrections* will come via a cooperative arrangement between offenders and correctional agents [presumably in a caseworker situation.] A naive article like Greenberg's is *dangerous*; it *separates* the two parties that have a *vested interest* in correction.[52]

It is indeed dangerous since it assumes *volition* (hence a new status) on the part of the offender. Volition is subversive of the foundation of the clinical model because the offender exercises independence of choice and may therefore not select the clinician as his choice of treatment. The person troubled or in trouble has to want something to happen. The best way to engage him is to treat him with dignity. *Administrators should immediately begin to zero-base budget all such program services not voluntarily chosen by inmates.*

> *The postulate of normality, competence, and worth.* If offenders are to be dealt with as human beings, it must be assumed that they are basically like everyone else, only their circumstances are special. Every administrative device that negates this principle, and any therapy that ignores it, must be questioned and, if possible, set aside.[53] (Selznick, 1968)

We will shortly elaborate a prison mission of justice for our current fortress prison environment—but the fortress prison system must be ended if we are to expect further rationality in correctional development.

MIDDLE RANGE

There are three elements which should govern the middle

range strategy which will be elaborated later: (1) a return to flat time sentences with procedural rules in law governing sentence selection; (2) the elimination of both parole boards and parole agencies as we have known them; and (3) the transformation of the fortress prison into institutions for no more than 300 persons, further divisible into sub-units of 30. The institutions will contain people sentenced to similar terms. Release will be determined by a narrow and reviewable system of vested good-time rules. We turn first to those elements of a short range which can be immediately implemented by administrators.

A JUSTICE MODEL FOR THE PRISON

The period of incarceration can be conceptualized as a time in which we try to reorient a prisoner to the lawful use of power. One of the more fruitful ways the prison can teach non-law-abiders to be law-abiding is to treat them in a lawful manner. The entire effort of the prison should be seen as an influence attempt based upon operationalizing justice. This is called the *justice model.*

It begins, not by moralizing, but by recognizing what the prison stay is about. Simply stated, it is an enforced deprivation of liberty, the taking of some or all of the days of a person's life and his confinement within an area. When men are confined against their will in this country, the bottom line of the arrangement of life for both the keeper and kept should be *justice-as-fairness.* Opportunities for self-improvement should be offered but not made a condition of freedom.

Confinement and compression, in a human zoo, of large numbers of men who in the past have frequently resorted to the use of force, fraud and violence is at best a precarious venture. James Q. Wilson said: "We have imposed the rehabilitative philosophy in a way that offends simple justice . . . when it is possible for one person, by manipulating the system, to go free while another, convicted of the same crime, remains in prison for a long term."[54] Prison administrators should not further confuse their staff with a mission either claiming moral or psychological redemption or with one that leans on brutality to create a Lyndsian type of orderliness. Selznick, writing about the "poverty of power," states:

. . . an administration that relies solely on its own coercive resources can make little contribution to the reconstruction of prison life or to the creation of environments that encourage autonomy and self-respect. [On achieving order he states:] Quiescent conformity imposed from above is a parody of social order, not its fulfillment. A system that validates the humanity of its participants, and engages their full resources, accepts the risk of disorder and even, from time to time, of searing confrontations.[55]

Herman Schwartz makes a similar point (1972):

. . . part of the prison's failure as a rehabilitational technique is that it denies prisoners any responsibility, any real control over their destinies. Yet having responsibility is indispensible to acting responsibily—prisoners cannot be expected to live responsibly in a free society if we permit prisons to atrophy all the skills, habits and attributes that are necessary to such behavior.

. . . it is an axiom of social dynamics that no respect will come except in response and reaction to power. Openness and the development of prisoner power of course appall and frighten traditional prison administrators.[56]

Life in prison can be made saner and safer for the keeper and kept by reconceiving its meaning. The justice model calls for all the ingenuity an administrator can muster to place the inmate population and staff within a lawful and rational arena. It appeals to both resident and worker to rationalize their stay in prison in a context of fairness.

Justice-as-fairness provides the keeper and the kept with a rationale and morality for their shared fates in a correctional agency. Considering the failure of most treatment methods within our current operating structure—the fortress prison—the justice model holds some promise, if not to cut recidivism, then to more decisively preclude Atticas. This model purports to turn a prison experience into one which provides opportunities for men to learn to be agents in their own lives, to use legal processes to change their condition, and to wield lawful power. *Men who can negotiate their fates do not have to turn to violence as a method of achieving change.*

It is a sad irony in our system of criminal justice that we insist on the full majesty of due process for the accused until he is sentenced to a prison; then justice is said to have been served. Consider that our criminal codes make it mandatory that before a criminal sanction may be imposed there be a finding beyond stringent levels of doubt that the accused's behavior was a union of *act* and *intent*—it was volitional. We will reduce degrees of responsibility for the alleged act if the behavior was adjudged non-volitional. We are tough in standards of arrest, most stringent in the finding of guilt. The defendant is protected under the mantle of the presumption of innocence. The state must prove its allegations "beyond a reasonable doubt." The defendant can stand mute in court and is protected from conviction out of his own mouth. Anything brought before the court to support a prosecutor's claim may be challenged. We believe that this system is civilized and protects us from star-chamber injustices. We strain to protect the lowliest from the capriciousness of legally constituted authority. The great irony occurs after a conviction when the judge commits a guilty offender to prison. It takes a great flight of imagination or studied neglect to include the current prison experience in a system of justice. The entire case for a justice model rests upon the need to continue to engage the person in the quest for justice as he moves on the continuum from defendant to convict to free citizen.

Our traditions and statutes support dysfunctionality. They first insist, in effect, that only volitional actors be sent to prison. Then corrections support treatment regimens which assume non-volitional behavior on the part of prisoners. On one level, the courts are increasingly aware of this dysfunctional aspect of the justice system and are responding by making themselves available as arbiters of predictable clashes between the keeper and the kept, as we have seen in Chapter III.

The proponents of the psychiatric or medical model visualized themselves as reformers. They grasped the prisoner from the onerous custody staff which meted out punishment for prison rule infractions. The clinicians viewed the prisoner as sick while custody staff saw him as bad. Both operated, until most recently, in an environment of low visibility and wide discretion. But the convict, it appears, would rather be bad than sick. He can hang onto a soft determinism and still be volitional. The clinicians didn't permit him much room for responsible behavior. One needs only to look at the extremes of either style to see their similarities and illogical conclusions from Arkansas to Patuxent. Speaking to "justice as therapy," Selznick observes (1968):

A concern for fairness and civic validation should permeate the entire administration of criminal law, including the daily life of the prisoner. That treatment will be most effective which does the most for the inmate's sense of self-worth and responsibility. Nothing contributes more to these feelings than a social environment whose constitutive principle is justice, with its corollaries of participation, giving reasons, and protecting personal dignity. . . .

Without questioning the worth of these objectives, it may be asked: Is it the public policy to punish offenders, especially young offenders, beyond the fact of imprisonment itself? If not, does humane and respectful treatment, not as therapy but as civilized conduct, require a special justification?[57]

The justice model seeks to engage both the keeper and the kept in a joint venture which insists that the agencies of justice shall operate in a lawful and just manner. It simply means that we believe that the prisoners did not use lawful means to guide themselves outside the prison and should therefore be provided greater (not lesser) opportunities to learn lawful behavior while in the institution. The staff effort should be turned to teaching a prisoner how to use lawful processes to achieve his ends. This also implies that the convict accepts the legal responsibility for the consequences of his behavior. In the absence of a continuum of justice in the prison, most ends are reached unlawfully. When unlawful behavior is detected, it is frequently dealt with in the absence of the very standards of due process we insist upon outside the prison. The result is a further indication to the convict that lawful behavior has little pay-off. He can be dealt with arbitrarily and usually responds by treating others in the same manner.

The justice model insists that, at least during the period of incarceration, the prisoner and the staff, as society's agents, will deal with problems in strict fairness—something we expect of each other outside of prison. Further, it points to a way of engaging both the keeper and kept in a rhetoric-free, manageable prison experience.

OPERATIONALIZING JUSTICE IN THE PRISON

The model of justice we propose affects several aspects of prison life. It attempts to create a lawful and rational arena for dealing with problems arising from an artificial environment which charges one group of men with forcibly restraining the mobility of another group of men. While this can probably never be voluntarily achieved, there are some immediate short range goals which we believe are realizable: (1) a mitigation of harshness, (2) peaceful conflict resolution, and (3) a safer staff work environment; these will emerge from the operationalization of fairness in prison life. What follows are some crucial aspects of the organization of prison life which, if reconceived and transformed, could be put in the service of reaching the previously cited short range goals. We will be concerned with the micro-world and macro-world concerns of prison administration. There is nothing contained in the programs offered with which the author has not already had an administrative experience.

I. JUSTICE IN THE MICRO-WORLD

Salience of the micro-world. Men live out their lives in specific settings, and it is there, in the crucible of inter-action, that potentialities are sealed off or released. The micro-world is the world of here-and-now, if an inmate's future is to be affected, that future should have a dynamic, existential connection with the experienced present.[58] (Selznick, 1968)

Citizens in a free society understand that the problems of everyday living in the home, marketplace, work, school, and church produce different perceptions of turf, claims, preroga-tives and rights. Accordingly, society attempts to organize orderly processes for conflict resolution. Conflict neglected may explode into violence. Conflict, to be resolved, must be trans-formed into negotiation, a form of diplomacy. However, the same problems that present themselves in free society are grossly magnified in a prison. Here the least significant micro-world event can, in the absence of conflict resolution mechanisms, escalate aimlessly into major disturbances, violence and death. Memoranda and directives clarifying expectations are helpful but do not settle hotly disputed claims. We offer a few alterna-tives.

1. Self-Governance

Two groups of people have historically been neglected in prison decision making—the guard and the convict. We begin with the premise that the prison is not an ideal setting for a democracy, but that it could be more democratized. While the "command of the sovereign" is louder inside a prison, there is no reason, as in the case outside the prison, why we cannot try to deepen the engagement of the governed in their own govern-ance.

One of the most strongly debated aspects of prison life is inmate self-governance. Experiments have been carried out sporadically over the entire history of corrections. They can be fairly categorized as having been both poorly executed and poorly documented. The arguments arising over forms of inmate self-governance represent historical reflections of the differing views of the purpose of prison. J.E. Baker finds few neutrals on the issue of inmate self-governance:

> Positive: Inmate self-government or inmate council systems are a part of the 'new penology' hence are therapeutic in nature. Since we are nothing if we are not therapeutic, then we are 'for' self-government. We know self-government will work if insidious forces do not undermine it.

> Negative: The entire history of self-government proves how unsound it is. It never lasted anywhere. That is proof enough of its unworthiness. If inmates were smart enough to govern themselves, they would not be in prison in the first place.[59]

Although many of the earliest forms of self-governance were found in homes for delinquent and orphaned children, Thomas Mott Osborne, Hiram Hatch and Howard B. Gill are among the most widely-acclaimed innovators of adult inmate self-governance. Osborne of Sing-Sing (1914) claimed: "These criminals were actually learning obedience to law, by practicing it; and insisting that everyone should obey."[60] Osborne's "Mutual Welfare League" was preceded by Zebulon R. Brockway, who over 40 years earlier had set up a plan for inmate self-government in the Detroit House of Corrections. Brockway's plan was based on Alexander Maconochie's Norfolk Island program.[61] Brockway's experiment used inmates in positions usually held by civilian officers. Helfman points out, "This promotion of inmates to semi-official relations and duties differed from the orthodox use of 'trustees' in local jails since the new duties were less servile and the institutional social status of the prisoners thus engaged was more elevated."[62] As with most experiments in inmate self-government, when Brockway resigned in 1871, the program came to an end.

The next major use of self-government was under Hiram F.

Hatch at the Michigan State Prison at Jackson; this program for "the adaptation of character to circumstances, the training to self command" ran from 1888 to 1891 when Warden Hatch resigned.[63]

An unsupervised group of convicts in Michigan drew up a constitution which read in part:

> The objects of this league shall be: by social intercourse to improve ourselves, and to aid in the moral, intellectual, physical and financial advancement of our fellowmen. To inculcate a higher appreciation of the value and sacred obligations of American citizenship, and the necessity of unconditional loyalty to the Federal and State government, as exemplified by a strict maintenance of the laws by them promulgated. To resist and oppose corruption and dishonesty in all forms and places and to promote honesty and efficiency in the discharge of all labor, tasks and duties assigned. To respect and aid by personal discipline, in the maintenance of all rules and regulations necessary to the discipline and good order of the prison.[64]

The Hatch program, called "The Mutual Aid League of MSP," had a close resemblance to Osborne's Mutual Welfare League pioneered a quarter of a century later.° Upon Hatch's resignation, all traces of the league were excised from the prison's history.°°

Osborne's plan, however,. was well documented. The convicts elected two representatives from each shop, they in turn elected

---

°Helfman points out that the closeness of the names, Mutual Welfare and Mutual Aid Leagues, and the similarities in the Brockway-Hatch structures probably precludes historical accident. They must have studied each other's forms. But we conclude from this that they all imitated Maconochie who pioneered inmate self-governance much earlier than Brockway, Hatch or Osborne.

°°An official state history "The Prison History: An Account of the Penal and Penitentiary System and Institutions of the State of Michigan. . ." (Lansing, 1899) makes no reference to Hatch's attempt at inmate governance.

a nine-member board of delegates. This board selected a sergeant-at-arms and set up judicial machinery to "try" cases of misconduct among the inmates. The elections were held at regular intervals, and the inmates who acted as judges were regularly rotated off the bench. As with other attempts at inmate self-governance, Osborne's League ended soon after he left the prison. He was viciously attacked for his reforms, indicted (the indictment was later dropped), and driven from office after two years.[65]

In 1927, Howard B. Gill of Massachusetts initiated what was to be known as the Norfolk Plan (Norfolk, Massachusetts, not to be confused with Maconochie and the Norfolk Island penal colony). It contained an inmate classification scheme, a group-based residence and supervision plan, the organization of prison life as a community assigning responsibilities to its citizen-convicts, and a series of individual treatment programs.[66] It was the housing units which furnished the constituencies for the inmate council. Of this system Gill said (1930):

> This is not to be confused with the strictly penal administration of the Colony [the prison itself] which is in the hands of the Superintendent and his assistants. Also in contrast to inmate organizations in some institutions which are founded on the principle of self-government in the hands of inmates only, this community organization operates on the principle of joint responsibility in which both officers and inmates take part. . . . Neither officers nor men give up their independence or their responsibilities, and each continually checks the other to insure square dealing; but both agree that cooperation works better than opposition where men must work and eat and live together, whatever the circumstances.[67]

J. E. Baker points out that many wardens simply regard any inmate council as a "gimme group."[68] A "gimme" group is one which, having achieved one level of aspiration, simply moves to attempt a higher one, not unlike life in the free world except for the narrow range of available levels attainable. Wardens, feeling that there is a finite limit though not able to calculate it, eventually call a halt to the "gimme" process; hence the demise of all councils sooner or later. One of the central reasons for failure according to Baker is that they depended too much on charismatic leadership and too little on institutionalization efforts requiring training others and instilling feelings of acceptance by lower echelon staff.[69]

> Two features of these past experiments stand out, both containing the seeds of self-destruction—inmates functioning as disciplinarians, and the dependence of the systems on a lone individual for sponsorship. . . . As administered, most of the past experiments in inmate self-government were inadequately structured and implemented arrangements superimposed on an untrained staff by individuals whose zeal far exceeded their correctional management ability. All of the self-government systems reviewed depended on a central figure and rapidly expired when that person departed. Apparently little, if any, effort was made to indoctrinate the staff and lead them to an acceptance of this concept of managing prisoners.[70]

More recently however, when staff is involved and has its role clearly defined, other results may be expected, as Studt, Messinger and Wilson found. (1968)

> When staff opened communication channels to a degree but continued to function without self-direction, inmates assumed the stereotyped 'gimme' approach customary when inmates are offered undefined access to discussion with officials. When staff themselves became a task-focused work group, inmates responded by becoming task-focused.[71]

The first element of the prison justice model is self-governance, but not in the historical sense of the "inmate council" or the "gimme group." Rather we suggest the joint venture model closer to Gill's idea of an inmate-staff governance group. Both groups of men should be heard, should be involved and thereby form a constituency inside the walls with the purpose of improving the quality of life and work in prison. The formats can vary, but the linkage of the inmates and staff is crucial to the sense of fairness herein proposed. The warden, with staff on the council, can feel easier about the "gimme" quality previous inmate council formats exhibited. Requests for programs and changes, he will realize, have been filtered through a staff prism. Inmates' perspectives will have been moderated by guards. Guards may finally become involved in program innovation, but more significantly, a forum for communication with the central actors present is created. The seats on the council may be filled in several different elective and elective-appointive formats. Several prisons might experiment with different formats.° The inmate-staff serves as a program planning and grievance mechanism. It is not, as were some earlier models, an internal court. The administration retains its veto power over proposals brought to it from the council.

A reasonable expectation for this type of council, with its thrust toward making behavior public on the part of both groups involved, is that it might serve as an early warning mechanism for the future problems. If such proves to be the case, then timely defusing (perhaps using other conflict resolution processes soon to be discussed) may help the administration avoid escalations leading to massive problems.

A program of self-governance does not mean that the council will be involved at the level of choosing the school colors. Its vitality and credibility will be established by the range of tasks with which it is permitted to deal. The President's Commission on Law Enforcement and the Administration of Justice has warned that ". . . Sometimes inmate cliques have controlled

---

°Stillwater Prison, Minnesota, is the only one, to the author's knowledge, with an inmate-staff council currently in existence with a three-year history.

elections to councils or have put pressure on those elected to reduce their orientation to staff objectives."[72] Because of the *inmate* council's weak historical past, the *inmate-staff* council may have difficulty in finding sympathetic adherents. However, the changed format of the inmate-staff council, placing both groups in the same boat, now permits it to undertake new tasks not previously available to the inmate councils of the past. The new format should not be brushed off with tired arguments about the older inmate council's shortcomings.* Unlike other attempts we do not visualize the council as a group of the "warden's boys" or an internal court for trying rule infraction cases.

2. Conflict Resolution

One of the new tasks a council may perform is that of conflict resolution through a formal procedure. As long as we are in the fortress prison we will have to assume that it will continue to be hazardous to the physical and emotional health of inmates and staff, that conflict is a normal ingredient of such compressed and pressured life, and that the participants in this abnormal prison society will need a machinery for peacefully settling such predictable and inevitable conflicts. Again, formats may differ, but the central point to be considered is that the new council might be entrusted with the prisons' formal grievance procedure, thereby becoming a vital agency in conflict resolution.

There is mounting evidence that now links weak inmate organization with rioting. Not permitting a formal public arena for negotiation (a sharing of power) forces inmates to withdraw to their own initiatives to ward off perceived assaults on their status. In general, Wilsnack and Ohlin** argue that institutions

---

*In 1960, the Wardens' Association, by resolution, opposed inmate self-government. (J.E. Baker, *Inmate Self-Government*, p. 47)

**Richard Wilsnack and Lloyd E. Ohlin in current research on *Prison Disturbances (Winter 1973-74)* pp. 1-41, unpublished manuscript, 1974 p. 28. (Harvard Law School, Center for Criminal Justice.)

permitting negotiation will experience disturbances of a non-riotous character (if experiencing any at all). Those prisons not permitting inmates the opportunity to make life more tolerable force prisoners to go beyond the prison walls to reach the public with a political message—the riot. Where prisoners learn that negotiation can make life tolerable, they tend to use it as a vehicle and have no need to resort to violence. An inmate-staff council increases communication, provides a negotiative model, and serves as an early warning system to guide preventive action. Convicts fully understand their less-than-equal power status when negotiating across the table from the administration, but elsewhere negotiation partners are rarely truly equal. It is the negotiation model, however, that does offer the prisoner status enhancement. In the absence of official (lawful) validation of such status, the prisoner seeks it unofficially (and frequently unlawfully). In the latter sense, inmate organization is said to be weak, fragmented, and in the hands of charismatic leaders who crystalize predictable discontent—all are the preconditions associated in current research with rioting.

Other findings concerned with attempts at violence reduction point out that honest communication with prisoner groups in efforts to quell violence *already underway* are doomed if they *did not previously exist.*[73] Speaking to prevention, rather than negotiations during a riot, Wenk and Moos state (1972):

It seems especially important to draw attention to the need for preventive measures in correctional institutions. Acute crisis situations almost always result in physical and psychological damage to the persons involved and in program deterioration because of stricter custodial management which usually follows. Even if a crisis situation arises in an institution with a basically benign social climate, the defusing of the tension will be within reach. In an institution where the pre-crisis conditions were already comparable to the latent crisis of long standing, the defusing may be a very difficult, if not impossible, task.[74]

The A.C.A.'s *Riots and Disturbances* report spoke to the need for communications and involvement of staff and inmates in implementation of new programs, but stopped short of recommending inmate councils except on an *ad hoc* basis for particular problems.[75] Fearful of sharing power and regularizing ongoing dialogue, it concluded in 1970:

> These groups would serve in an advisory capacity only, and the advisory group would be dissolved as soon as the particular problem or issue had been resolved. This practice should ensure inmate involvement and at the same time prevents selected inmates from capitalizing on their tenure on an advisory panel to exploit other inmates.[76]

But three years later the same investigators who prepared the latter report (Leeke and Clements) found, in a new report entitled *Inmate Grievance Procedures* (1973):

> . . . our present review of a variety of constructive approaches to the problem of inmate grievance resolution shows that a growing number of correctional systems are seeking (and implementing) tentative solutions in this area. For example, many systems publicize the right of inmates to communicate freely with supervisors, administrative staff, top officials, judges, and elected representatives. Some allow for direct contact with newspapers and other media representatives. From the point of view of improving communications between the inmate population and both line and staff personnel, the use of in-house publications by a growing number of correctional agencies may prove to be the most effective method of at least airing basic inmate complaints.

> We have noted that the Ombudsman concept has received a good deal of study by correctional administrators, although only a few have initiated modified Ombudsman programs within institutions. More attractive at the moment is the investigative approach where initiative for determining inmate grievances lies with correctional officials assigned

such responsibility. *Inmate councils have also received broader support from administrators, and their implementation would seem to be a growing trend. In terms of the general articulation of broadly-based issues causing discontent, the inmate council, if truly representative of the population at large, can provide a satisfactory method of achieving inmate input into the decision making process governing an institution.*[77]

Attica (1971) may have stimulated such widespread interest in the above procedures so vigorously rejected in previous official reports (between 1970-1973). In an article under the monograph title *Prevention of Violence in Correctional Institutions,*° Jack Brent of the Federal system suggested:

Constructive change can occur only if prisons officials are not hoodwinked into believing the notion that they can still get away indefinitely by manipulation. The times will not allow it. . . . If administrators know their facilities, inmates, and jobs, they can constantly readjust the institutional climate in order to bring out the best. Our object is to meet needs. For example, one component of inmate sentiment is to exert some control over the decisions that affect their lives.[78]

In order to reduce violence, Walter Dunbar proposed that we recognize and place emphasis on inmate rights and responsibilities.[79] But two other papers in this monograph still focused on the "new breed" of inmate. Flynn argued that

racial militants . . . are more likely than non-militants to endorse the advancement of their cause by any method necessary, including violence as a legitimate last resort°°. .

° *Prevention of Violence in Correctional Institutions,* Criminal Justice Monograph, Government Printing Office, Washington, D.C., June, 1973.

°°This is contradicted in a carefully documented empirical study by Ellis, Grasmick and Gilman, "Violence in Prison: A Sociological Analysis," *AJS,* July,

There can be no doubt but that the current composition of inmate population in our institutions of radical idealogists [sic] with *common criminals* has accelerated the politicalization of minority members, to the detriment of the goals of rehabilitation and reintegration. . . . Therefore it is necessary to refute categorically any notion or suggestion on the part of inmates, or vested interests outside, that *ordinary criminal* behavior should somehow be rationalized and dignified by labeling it political activity. The information exchange between the *ordinary criminal* and the *radical ideologist* results in the worst possible combination for society. Whereas *radical ideologists* absorb the criminal technology of *common criminals*, the latter are furnished with a ready-made critique of society and a complete set of relationalizations [sic] for their predatory activities. It is obvious that programs and rehabilitative efforts under these circumstances will be futile. In addition, this peculiar mixture of prisoners is probably one of the most *unholy alliances* and explosive combinations to be found anywhere in the world.[80]

Barton Ingraham inquiring, "Will Legal Relief from Inmates Prevent Violence in Correctional Institutions?" partly responds to his own question noting: " . . . effecting change through court

---

1974, pp. 16-43, which found that race was not a factor in reported aggressive transgressions in prison; rather, high proportions of inmates in a prison population with no fixed parole date leads to tensions.

In another study on prison violence, a California Task Force noted that violence could be reduced through certainty of release date: "Specific recommendations of the Task Force pertain to safety and security, improving the institutional environment, and increasing inmate self-determination. *The inmate's ability to predict and modify the length of sentence must be increased; each inmate should have a written statement of the steps he can take to retain, advance, or lose his release date.*" California Corrections Department, *Report and Recommendations*, by the Task Force to Study Violence, Sacramento, 1974.

The Attica Commission found "parole had become *by far the greatest* source of inmate anxiety and frustration. There were very few inmates interviewed . . . who did not list parole and 'CR' [conditional release] among their chief grievances." (*Attica Commission Report*, 1972, pp. 91-92.)

For further elaboration of this point, see Appendix V.

proceedings is a sedate and well-mannered way of bringing grievances to public attention, *one hardly in keeping with the personality characteristics of violence-prone inmates.*" [81] And in a confusing statement mixing his notions of a sort of subversive "new liberalism" with "classical liberalism" Ingraham concludes:

> There has been a movement growing in legal circles during the last ten years which might be called the school of 'new liberalism,' in order to distinguish it from the *classical liberalism* of such early penal reformers as Becarria and Bentham. New liberalism is anti-corrections, hostile to the whole idea of *scientific modification of human behavior,* and fanatical on the issue of extending legal due process into areas which were once considered reserved for the exercise of knowledgeable administrative discretion. . . . I submit that this *alliance,* [courts and "new liberals"] if there is one, can be no more than a marriage of convenience; one which will end in divorce once it becomes apparent that their goals and the goals of new liberals are incompatible. For the latter aim at nothing less than the *total dissolution of the experiment* in corrections which began two hundred years ago with the Walnut Street Jail.[82]

We conclude that the practitioners moved successfully, in the literature at least, from the conspiratorial notion of insidious forces to the hard facts of prison life to explain riots and seek prevention solutions while some academicians have ideologically refocused the new breed-conspiracy theme. These contributions, loosely cast in a 19th century tone, "common criminals," "new liberalism," "unholy alliance," "judicial activism" and "the true revolutionary of the New Left or similar orientation . . ." [83] could hardly be in the service of tight reasoning in a field so desperately in need of it. Later academic contributions, based upon empirical evidence, point in other directions: (1) liberalization of prison visiting reduces reported violence; (2) blacks and whites transgress violently at equal rates; (3) more severe punishment serves to increase the overall levels of prison violence; and (4) high aggression levels are most frequently related to high percentages of convicts with one year or more extensions of parole board dates and no visits.[84] No empirical evidence linking black militant conspiracies to riots (of the 1920s, 1950s or 1970s) has been reported, although there is much evidence of persistent institutional racism. Administrators should more fruitfully concern themselves with the abnormalities of *prison life* rather than the political abnormalities of *prisoners.* °

The inmate-staff council and other open communication vehicles suggested form one strata of a multi-tiered strategy for reducing tension, redressing grievances, and using lawful means for change which modern correctional administrators need to consider; others follow.

3. Legal Aid in Prison

In 1969, Chief Justice Warren Burger spoke to the American Bar Association's Annual Meeting in Dallas, Texas. In what was to become known as the "Dallas Speech," Burger urged the A.B.A. to take an active role in prison reform. Responding to Burger's plea, the A.B.A. formed the *Commission on Correctional Facilities and Services*, a 26-member inter-disciplinary group representing the fields of criminology, psychiatry, business, labor, government, and law. In the six years since the Dallas Speech, the Commission has been working on correctional reform through a number of specialized programs, funded by both government and private sources. Currently, the A.B.A. operates the following projects: the National Volunteer Parole

---

° In another sense, Cressey points out that our modern riot is a Chinese import: "The contemporary pattern of riots in American prisons was established about twenty years ago. It became common shortly after Chinese prisoners of war held by Americans during the Korean War seized hostages and made demands of their captors." Cressey further points out that the "new militancy [as] a sign of new prisoner power is hardly new. Inmates have dominated the internal affairs of prisoners during most of their two-hundred-year history." He sees a shift in leadership crystallizing around the aggressive leader who these days is more political. (Sutherland and Cressey, *Criminology* (9th Edition), 1974, pp. 550, 552, 553.)

Aide Program, in which young lawyers work with parolees on a one-to-one basis; the National Clearinghouse on Offender Employment Restrictions, working toward removing unreasonable obstacles to the employment of ex-offenders; the Correctional Officers Education Program, cooperating with junior and community colleges to develop degree programs for guards and line officers; the Resource Center on Correctional Law and Legal Services, preparing manuals and monographs on prisoners' rights as well as submitting briefs in suits affecting correctional law; the Bar Activation Program for Correctional Reform, encouraging the formation of local and state bar committees to work on penal reform; the National Pretrial Diversion Center, assisting in developing alternatives to incarceration; the Statewide Jail Standards and Inspection Systems Project, drawing up minimum standards for the operation of jails; the Clearinghouse for Offender Literacy Programs, producing handbooks and materials for the teaching of reading in prison; and the Correctional Economics Center, studying the cost and resource allocation problems in achieving prison reform. In addition, the Commission and the Young Lawyers Section of the A.B.A. publish the *Prison Law Reporter*, a monthly account of decisions in correctional law. In 1973-74, the Commission inaugurated two new projects: BASICS, which gives grants to state and local bar associations for the purpose of achieving specific correctional reform goals; and a magazine, *Corrections*.

Since the start of the *Commission on Correctional Facilities and Services*, there has been extensive work done to involve the law profession in the operation and day-to-day functioning of the prisons. Much of the work has been to clarify administrative procedures and to create model correctional legislation and standards. Some of the more important work concerning the legal aspect of prisons is being carried out in the Resource Center on Correctional Law and Legal Services. It has produced a training handbook on prison law to be used by correctional workers. Monographs outlining rights to medical care, censorship, disciplinary due process and prison law libraries have been prepared, as have materials on the use of ombudsmen and grievance mechanisms for dealing with inmate complaints and problems.

Though prisoners clearly need legal advice in seeking post-conviction remedies or in dealing with the conditions of confinement, many of their legal problems are civil. Divorce, child custody, the protection of property—all these are matters of deep concern to the prisoner. It seems clear that the civil legal assistance currently available to inmates is inadequate. A study done by Marvin Finkelstein of the Boston University Center for Criminal Justice (1972) indicated that 76% of the corrections personnel and eighty-seven of the eighty-eight law schools surveyed thought that prison legal services are not sufficient at present.[85] Existing programs tend to focus their energy on criminal law; of the law schools with prisoner legal assistance programs surveyed, 83.3% directed more than half their activities toward criminal law.[86]

Nevertheless, requests for civil legal assistance form a significant portion of the caseloads of legal aid programs. In a six-month period, 19.7% of the requests for assistance received by the Boston University program were for civil legal aid.[87] A similar program at the University of Minnesota reported 23% of its caseload as dealing with divorce and annulment (the second largest category of requests in the entire program, the first being appeals from conviction and the third largest category being other domestic relations problems.)[88] The University of Wisconsin Law School student interns found that the most common civil legal problems were domestic relations, financial matters such as insurance and the repossession of property, dealings with government agencies, and complaints against the institution.[89]

Lawyers can also play an important role in helping to create structures for the orderly handling of grievances. A Minnesota report on model grievance procedures points to the importance of such a program.

It seems essential, too, that the corrections field move toward organizing procedures and channels of communications which will give more tangible form to the due process principles which are relied upon to assure fair treatment in our society. Such development would seem not only to fit into sound criminal justice practice but might forestall need for the courts to prescribe such measures and procedures from outside the correctional system.[90]

In the long run, the changes in prison will come from properly functioning administrative procedures, not court-ordered reversals of administrative decisions or individual cases. This is pointed out by Turner (1971):

> ... As a matter of strategy, however, the prisoner's lawyer should not ask the court to review a number of individual administrative decisions; rather, the court should be asked to strike down the decision-making process itself and require of the prison officials procedural fairness.[91]

Legal aid for prisoners is becoming not a privilege but a right that society has an obligation to provide if it expects the prisoner to improve his circumstances lawfully. "Now there is a growing conviction that not only are people entitled to equal. protection under law but that society must insure that they have equal opportunity to invoke its protection."[92]

Failure to meet the legal needs of inmates simply adds problems to the already burdened existence of the prisoner. "Inability to do anything effective about their legal problems results in added frustrations for the inmates and reinforces resentment towards the institution and the law in general."[93] Events outside the walls often have considerable impact on the inmate or his family, but he usually has no means of influencing them. With legal advice, he can bring some leverage to bear on these events, lessening his sense of impotence. This is one sense in which Selznick pointed out that justice serves as therapy. Dawson also calls this to our attention: "Indeed, the cultivation of a sense of fair dealing in the offender would appear to be helpful, if not essential, in attaining one of the principal goals of these correctional processes, the rehabilitation of the offenders."[94] Furthermore, resolution of potentially troublesome legal problems before release can make the ex-inmate's re-entry into society smoother.[95]

The role of the lawyer in a prison also extends to service for the guard. Usually the warden can call upon the state's attorney to represent the institution or himself against a legal attack, but the guard is not, as we have seen, completely absolved of legal responsibility. He may have questions about the extent of his liability when he is called upon to dispense medicines, break up fights, pursue an escapee, deny a privilege, or fails to warn a prisoner of an impending action. °

Finally, legal aid programs can assist in ways other than either reviewing practices in the prison or assisting inmates with legal problems. The President's Commission (1967) pointed out that: "They can provide increased visibility for a system that has generally been too isolated, helping to mobilize public opinion and bring political pressure to bear where needed for reform. The mere presence of outsiders would serve to discourage illegal, unfair or inhumane practices."[96]

4. The Justice of Administration

Corrections, as a public agency, represents an official governmental service of considerable power. It cannot escape its responsibility to provide administrative due process. Robert Dawson states: "In the exercise of broad governmental power there must be assurances of fairness and consistency."[97] One repeatedly hears the argument that correctional administrators are professional, that the broad discretion they exercise is necessary,

---

° The National Association of Attorneys General published a *Special Report on Corrections*, January 18, 1974, which lists some 75 different kinds of prisoners' suits calling prison officials' attention to the burgeoning of correctional case law and the variety of potential liabilities.

and that review or a narrowing of such discretion would place undue restraint upon them. In response, we point out that administrators come from many different professions; that we are not interested in eliminating discretion but rather having it put under a public spot-light; and that in a democracy no public agency can safely enjoy unbridled discretion.[98]

> In other words, the prison administration should not be permitted to act in a standardless, arbitrary, or capricious way; it should be required to have valid rules that are fairly communicated to the persons who risk sanctions for violating them. [99]

We are not sure that a tight set of procedures for correctional administrators' use in fair decision making can or even needs to be compiled.

> What is needed is to provide offenders under correctional authority certain protections against arbitrary action, not to create for all correctional decision making a mirror image of trial procedures. What sorts of protections are proper will depend upon the importance of the decision. For some kinds of decisions, such as decisions to revoke probation or parole, offenders should be accorded the basic elements of due process, such as notice, representation by counsel, and opportunity to present evidence and to confront and cross-examine opposing witnesses. For other less important decisions it might be enough simply to allow offenders a decent opportunity to hear the basis of an official's proposed decision and to present any relevant opposing facts and arguments. [100]

This is simply a different way of reflecting back Edmond Cahn's "consumer" and our "justice" perspective. It means that the administrator recognizes himself and his agency to be located on a continuum of justice. The demand for making public the basis upon which he makes decisions is not a challenge to his professional judgment, although sometimes it might be, but rather is a legitimate demand by the public upon one of its servants for information.

... Because the correctional process involves the use of governmental authority over the liberty of individuals, it must be fair as well as effective, that is, it must conform to notions of decision-making regularity and responsibility that normally accompany governmental action of a coercive nature ... [the] same safeguards against unfairness that characterize the criminal trial and, increasingly, pretrial decision making, should be imposed upon the correctional process ... the correctional process is so important to offenders and the community alike that it should be the object of continued attention.[101]

Discretion is a central problem in corrections, affecting its entire structure from the administrators to the convict. Its successful harnessing could go a long way toward instilling a sense of fairness to all concerned. More significantly, perhaps it would free the administrator from bondage in the rhetoric of the imperial perspective and permit him to take a position more suitably appropriate for an agent of justice. In this sense, freedom for the correctional administrator lies in the direction of voluntarily adopting a model based on justice for administering his official affairs. How may this be done? Professor Kenneth Culp Davis suggests several ways of structuring discretion.

The seven instruments that are most useful in the structuring of discretionary power are open plans, open policy statements, open rules, open findings, open reasons, open precedents, and fair informal procedure. The reason for repeating the word 'open' is a powerful one: Openness is the natural enemy of arbitrariness and a natural ally in the fight against injustice.[102]

Properly understood, this discussion is limited to the elimination of unnecessary and arbitrary discretion. It does not imply the total elimination of discretion, rather a lifting of the veil so that fairness can creep in to protect those affected. We all respond more positively to fair treatment and even to a punitive action when it is accompanied by a precise explanation of the violated norm.

In the context of prison, justice-as-fairness means having clear rules, insuring their promulgation, and following a procedure for determining and punishing rule infractions rooted in due process safeguards (for example: statement of the allegation, notice, counsel substitute, a hearing, the chance to cross-examine, written findings, appeal.) Further, it means giving up the foot dragging which the litigation so vividly bares (see Chapter III.) Correctional administrators should not have to be brought to court to provide adequate law libraries and access to them, to provide more than ten sheets of paper for legal research, or for punishing by segregation those who exercise their right to access to the court, the press or the public. A justice perspective assures that expressions of racism will be fought. We should be in the forefront of exposing the indignities of poor medical care, inadequate diets, servile labor, absence of recreational programs and inhumane segregative facilities. The record shows that in court we appear to be alibiing for the existence of such conditions instead of agreeing to seek remediation. The public and court will permit us reasonable precautions concerning what may freely enter prisons, but they look askance at the broad prison regulations surrounding mail, publications and visitors. Administrators need to make a dramatic break with the vestiges of the nineteenth century "buried-from-the-world" philosophy. Courts should not have to *force* modern administrators to adopt any of the above procedures. Quite aside from the embarrassment it brings to us as agents of justice, it embarrasses our claims to professionalism.

In our justice perspective, the guard must be treated fairly as well. Our study of guard turn-over rate at Stateville prison (102%) also revealed some unexpected outcomes which have fairness implications. A substantial percentage of a sample of dropouts reported taking new jobs at the same or *lower* wages elsewhere. One might assume that fear, abuse from convicts, and other hazards attendant to being a guard would drive many from the work. The research shows, however, that a prime reason for leaving was instead *abuse from superiors*—sergeants, lieutenants and captains. There were other reasons as well, but *working with criminals* did not surface high as a negative factor. * Fairness recognizes the quality of the work environment and takes steps to improve it. An agenda for fairness should include: clearly drawn work assignments, employment standards and salary on par with the state police, hazardous duty and malpractice liability insurance, a dignified but mandatory early (age 55) retirement, special family benefits for duty-related death, the right to organize and bargain collectively, involvement in program planning, a grievance procedure, freedom from partisan political pressures,** merit procedures for promotion, and mandatory training that is unambiguous about the guards' work role and focuses on procedures of justice-as-fairness in addition to traditional custodial concerns.

In the micro-world of the prison, the justice perspective calls upon the maker of rules to share legitimate power with the enforcers and consumers of the rules. It also urges that all rules and rulings be required to stand the test of being the least onerous way of reaching a lawful end.

The days of hiding behind the wall are effectively over. Correctional administrators can undergo the turmoil of being forced to go public or can take the initiative and voluntarily begin playing a more open hand. By this we mean a checks and balances system of scrutiny—not another torrent of slick publications. For those who believe that such a course of action is a new or radical departure in thinking, we cite John Howard in his *State of Prisons* (1777):

---

*Derived from an attitude survey of guard employment attrition rates, "Dropouts and Rejects: An Analysis of Turnover Among Stateville Guards," by James B. Jacobs and Mary P. Grear, University of Chicago Center for Studies in Criminal Justice (Mimeo, p. 26), 1974. Some 26% of the sample of dropouts took higher paying jobs, 57% took jobs at lower salaries.

** At Menard prison in 1973, guards talked freely about purchasing and retaining their jobs, and being promoted as a function of routine payments to county party chairmen, ranging from $50 to $300.

Finally, the care of a prison is too important to be left wholly to a gaoler, paid indeed for his attendance, but often tempted by his passions, or interest, to fail in his duty. For every prison there should be an inspector appointed; either by his colleagues in the magistracy or by Parliament. . . . He should speak with every prisoner, hear all complaints, and immediately correct what he finds manifestly wrong.[103]

5. Overseeing Fairness—The Ombudsman

In response to public pressure for civilian review boards in the last decade, police uniformly asked "why us?" A fair question. We agree with the police, even though we are sympathetic to the argument that all low-visibility public agencies need public oversight. The police should not be singled out. Correctional practice needs to be brought under the umbrella of public scrutiny as well.

. . . We must make a greater attempt to preserve adversary safeguards in quasi-judicial decision-making as well as in the courts—or to find approximations that assure intelligent inquiry. Commissions, *ad hoc* tribunals, administrative courts, Ombudsmen—none of these are panaceas for any problem in public administration, but all can help make the values of truth, freedom, and justice less precarious.[104] (Wilensky, 1967)

The Ombudsman has been an accepted institution in Sweden's civil administration since 1809. The concept has only recently been recognized in the United States and even more recently put into practice.

An ombudsman is an independent, external, impartial, and expert handler of citizens' complaints against governmental agencies who is easily accessible by the citizenry. He is an individual generally appointed by the legislature, who, upon receiving a complaint from a citizen alleging government abuse or occasionally upon his own motion, investigates and intervenes on behalf of the citizen with the governmental authority concerned.[105] (Tibbles, 1972)

The prison is an eminently well-suited setting for the Ombudsman. His clientele, by definition, is frequently cut off from opportunities to carry their complaints beyond their keepers.

Administrators' most frequent objections to the use of an Ombudsman are: (1) existing methods of complaint hearing are adequate; or (2) if inadequate, the agency should be able to modify its practices without outside oversight which leads to dichotomized authority. In corrections, both have proven wrong. Complaints continue to pile up at an increasing rate, and, because of non-resolution, pour over by way of litigation into already overloaded courts. The American experience with the Ombudsman, as meagre as it is, shows no cause for alarm with the dichotomization-of-authority argument. The earliest Ombudsman type program dates from 1777 when the Continental Congress established the Inspector General of the Army.° The well-known General Accounting Office and auditors perform similar services in other settings. Bureaucrats used to these oversight agencies accept them without arguing the erosion of their authority. Corrections, for the most part, has not had an experience with oversight and like the police wants to know "why us!" A continuous history of conflict, brutality, rioting and killings simply requires a mechanism of public oversight. Several states have already adopted some form of the office of Ombudsman for all its citizens. Minnesota is the first to have an independent statutory Ombudsman for its prisoners, parolees and correctional staff.°°

°The Inspector General of the U.S. Army testified in favor of an Ombudsman for the Department of Corrections in Sacramento in December, 1970.

°° "In the last session of Congress, the late Congressman William F. Ryan unsuccessfully introduced a bill that would have withheld L.E.A.A. funds from any state that failed to establish an ombudsman for prison." (Linda Singer and J. Michael Keating, "Prisoner Grievance Mechanisms," *Crime and Delinquency*, July, 1973, p. 373)

At the request of the Department of Corrections (1971), the University of Minnesota Law School drew up an initial proposal which was first funded as an L.E.A.A. project, and ultimately found statutory authority in 1973. The basic purpose for the office of the Ombudsman was to permit " . . . the release of inmate frustration by opening communication . . . [and] to insure procedural safeguards which are so fundamental to our system of justice, [that is] . . . due process."[106]

More specifically the Ombudsman would seek to fulfill the following ends:

(1) The improvement and clarification of administrative procedures and regulations.

(2) Reorganization and revitalization of internal prison review procedures.

(3) Increased access to judicial review by cooperation and coordination with the various legal aid services.

(4) Encouragement of more active involvement of private and governmental agencies and interest groups in alleviating the grievances.

(5) Coordination of overlapping governmental agencies by means of increased flow of information from the agencies to inmate and staff regarding functions, programs, and procedures.

(6) [Seek] strengthening and corrective legislation by providing the Legislature with information and recommendations regarding the correctional institutions.

(7) Improving the relationship between staff and inmate by providing the inmates with information on the actions, motives, and design of administration actions.

(8) Alleviation of tension within the prison by means of more open communication, i.e., a 'release valve.'[107]

Initial anxiety melted when each of the state's institutional administrators and their executive staff met, analyzed, and modified the proposal. They in turn trained their staffs and by written notice informed all inmates, parolees (and their families), guards, and the department's field services of the new program.

Perhaps the key to successful initiation and operation of an Ombudsman program is the credibility the office attracts. Given centuries of mistrust, it is of crucial importance that the Ombudsman be independent of the department of corrections. If it is this political distance which initially produces confidence in the Ombudsman, then it is his ability to meet the needs of his constituency which assures continuing success. *

What should be obvious to correctional administrators is that an Ombudsman can help bring change which they find difficult to manage themselves because "an administrative agency head has difficulty investigating and criticizing his officers and employees while continuing to keep their loyalty and confidence."[108]

Administrative fears ease, as more states** adopt variations on the correctional Ombudsman theme and as research and the literature grow.*** If the Ombudsman office is statutory and

---

* A.B.A., after studying the Minnesota Ombudsman office concluded (after one year) that among its accomplishments were the following:

— passage of legislation authorizing the Ombudsman following initial establishment by executive order;
— clarification of disciplinary policies and procedures at the state's largest prison;
— agreement by the Parole Board to give reasons for parole denials in writing;
— provision of financial accounting to inmates on their welfare fund;
— creation of inmate/staff advisory councils as a grievance mechanism;
— recommendations and establishment of a timetable for improvement of grievance and disciplinary procedures at the state's largest prison; and
— assumption of state liability and processing of claims for destruction and loss of prisoners' property during a shakedown.

(The Minnesota Correctional Ombudsman, A.B.A., 1974, p. 9)

**Correctional Ombudsmen programs now exist in Minnesota and Kansas (by statute, 1974), South Carolina, Ohio, Michigan, Pennsylvania, Hawaii, Indiana, Connecticut, Oregon, Iowa, and others are planned.

***For example: L. Tibbles, Ombudsman for American Prisons, 48 N.D.L. Rev. 166 (Spring, 1972); B. Taugher, A Penal Ombudsman: A Step Toward Penal Reform, 3 Pac. L. Jour. 166 (1972); T. C. Fitzharris, The Desirability of a

independent of the corrections department, it will have a life of its own. A Governor's Executive Order is a good mechanism for commencing an "experiment" but is too politically vulnerable for permanency given the "two-year perspective." The "two-year perspective" refers to the political timidity which usually accompanies correctional innovation each time either a legislature or a governor stands for election. Since most major correctional program changes require at least a two-year lead time, it takes an extraordinary coalition of political forces to carry it, assuming the program itself does not collapse as a result of internal shortcomings. Bright, creative people enter this milieu anxious to bring about change and find themselves with one foot in the quicksand of state government inertia and the other groping for a toe-hold onto the few human and other resources available. Legislation is superior to the Executive Order and provides a firmer foundation for institutionalizing an Ombudsman program and retaining forward looking personnel.

Legislative endorsement of an Ombudsman program could even begin the process by which the correctional system is made more effective and less dependent upon benign political leadership. Since corrections by definition is a political process, one cannot naively assume that "depoliticizing" is an answer (i.e., a sort of regency-model of administering corrections.) Yet this may take us on the road to a partial solution. Most jurisdictions now have the administrator of their corrections system appointed by the governor. Even the most reform-minded governors eventually have to back away from the political heat engendered by periodic but natural explosions caused by operation of the fortress prison. Governors who are genuinely interested in re-

---

Correctional Ombudsman, Report to the California Assembly Interim Committee on Criminal Procedure, revised edition, University of California Institute of Government Studies, 111 pp., 1973; Goldfarb & Singer, *Redressing Prisoners Grievances,* 39 Geo. Wash. L. Rev. 175, at 304-316, (1970) (Section on "Non-Judicial Alternatives for Resolving Grievances"), updated in *After Conviction* at 506-522 (1973); South Carolina Collective Violence Research Project, *Inmate Grievance Procedures,* ch. 3 on "The Role of the Ombudsman in Corrections," at pp. 11-14 (1973).

form (the less politically-charged word is "modernization") have two basic styles of operation. On one hand, they appoint an administrator in whom they have confidence and give him/her enormous latitude. The governor can then give the impression of entering the scene to lend stability in times of crisis by applying the brakes and calming public fears. The other method is to take on the forceful leadership role himself, but there is not much successful history with this style to date. Most who have a modicum of interest in corrections talk custody and try to bootleg humaneness. In other jurisdictions, not really interested in risking change, they may talk rehabilitation but act custody. In any event, custody and rehabilitation in the fortress prison are for the most part different sides of the same "imperial perspective" coin.

An Ombudsman is still another stratum of the multi-tier conflict resolution system we are constructing in this chapter. Staff-inmate governance operates at the level of program innovation, grievance and dispute settlement, and concerns about overall conditions of confinement. It brings the two major groups into a public arena for communication and problem solving purposes. The introduction of legal services assists both groups in seeking redress, but also distinguishes and seeks local remedies before involving the courts. Through assisting the individual prisoner with civil legal aid, the prison itself is removed as an obstacle for the convict to continue to be an agent in his own life. Lawyers also assist in establishing due process mechanisms for the internal court and other procedures. Finally, their presence has a salutory effect in a largely invisible agency. The introduction of an Ombudsman assures that the entire process operates fairly.

> Yet an ombudsman system cannot be a substitute for competent administration, for conscientious personnel, for adequate supervision of public employees by superiors, for administrative appeals, or for judicial review of administrative action. An ombudsman system should be added to such protections and should not be regarded as a substitute for them.

The long-term objective should be effective criticism of administrators by independent officers who have no stake, direct or indirect, in any particular results.[109]

II. JUSTICE IN THE MACRO-WORLD

The prison's macro-world is comprised of confusing forces and attitudes which act as constraints on modernization. We cite some and offer some tentative answers which might rationalize and bring justice-as-fairness into operation: (1) we will first move outside the prison to discuss some other neglected areas of justice—the victim, witness, and juror—as they affect prison life, and (2) sentencing practices and parole granting. In discussing these factors which heavily impinge upon prison life, we will keep an eye on how the convict is viewed by the major actors in criminal justice.

1. The Victim-The Witness-The Juror

Historically the criminal law replaced earlier known kinship group settlements of wrongs. The consolidation of political power in a jurisdiction changed private vengeance-seeking (vendetta) in a variety of forms into collective order. When one party's wrong against another was transformed from a personal injury to a disturbance of the "King's peace," distance was created between the victim and the offender (and the administration of justice was insulated from the people). Crime came to be seen as a harm to the state (society). Today, private vengeance may itself be a crime. If A harms B, it is transformed into the "People v. A," and B is mainly a harmed spectator to the trial. The state retains a monopoly of power to exact a *public* restoration of the disturbed balance although it is B's life which was upset. But it does so unsatisfactorily:

The State cannot prevent crime, cannot repress it, except in a small number of cases, and consequently fails in its duty for the accomplishment of which it receives taxes from its citizens, and then, after all that, it accepts a reward; and over and above this, it condemns every ten years some 3,230,000 individuals, the greater part of whom it imprisons, putting the expense of their maintenance on the back of the honest citizen whom it has neither protected from nor indemnified for the harm alone by the crime; and all this in the name of the eternal principles of absolute and retributive justice. It is evident that this manner of administering justice must undergo a radical change.[110] (Enrico Ferri, 1917)

Currently there is a major revival of interest in offender restitution and victim compensation occasioned largely by Margery Fry's essay "Justice for Victims" in the *London Observer* in July 1957. * However, our immediate interest in the subject is in how the isolation of the victim creates a sense of injustice resulting in resentment and further cries for vengeance.

When a crime is committed, the *state* (having assumed the burden) has failed to keep the peace. If we expect the private citizen to assist the state in prevention, detection, and suppression of crime, a certain amount of jeopardy attends such a commitment. Assuming the citizen's readiness to accept it, should he not be insured against duty-related injuries? Remembering that the state prohibits private vengeance, the responsible citizen must seek to "right the wrong" through the criminal justice system. But this is not a satisfactory outcome since it effectively cuts off a civil remedy. A prison sentence simply represents the state's intervention—not the victim's. The victim, now in his role as taxpayer, will become a double victim and, in consequence of

---

* A new work by Burt Galoway and Joseph Hudson, *Considering the Victim: Readings in Restitution and Victim Compensation* (1975), is the most comprehensive multi-discipline perspective available on the subject. For their thoughts on operationalizing a restitution program, in which they have had experience, see Fogel, Galoway and Hudson, "Restitution in Criminal Justice: A Minnesota Experiment," *Criminal Law Bulletin* Vol. 8 (1972), and Galoway and Hudson, "Issues in the Correctional Implementation of Restitution to Victims of Crime," *American Society of Criminology*, N.Y. (Nov. 1973).

the offender's ineffective prison experience, may yet again be victimized either generally or specifically.

A reading of Galoway and Hudson is convincing proof that victim compensation through offender restitution holds much promise as a possible rehabilitative and reconciliation tool, but our interest is limited to fairness. If we expect an involved public (with a sense of justice), then we need to offer civil remedies when, in chancing involvement, some become innocent victims. This notion extends to the witness who is treated in largely a shabby manner and the jury member who gives much in return for a pittance. Our proposal would lead to state reimbursement for the latter two at least on the level of the minimum wage law.

In a concern for a rational prison and fairness to the major private actors in criminal justice, we can perceive of a strategy linking both. It is our belief that adequate compensation to the victim of crime, the witness and the jury panelist *is right in itself*, and as a matter of fairness, requires little justification. If victim compensation and offender restitution beyond this were widely implemented, it might lead to an atmosphere in which rational prison planning could progress or at least might mute the cry for further escalations of harshness. In a "pocket-book culture" where money is so important, one might reasonably assume that reimbursement for injury could quell the urge to retributively punish. If a successful renaissance of restitution were to occur, more offenders would by definition have to be kept out of prisons, at work repaying their victim. If money is a plausible nexus between the exploitive offender and the isolated victim, and if it can engage both in a vengeance-free relationship, then its expenditure may create a just and inexpensive path to restoring the balance without further deepening the sense of injustice for either.

2. Sentencing and Parole—Some Alternatives

We have already examined the maze of sentencing patterns which exist in the nation. We have an idea of the disparities which arise as a result of lawlessness in sentencing procedures.

In the area of sentencing we are a government of men, not law. Prisoners entering our institutions burdened with a sense of injustice, living in its compressed tension, and frustrated by ruleless procedures for parole, make the entire prison venture unsafe for all. Yet we will need some form of separation of the dangerous for the foreseeable future. But sentencing, which is the separation mechanism, can be accomplished more sensibly and equitably.

The indeterminate sentence is now experiencing the beginning of its end. Recently, a group of informed leaders have begun sounding the death knell for the rehabilitation model and its powerful tool—the indeterminate sentence. ° Judge Laurence W. Pierce (U.S. District Court) states in relation to the rehabilitation model: "I join the chorus of those who are suggesting that this commitment be reassessed."[111] Judge Frankel finds the indeterminate sentence is frequently "evil and unwarranted." [112] Judge Constance Baker Motley has suggested a system of graduated sentences of a mandatory nature for the repetitive offender but no prison for most first offenders.[113] Dr. William E. Amos, Chairman of the Youth Corrections Division of the U.S. Board of Parole, took the following position:

(1) We should confine fewer people.
(2) The philosophy of confinement should be deterrence, accountability, and the protection of society—*not rehabilitation.*
(3) Adequate training or rehabilitation centers should be operated by *other agencies* to serve those offenders whose offenses are directly related to educational, physical, or psychological deficiencies. These agencies may be vocational rehabilitation, welfare, educational, or even private agencies.

° "Now both the public and the correctional staff expect prisoners to be, at least, no worse for the correctional experience and, at most, prepared to take their places in society without further involvement with the law." (National Advisory Commission on Criminal Justice Standards and Goals, 1973.)

(4) Whenever a person is confined he should be provided the protection, services, and opportunities that would reflect our belief in the dignity and nature of man. I would further propose that a National Inmate Bill of Rights be prepared, and all states be urged to adopt and implement it.[114]

Allen Breed, Director of the California Youth Authority, has come to the position that our "goal may [have] to be to make rehabilitation fit the crime."[115]

But we should not confuse the public or ourselves on what we are doing. If we send offenders to prison we do so to punish them, not to rehabilitate them. Hopefully, we can carry out our punishment in humane and sensible ways—and long sentences for offenders who are not dangerous can hardly be called sensible.

The method would vary with the offender. Dangerous offenders must be kept in secure institutions—for the protection of society—for this must remain our primary consideration. The vast bulk of offenders need not be incarcerated at all, or for as short a time as possible, *and always for periods that are specified in advance.*[116]

The AFSC Task Force also called for the reduction of discretion in sentencing and an end to reliance on rehabilitation as a goal in corrections.[117] Richard A. McGee, president of the American Justice Institute and perhaps the nation's most prestigious correctional figure, has after over 40 years of practice concluded:

The divergence of views with respect to the purposes of criminal justice administration on the part of police, courts, corrections, legislature, significant citizen groups, politicians and the communication media gives rise to a total picture of confusion, capriciousness, and injustice, if not irrationality. A system needs to be devised and put into operation which will (a) protect the public, (b) preserve the rights of individuals, and (c) satisfy reasonable men that it is fair, consistent, intelligent, and incorruptible. Such a system must be capable of adapting to the advancement of human knowledge and to the changing social and economic needs of the total society. That such a system of criminal justice does not exist in America today except as an unrealized ideal is scarcely open to argument. This void is more apparent in sentence determination than in most other phases of our present 'non-system.' . . . The time for change has come. The question in most jurisdictions now is not do we need change but change to what and how to bring it about. Whether to muddle along responding to unsystematic political sharp-shooting or to make fresh plans for orderly legislative enactment—that is the choice. Simple logic dictates the latter course. As a point of departure, this writer after years of frustrating experience and informal consultation with numerous practitioners and students of the problem has devised an alternative sentencing system. . . . [118]

McGee urges *inter alia* the (1) end of indeterminate sentencing; (2) a return to flat time sentencing; (3) procedural criteria for sentencing; (4) sentencing review procedures; and (5) an end for both parole boards and parole * itself.[119]

An important chorus, as Judge Pierce noted, is developing, but at least eight additional widely respected reports must be added to the chorus seeking a sensible sentencing scheme: (1) The National Council on Crime and Delinquency's *Model Sentencing Act* (1972); (2) The American Law Institute's *Model Penal Code* (1963); (3) The ABA's *Standards Relating to Sentencing Alternatives and Procedures* (1969) and their *Standards Relating to Appellate Review of Sentences*; (4) *The National Advisory Com-*

---

* Milton Rector, Executive Director of the NCCD, looking to "Corrections in 1993," also urges the elimination of parole boards and parole. He suggests the periodic mandatory release of prisoners with assessments of how the prisoner fares on these furloughs as determinative of readiness-for-release decisions. (Harleigh B. Trecker, editor, *Goals for Social Welfare 1973-1993: An Overview of the Next Two Decades*, 1973)

mission on Criminal Justice Standards and Goals' Report;
(5) The President's Commission on Law Enforcement and Administration of Justice; (6) The New York State Citizens Inquiry
on Parole and Criminal Justice; (7) The Committee for the Study
of Incarceration; and (8) The Group for the Advancement of
Corrections, Toward a New Corrections Policy. * All have a
common thrust in relation to sentencing best described by the
ABA in a commentary, "Perhaps no single process or series of
processes in the criminal justice system is more chaotic than the
act of sentencing."[120] Although each report represents a variation on a similar theme—the emergent consensus seems to be:

1. Sentencing criteria should be statutorily required. **

---

* Consisting of "Two Declarations of Principles": one by correctional administrators, and a second by the Ex-Prisoners Advisory Group (sponsored and
published by The Academy for Contemporary Problems, 1501 Neil Avenue,
Columbus, Ohio, 1974).

** Richard McGee states:

Under American concepts of fairness and due process, and in view of the
present trends of higher court decisions, one can confidently predict
more and more judicial intervention in a system that permits a nonjudi-
cial board in the executive branch to exercise this kind and degree of
discretionary power over other human beings without judicial review.
The system is being revised now chiefly by the appellate courts on an unplanned piecemeal basis. It seems far more rational to plan a new system
to be installed by legislative enactment. ("A New Look at Sentencing:
Part II," Federal Probation, Sept. 1974.)

Well over a century ago Iowa's former Criminal Code required judges to
consider the following criteria:

After a plea or verdict of guilty in any case where a discretion is conferred upon the court as to the extent of the punishment, the following
are to be considered by the court as circumstances of aggravation in pro-
nouncing the sentence upon the defendant:

First—If the person committing the offense was by the duties of his
office or by his condition, obliged to prevent the particular offense committed or to bring offenders committing it to justice;

Second—If he holds any other public office, although not one requiring
the suppression of the particular offense;

Third—Although holding no office, if his education, fortune, profession or reputation, placed him in a situation in which his example would probably influence the conduct of others;

Fourth—When the offense was committed with premeditation in consequence of a plan formed with others;

Fifth—When the defendant attempted to induce others to join in committing the offense;

Sixth—When the condition of the offender created a trust which was broken by the offense, or when it afforded him easier means of committing the offense;

Seventh—When, in commission of the offense, any other injury was offered than was necessarily suffered by the offense itself—such as wanton cruelty or humiliating language in case of personal injury;

Eighth—When the offense was attended with a breach of any other moral duty than that necessarily broken in committing it—such as personal injury accompanied by ingratitude;

Ninth—When the injury was offered to one whose age, sex, office, conduct, or condition, entitled him to respect from the offender;

Tenth—When the injury was offered to one whose age, sex, or infirmity rendered him incapable of resistance;

Eleventh—When the general character of the defendant is marked by those passions or vices which generally lead to the commission of the offense of which he has been convicted.

The following circumstances are to be considered in alleviation of the punishment:

First—The minority of the offender, if so young as to justify a supposition that he was ignorant of the law or that he acted under the influence of another;

Second—If the offender was so old as to render it probable that the faculties of his mind were weakened;

Third—Those conditions which suppose the party to have been influenced in committing the offense by another standing in correlative superior situation to him;

Fourth—The order of a superior officer is no justification for committing a public offense, but under circumstances of misapprehension of the duty of obedience may be shown in extenuation of the offense;

Fifth—When the offense has been caused by great provocation or other cause sufficient to excite in men of ordinary tempers *such* passions as require unusual strength of mind to restrain.

(as cited in Sol Rubin, *The Law of Criminal Corrections*, 1974, pp. 131-132).

2. Sentencing should be based upon classification of offenders into risk categories.***

3. Sentences should be more definite, (there are fairly broad variations but indeterminancy is substantially rejected) or fixed and graduated by seriousness of the offense.

4. Sentences should be reviewable.

5. Sentences of imprisonment should be substantially reduced.****

6. Sentences of imprisonment should be justified by the state after an exhaustive review fails to yield a satisfactory community-based sanction.*****

***Speaking to the provisions of the *Model Penal Code and the Model Sentencing Act* in relation to risk categories, the President's Commission (1967) notes:

The enactment of statutory criteria provides a way of directing the judge's attention to those factors which the legislature has determined to be relevant to the sentencing decision. Both the Model Penal Code and the Model Sentencing Act employ statutory criteria in conjunction with separate sentencing provisions which attempt to discriminate between offenders who require lengthy imprisonment and those who are likely to be released after relatively brief periods of custody. . . . Under the Code, for example, the court may impose an extended term only if it finds that lengthy imprisonment is necessary for the protection of the public because the defendant is a persistent offender; a professional criminal; a dangerous, mentally abnormal person; or a multiple offender whose criminality was so extensive that an extended term is warranted.

****The President's Commission (1967) further notes:

An enlightened sentencing code, therefore, should provide for a more selective use of imprisonment. It should ensure that long prison terms are available for habitual, dangerous, and professional criminals who present a substantial threat to the public safety and that it is possible for the less serious offender to be released to community supervision without being subjected to the potentially destructive effects of lengthy imprisonment.

*****The American Law Institute's *Model Penal Code* suggests the judge weigh the following grounds in favor of a non-incarcerative sentence:

(a) the defendant's criminal conduct neither caused nor threatened serious harm;

Others have urged Commissions on Sentencing,[121] sentencing review councils,[122] separate sentencing hearings,[123] an end to plea bargaining (because it limits all other sentencing alternatives),[124] statutory authority for non-incarcerative sentences,[125] an end to the capriciously excessive "emergency laws" which periodically panic legislatures,[126] and for sentencing decisions to be weighted in favor of promoting a concept of individual liberty.[127]

The current and persistent thrust may be fairly characterized as a *neo-classical consolidation* of penal sanctions. We add the perspective of justice-as-fairness which insists upon tight procedural regularity, hence a narrowing of discretion, for the agencies of the criminal law.

A Return to Flat Time

All this leaves the problem just where it was. The irresponsible humanitarian citizen may indulge his pity and

---

(b) the defendant did not contemplate that his criminal conduct would cause or threaten serious harm;

(c) the defendant acted under a strong provocation;

(d) there were substantial grounds tending to excuse or justify the defendant's criminal conduct, though failing to establish a defense;

(e) the victim of the defendant's criminal conduct induced or facilitated its commission;

(f) the defendant has compensated or will compensate the victim of his criminal conduct for the damage or injury that he has sustained;

(g) the defendant has no history of prior delinquency or criminal activity or has led a law-abiding life for a substantial period of time before the commission of the present crime;

(h) the defendant's criminal conduct was the result of circumstances unlikely to recur;

(i) the character and attitudes of the defendant indicate that he is unlikely to commit another crime;

(j) the defendant is particularly likely to respond affirmatively to probationary treatment;

(k) the imprisonment of the defendant would entail excessive hardship to himself or his dependents.

(ALI *Model Penal Code* § 7.01 1962.)

sympathy to his heart's content, knowing that whenever a criminal passes to his doom there, but for the grace of God, goes he; but those who have to govern find that they must either abdicate, and that promptly, or else take on themselves as best they can many of the attributes of God. They must decide what is good and what evil; they must force men to do certain things and refrain from doing certain other things whether individual consciences approve or not; they must resist evil resolutely and continually, possibly and preferably without malice or revenge, but certainly with the effect of disarming it, preventing it, stamping it out and creating public opinion against it. In short, they must do all sorts of things which they are manifestly not ideally fit to do, and, let us hope, do with becoming misgiving, but which must be done, all the same, well or ill, somehow and by somebody.

If I were to ignore this, everyone who has had any experience of government would throw these pages aside as those of an inexperienced sentimentalist or an Impossibilist Anarchist.[128] (George Bernard Shaw, 1922)

Richard McGee's alternative for California returns to flat time sentences in a five degree felony plan ranging from a minimum of three months to three years in the 5th degree to seven years to life (and death, if lawful) for 1st degree felonies. Considerable discretion is left to judges (with a built-in appellate review council), and state parole is collapsed into the existing probation system in the county in which the released convict is expected to dwell. The prison therefore receives no discretion other than through the residual good time law which is not eliminated. Our suggestion, although closely paralleling McGee's, calls for a total flat sentence for different classes of felonies mitigated by substantial vested good time credit. Both plans return power to the judiciary within statutory guidelines and eliminate parole boards. McGee observes:

The judicial system is uniquely equipped to manage the decision making process in accordance with law, if an

appropriate system were established to control capriciousness in subjective sentencing judgments. If judges are not
social scientists, we submit that most parole board members
are not either and even where some of them are, there is no
evidence that their decisions on balance are more wise and
appropriate than those of judges.[129]

We call for a system based upon a finding of *clear and present
danger* to be necessary for the imposition of a term of imprisonment. Imprisonment should be the courts' last available sanction
following an affirmative action by authorities seeking other
alternatives. When a finding of clear and present danger is
made, it should require incarceration. At this point we part with
McGee, who we believe leaves too much discretion to the courts
(even with the appellate review council, which we do support).
If we can accomplish procedural regularity in sentencing, we believe a system based upon categories of *demonstrated risk* will
bring more certainty and fairness *to the prisoner.**

But the prison needs one other tool to make prison life more
rational. We propose that the length on the flat time sentence be
mitigated *only* by good time credit. This puts modest discretion
closer to the source which can most usefully employ it. It simply
says to the prisoner:

> Your stay has been determined to be four years, no more,
> you can get out in two years but that's up to you. We reduce
> your sentence one day for every day of lawful behavior. You
> can't get out any faster by making progress in any other
> aspect of prison life. Lawful behavior is the payoff. We
> trade you a day on the streets for every good one inside.
> For rule infractions which may lead to a loss of good time,
> you will be able to defend yourself at a hearing, safe-
> guarded by due process. We publish and issue a list of
> prison rules and the penalties for their violation. Our
> internal court does not deal with any actual crimes you may

---

*See Appendix I (A and B) for prisoners' views on certainty.

commit. If we have probable cause to suspect you committed a felony during your term with us it becomes a
matter for the local district attorney. This may lead to another prison consecutive sentence. The good time you earn
is vested. It's in the bank. Nobody can touch it. The internal
court can only take up to 30 days' time for an offense. You
can appeal to the warden and the director of the department.

The basic idea behind each of the leading sentencing revision
plans is a search for the classification of dangerous felons. They
presuppose tight sentencing procedures and they propose a
variety of ways of accounting for the more dangerous offender.
For example:

A. Model Penal Code*

Felonies	Ordinary Term Minimum	Maximum	Extended Term Minimum	Maximum
1st degree	1-10 yrs.	life	5-10 yrs.	life
2nd degree	1-3 yrs.	10 yrs.	1-5 yrs.	10-20 yrs.
3rd degree	1-2 yrs.	5 yrs.	1-3 yrs.	5-10 yrs.

B. Model Sentencing Act**

	Ordinary Offender Minimum	Maximum	Dangerous Offender Minimum	Maximum
First degree murder	none	life	none	life
Atrocious crimes***	none	0-10 yrs.	none	0-30 yrs.
Ordinary felonies	none	0-5 yrs.	none	0-30 yrs.

---

*Model Penal Code §§ 6.06-.09.

**Model Sentencing Act §§ 5.7-9.

***optional

C. McGee's Plan

5th degree—3 months to 3 years
   These in most cases may be reduced to misdemeanors of the first degree in the discretion of the court.
4th degree—6 months to 5 years
3rd degree—12 months to 12 years
2nd degree—18 months to 20 years
1st degree—7 years up to life, or death, if the law permits[130]

Proposed Flat Time System

Using the author's home state as an example, Illinois currently provides for four classes of felony sentencing and for murder separately.° The law requires the court to impose an indeterminate sentence of imprisonment in most instances, by specifying both a minimum and a maximum term of imprisonment, each within certain specified statutory limits. In most instances, the minimum term imposed also may not exceed one-third the maximum term imposed.

The present schedule of offenses is as follows:

Offense	Maximum Term Range	Minimum Term Range
Murder	Death, or any term in excess of 14 years, if compelling reasons for mercy are shown.	14 years, unless the court sets a higher term
Class 1	Any term in excess of 4 years	4 years, unless the court sets a higher term
Class 2	Any term in excess of 1 year, not exceeding 20 years	1 year or more, up to one-third of the maximum term set by the court

°Illinois Code of Corrections, Article 8, § 1005, 8.1.

| Class 3 | Any term in excess of 1 year, not exceeding 10 years | 1 year or more, up to one-third of the maximum term set by the court |
| Class 4 | Any term in excess of 1 year, not exceeding 3 years | 1 year in all cases |

Under this system, a convicted person gets a "bracketed" term of imprisonment—2 to 7 years, 1 to 10 years, 15 to 60 years, etc. His sentence is "indeterminate" in that he has no idea of how much of the range between his minimum and maximum sentences actually will have to be spent in custody.

Type A Sentences

It is first important to understand what is *not* recommended by our flat time proposal. We do *not* propose that all offenders committing felony offenses go to ·prison. Such a draconian measure would run afoul of the provision of Article I, Section 11 of the Illinois Constitution of 1970 which requires that "all penalties [must] be determined both according to the seriousness of the offense and with the objective of restoring the offender to useful citizenship," as it would in many other states with similar provisions.

Instead, our proposal broadens the flexibility available to the trial court in many respects. We anticipate a broadening of the court's power to employ mandatory supervision (probation), conditional discharge, periodic imprisonment, restitution and fines as sentencing alternatives—both alone and in combination. As part of a mandatory pre-sentence investigation, we would require an affirmative showing by the state that the felon could not be safely supervised in a non-incarcerative program before permitting the imposition of a prison term. Draft legislation spelling out such a standard parallels the ALI *Model Penal Code* § 7.01. To structure the discretion of the court in that regard, our proposal sets forth standards in mitigation and aggravation for the court to apply in each case.

Factors in Mitigation

The following grounds shall be accorded weight in favor of withholding a sentence of imprisonment:

(1) the defendant's criminal conduct neither caused nor threatened serious harm;

(2) the defendant did not contemplate that his criminal conduct would cause or threaten serious harm;

(3) the defendant acted under a strong provocation;

(4) there were substantial grounds tending to excuse or justify the defendant's criminal conduct, though failing to establish a defense;

(5) the victim of the defendant's criminal conduct induced or facilitated its commission;

(6) the defendant has compensated or will compensate the victim of his criminal conduct for the damage or injury that he sustained;

(7) the defendant has no history of prior delinquency or criminal activity or has led a law-abiding life for a substantial period of time before the commission of the present crime;

(8) the defendant's criminal conduct was the result of circumstances unlikely to recur;

(9) the character and attitudes of the defendant indicate that he is unlikely to commit another crime;

(10) the defendant is particularly likely to comply with the terms of a period of mandatory supervision;

(11) the imprisonment of the defendant would entail excessive hardship to him or his dependents.

If the court, having due regard for the character of the offender, the nature and circumstances of the offense and the public interest finds that a sentence of imprisonment is the most appropriate disposition of the offender, or where other provisions of this Code mandate the imprisonment of the offender, the grounds listed above shall be considered as factors in mitigation of the term imposed.

While we see the availability of a wide range of sentencing alternatives to the court as essential, we do not believe that a comparably untrammeled degree of discretion in deciding on the range of time a person should serve *in prison* is desirable. To illustrate, if two judges were asked to impose sentence on a burglar under current law, one might decide on a sentence of 1 to 4 years while the other might elect 2 to 6 years. In so doing, each judge might have had the same degree of culpability in mind. Indeed, on any given day, each might have elected to use the other alternative. No standards can be devised to assess the correctness of such determinations, except within very broad limits. Yet that decision can cost a person two years of his life. Far more extreme examples easily come to mind.

Type B or C Sentences

Types B and C are distinguished by length and the standard required for enhancement of the prison term. Type B is the ordinary term, Type C is the enhanced term. The standard for the imposition of a prison sentence (paralleling sections of the previously cited Iowa statute) follows:

Factors in Aggravation

The following factors shall be accorded weight in favor of imposing a term of imprisonment, and in the instances specified shall mandate a term of imprisonment.

(1) that in the commission of a felony offense, or in flight therefrom, the defendant inflicted or attempted to inflict serious bodily injury to another. Serious bodily injury as used in this Section means bodily injury which creates a substantial risk of death, or which causes death or serious disfigurement, serious impairment of health, or serious loss or impairment of the function of any bodily organ.

(2) that the defendant presents a continuing risk of physical harm to the public.

If the court so finds and in addition finds the factors specified in subsection (1) of this Section, and that an additional period of confinement is required for the protection of the public, the defendant may be sentenced as provided (see below for sentencing schedule) in this Code whether or not the defendant has a prior felony conviction. However, a sentence under this Section shall not be imposed unless the defendant was at least 17 years of age at the time he committed the offense for which sentence is to be imposed.

(3) that the defendant is a repeat offender whose commitment for an extended term is necessary for the protection of the public. A defendant of this type shall have sentence imposed pursuant to (the sentencing schedule of) this Code. Provided, however, a sentence shall not be imposed pursuant to this Section unless:

(a) the defendant was at least 17 years of age at the time he committed the offense for which sentence is to be imposed;

(b) the defendant has been convicted of at least one other Class 1 or Class 2 felony or two or more lesser felony offenses within the 5 years immediately preceding commission of the instant offense, excluding time spent in custody for violation of the laws of any state or of the United States.

(4) that the defendant committed a felony offense that occurred under one or more of the following circumstances:

(a) the defendant, by the duties of his office or by his position, was obliged to prevent the particular offense committed or to bring the offenders committing it to justice;

(b) the defendant held public office at the time of the offense, and the offense related to the conduct of that office;

(c) the defendant utilized his professional reputation or position in the community to commit the offense, or to afford him an easier means of committing it, in circumstances where his example probably would influence the conduct of others;

(d) if the court, having due regard for the character of the offender, the nature and circumstances of the offense, and the public interest finds that a sentence of imprisonment is not the most appropriate disposition under this Code, the grounds listed in paragraphs (1) and (4) above shall be considered as factors in aggravation of the sentence imposed (non-imprisonment).

We propose to inform the convict at the outset of the penalties for his crime. We would replace the present law with a series of determinate sentences, keyed to the present felony classification system. For each felony class, a fixed sentence is proposed, with a narrow range in mitigation or aggravation allowed around that definite figure to permit adjustments either for the facts of a particular case or for the seriousness of the offense as compared to others in the same class. In effect, then, a relatively small range of allowable prison terms would be associated with each offense. Whenever the court found imprisonment to be the appropriate disposition, it would select a fixed sentence from within that range and impose it. When a convicted person left the courtroom, he would know his actual sentence to be served less good time. A schedule of sentences could be as follows:

Type B

Offense	Flat-Time Sentence	Range in Aggravation or Mitigation	Range of Allowable Sentences
Murder A	Death or Life	—	Death or Life
Murder	Life or 25 years	± up to 5 years	Life, or any fixed term from 20 to 30 years
Class 1	8 years	± up to 2 years	Any fixed term from 6 to 10 years
Class 2	5 years	± up to 2 years	Any fixed term from 3 to 7 years

Class 3	3 years	± up to 1 year	Any fixed term from 2 to 4 years
Class 4	2 years	± up to 1 year	Any fixed term from 1 to 3 years

We do not propose mitigation reductions in the enhancement schedule because it appears to us to be contrary to the purpose of extending terms at all. We are mindful that good arguments can be made to adopt a mitigative schedule as well; however, we do not find such arguments persuasive.

In addition, enhanced sentences (extended terms of imprisonment) are available for especially dangerous or repeat offenders. A schedule of enhanced sentences appears below as an illustration:

Type C

Offense	Flat-Time Sentence	Range in Aggravation	Range of Allowable Sentences
Class 1	15 years	+ up to 3 years	Any fixed term from 15 to 18 years
Class 2	9 years	+ up to 2 years	Any fixed term from 9 to 11 years
Class 3	6 years	+ up to 2 years	Any fixed term from 6 to 8 years
Class 4	5 years	+ up to 2 years	Any fixed term from 5 to 7 years

A necessary corollary to this new sentencing structure is the vested good time credit provision. With the setting of a flat time sentence and the abolition of parole, the possibility of this day-for-a-day reduction in time served is essential to give prisoners a sufficient incentive to behave lawfully while in prison. Short of "maxing out," executive clemency is the only "escape hatch" for those serving life (or any other) sentences.

Aggravating and mitigating limits are purposively narrowly drawn since there is evidence that plea bargaining not only helps speed up "justice," but when it fails it also produces "retributive justice." Persons wishing to exercise their constitutional rights to a trial may be additionally punished. One study found: (Blumberg, 1967)

> In fact, the judges, the district attorney, and the probation report will, upon sentence of such an individual, explicitly note that the defendant has caused the state to go to the expense of a trial. In 1962 [in a large jurisdiction] the ... probation division investigated 3,643 out of 4,363 cases processed that year. . . . Of the number investigated, 1,125 were placed on probation; all but three of these pled guilty *before* trial. [131]

Nor does the problem simply turn on the question of probation sentencing.

> The concessions accorded by prosecutors to a defendant who pleads guilty are not the only sentencing advantages he may expect to receive. A Questionnaire sent by the Yale Law Journal to every federal district judge reveals that 66 per cent of the 140 judges replying consider the defendant's plea a relevant factor in local sentencing procedure. 87 per cent of the judges who acknowledged that the plea was germane indicated that a defendant pleading guilty to a crime was given a more lenient punishment than a defendant who pleaded not guilty. The estimates of the extent to which the fine or prison term was diminished for a defendant pleading guilty varied from 10 to 95 per cent of the punishment which would ordinarily be given after trial and conviction. [132]

Maximum sentence are further evaded by criminal defendants through deals with the prosecutor. There is evidence to suggest that defendants, unaware of actual sentencing patterns but informed of the maximums stated in the law, may be needlessly bargaining away their constitutionally protected right to trial since the actual time served is uniformly considerably less than provided by statute.[133] The question remains: do prosecutors actually attempt to punish those who seek a trial more so than those who plead guilty? In 1963, the *University of Pennsylvania Law Review* surveyed prosecutors and divided them into three groups: (a) those who *definitely* state that they seek out pleas of guilty through bargaining, (b) those who by some qualified answers *probably* seek pleas of guilty through bargaining, and (c) those who *definitely do not* plea bargain.[134] In response to following questions posed by the Law Review, the prosecutor's view concerning additional punishment emerges:*

(a) *Does* a defendant who pleads guilty generally receive a lesser sentence than a defendant who pleads not guilty and goes to trial and is found guilty?

(N = 65)	Percent of Prosecutors	
	Yes	No
Definitely Plea Bargain Group	62	38
Probably Plea Bargain Group	57	42
Do Not Plea Bargain Group	--	100
All Groups	55	45

(b) All other things being equal, *should* a defendant who pleads guilty receive a lesser sentence than a defendant who pleas not guilty and goes to trial and is found guilty?

(N = 70)	Percent of Prosecutors	
	Yes	No
Definitely Plea Bargain Group	71	29
Probably Plea Bargain Group	62.5	37.5
Do Not Plea Bargain Group	43	57
All Groups	67	33[136]

*See Appendix III for a public opinion poll finding on plea bargaining.

Even assuming the relevancy of our claim that the rationalization of parole along lines of a punishment-deterrence-justice model could bring more safety, sanity and fairness to prison life, some have argued: "Why mess with the system?" Some critics reason that even if the present anomie in sentencing and parole *appears* to be unjust, most prisoners average only a two year plus stay; and the more the appearance of unfairness is exposed, the more tightening up will be legislated. This might, in their view, bring more convicts into the system and keep them longer. Therefore, modernization may contain the seed of an unintended consequence which could operate against the cause of lower numbers of prisoners with relatively shorter average stays as compared to actual sentences. Hence the rationale becomes: "leave it alone, you can't really affect the onerousness of prison life anyhow, and you may open up a Pandora's Box for conservative legislators which will produce draconian prison stays (actual) rather than merely the semblance of long sentences as we have now." This is not unattractive. It is even a bit seductive. But it is not convincing on several grounds.

We find it difficult to avoid dealing with injustice in practice by simply assuming that the period of unfairness is relatively (if haphazardly) short. With the continuing expansion of non-incarcerative sentencing alternatives, we approach the irreducible minimum who will not be viewed as an attractive constituency for prison modernization by legislators. Legislatures are infrequently guided in their criminal justice decision-making by knowledge. Indeed, the usual process of law-making is fragmented, except for revisions of penal and correctional codes which occur with the frequency of one a century. Different constituencies in the system of criminal justice advance collision course bills which are not usually in tandem with each other. This process produces overload on one or another part of the continuum with little or no reference to the other parts. A simple example was the burgeoning undercover narcotics enforcement establishment. Without the necessary accompanying resources in jails, courts, clinics and prisons to absorb them, the street addicts were crowded into the system as a result of employing so many more police charged with the responsibility of simply arresting them.

Some academicians have argued that flat time at the level we suggest (2, 3, 5, 8 years) will never survive in a state legislature. Legislators will increase the flat rates, at least doubling the order of magnitude (4, 6, 10, 16 years). Having done several computer simulations with the proposed (2, 3, 5, 8) scheme, we believe that knowledge in this case *can* guide a legislature. As a matter of fact, the legislature using a flat time, no parole model can now predict with a higher degree of confidence: inmate populations, necessary bed space, staff coverage, etc., and, as a consequence, future costs and building needs.

We took the Illinois Department of Corrections population projections, without a change in the sentencing and parole laws, and found that in 48 months (using a straight line projection) the inmate population would rise from the current 7,000 (rounded) to 10,000. We then took the 1971 to 1974 intake population and had the computer "give" them 2, 3, 5, 8 year sentences, as appropriate. Further, we added multipliers for a bad economy and heavier intake, varying but conservative rates for the accumulation of good time, and a sped up process (another component of a broad legislative program calling for a 60-day fair trial law) of moving 7,000 jail prisoners (5,000 in Cook County alone) through the system.

The "2, 3, 5, 8" scheme produced an 11,500 population for the same period of time the "no action" indeterminate scheme projected a 10,000 population. But the flat time scheme was manipulable. If we reduced the five to four we "lost" eleven hundred prisoners from the population. When we dropped the eight to seven years we lost another thousand convicts. When we adopted the 4, 6, 10, 16 scheme, we tripled the population.

Several other simulations using expanded probation, periodic imprisonment, or decriminalization of certain crimes yielded different lower populations.°

We found that we could project pessimistic and optimistic world-views depending upon the sentencing scheme adopted. Perhaps most significantly, we found that it was now possible to predict with a high degree of reliability.

We now have the knowledge to confront the *realpolitik* of the legislative process, namely *prediction reliability* and *cost tolerance*. The flat time plan permits those interested in modernizing the system to forcefully enter the fray instead of sitting on the sidelines hoping for a semblance of sanity in the unpredictable whirlpool of current practice. We can point out to the public the intolerable costs which must be undertaken when you trade a 2, 3, 5, 8 plan for a 4, 6, 10, 16 plan. Legislators may have to calculate the political cost of their politicized calls for longer and longer sentences. The flat time program, while delivering a plausible sentencing format, may also have the broader appeal of muting the cries for retribution and vengeance when associated costs are apparent. In the author's experience with the proposal, he has found that police chiefs, for example, are more interested in certainty and swiftness of outcome than in severity, measured in length of years sentenced.

III. VOLITIONAL PROGRAMS AND CONVICT LABOR

Consistent with the neo-classic approach taken throughout this work, the organization of the justice-as-fairness prison is based upon the principle of maintaining that spark we all seek for validation of manhood (and womanhood)—responsibility. The prison sentence is punishment, but it is not to be vengefully

---

°See Appendix VI for methodology employed and results of simulations on the distributive effects of the 2, 3, 5, 8 year plan among the various Illinois felony classes.

executed. The conviction was based upon the offender's volition, and now this volition forms the basis for his treatment as a prisoner. The new prison program can offer a reasonable array of services beyond the food-clothing-medical-shelter needs. We see the need for educational, recreation, conjugal visitation, work and vocational programs.

We reject the idea of building a factory first (even one which pays prevailing rates), and then putting a prison around it. We are aware of its success in Scandanavia (and of the success of other nonexportable programs). The historical lessons of prison labor should give us pause for the concern in trying to operate a "free enterprise" system in a state prison. A few assembly type, collapsible work enterprises at prevailing rates are attractive. With such a system, when the market for the product dries up, we will not be left with an obsolete prison factory coupled with legislative demands requiring servile labor to produce revenue. Other collapsible or easy "turn around" formats may be conceived. All other prison support services requiring manpower should be paid for by convict or free labor at prevailing rates. When prevailing rates are obtained, the prisoner should be charged a reasonable rate for his stay, pay taxes, pay victim restitution if appropriate, have allotments sent to his family (so that he may remain head of household while doing a prison term). The convict, as a resident, should only be expected to take care of his immediate household chores without pay.

Education (academic and vocational) in our new prison program is akin to labor. There is no need for a full spectrum of remedial, elementary, high school and college programs. Prisons rarely have them anyhow. Education should be offered on a contractual basis after a prisoner (or group of prisoners) has selected a program he believes necessary for his own self-improvement. Counseling should be provided to assist in selection. New programs can simply be added and old ones discarded in response to need. Programs should not be retained for the purpose of keeping dozens of civil service academicians busy without reference to user or market needs.

All clinical programs can be dismantled as well. The spectacle of organizing inmates into therapy groups or caseloads is embarrassingly tragic. It is best described as a psychic lock-step. When the indomitability of the human spirit could not be crushed by our "break the spirit" forefathers, we relinquished the task to the technology of psychiatry. It is our belief that a conception of the prisoner as volitional and his assumption of responsibility for his behavior provide the best chemistry for good mental health. "To punish a man is to treat him as an equal. To be punished *for an offense against rules* is a sane man's right," said W.F.R. Macartney, an English ex-prisoner.[136]

All of this means that the prisoner has to be given opportunities to call some of the tunes. If he feels he has an emotional problem requiring professional assistance, the prison should make a timely response by providing a delivery system whereby private therapists are contracted for from the free world. J.D. Mabbott (1939) believed that:

> . . . it would be best if all such [clinical] arrangements were made optional for the prisoner, so as to leave him in these cases a freedom of choice which would make it clear that they are not part of his punishment. If it is said that every such reform lessens a man's punishment, I think that is simply muddled thinking which, if it were clear, would be mere brutality.[137]

The central point to be made is that *the prisoner chooses*° and

---

°A voucher credit system (a computerized account) might put on the "books"—$6.00 to $8.00 for each good day. A prisoner is free to use the credit (even borrow in advance) either inside for education and clinical services or upon release for "reintegrative" services. Reintegration is a term popping up more and more. It appears that rehabilitators, viewing the handwriting on the wall, are making still another rhetorical leap to save their empires. After decades of hiding, the U.S. Parole Board is now promising to be most visible. This welcome turnabout, however, comes at a time when the whole question of continuing parole boards at all is in question. Correctional agencies, like many other threatened governmental entities, have learned extraordinarily life-sustaining adaptive behavior.

his release is not a function of clinical progress. We wonder, in an atmosphere of real choice (in the sense of "free enterprise"), how many prison clinical programs would survive if survival turned merely on attendance and inmates were assured immunity for absence.°°

AN ALTERNATIVE TO THE FORTRESS PRISON

A diagrammatic outline of a new smaller facility is found on page 266. We recommend that such units be built in or close to urban centers because: (1) most prisoners come from urban areas and thus the maintenance of family ties is facilitated; (2) professionals we wish to attract (as well as industry) for the contracting of services are also urban-oriented; and (3) the new prison staff will have more in common with prisoners when both are selected from similar populations.

As the Twentieth Century comes to an end, the prison must act on the universally accepted axiom that the human animal is basically heterosexual and that deprivation of opportunities for sexual expression, in the best of circumstances, leads to distorted behavior. Dignified, private and extended visitation is a minimal standard in our new scheme. It is not a reward. Like medical and food services, it is minimally required for those from whom we expect responsible behavior.

These new facilities may be distinguished by degrees of security. Secure custody architectural treatment can now be accomplished mainly by perimeter security. The internal arrangements can be of the Vienna character. The National Clearinghouse of Correctional Architecture at the University of Illinois, Urbana, has developed several modern and more

---

°° A warden in Wisconsin, after reading this book in manuscript form, provided an excellent critique and raised the question: How can we be sure anybody [prisoners] would come to our therapy programs if we gave them a choice? He concluded in a postscript, stating: "and I don't mean this to be defensive."

humane formats as alternatives to the fortress prison. When a 300 person facility is sub-divisible into living units of thirty, other advantages arise: (1) the oppressive features of large congregate living (counts, group movements, routinization, etc.) are eliminated; (2) further refinements of classification (by work, education, or even treatment groups voluntarily devised) for residence selection are available; (3) staff can be assigned to manageable units and have their skills matched to the needs of the prisoners they supervise; and (4) finally, the guard as we have known him historically may find new roles for himself. In the last analysis, it may provide a safer work environment.

We offer no single scheme for the course of transition from the fortress prison to a new environment. It will take a state-by-state struggle for each to find their particular way.* Some states, not yet committed to the rehabilitation approach, might leap over the next two decades by moving to a justice model now. Others, having already become disillusioned with treatment approaches but trapped into strict custody arrangements, can begin a process of detente between the keeper and kept based on an agenda of fairness rather than one of increasing clinical services. And for the majority of states located somewhere in between, it will take searing self-analysis and hard-nosed administrative decisions to redirect their efforts toward justice in prisons.

Transformation of the fortress prison will be expensive, but not as expensive as building and operating new fortress prisons. There will be offsetting savings in locking fewer people up for less time, and further savings are realizable by the dismantling of archaic clinical, industrial and educational programs. Our conception of the prison stay as reasonable and certain (if austere) is based upon the premise that the pay-off will be an increase in the probability of safer streets.

---

*Richard McGee suggests a rational sentencing transition plan for California. With a history of strong commitments to county probation, California can reasonably collapse its state parole services into county operations. But there are too many variations in the U.S. to suggest (McGee does not) adoption of one transition plan for all or even many of the states.

Finally, we suggest a perspective that assumes crime and the criminal are not aberrations, that incarceration for some will be necessary, that in a democratic society the prison administrator's first priority is to accomplish it justly, and that we stop seeking messianic "treatments" as a way of "changing" people. David Rothman has some timely advice along these lines:

> Such millenial goals and the true-believer syndrome they engender have helped generate and exacerbate our present plight. But pursuing a strategy of decarceration might introduce some reality and sanity in a field prone to illusion and hysteria. Americans will not escape the tradition of reform without change by continually striving to discover the perfect solution. Rather, we must learn to think in tough-minded ways about the costs, social and fiscal, of a system that has flourished for so very long on the basis of fanciful thinking. If we talk openly and honestly about what we can and cannot accomplish, if we demolish the myths of incarceration, regardless of how convenient or attractive they appear to be, if we put adequate funds and support behind the pilot programs that, when evaluated carefully, should lead us to fund large-scale measures, then we may begin to reverse a 150-year history of failure.[138]

AN ALTERNATIVE FORMAT
TO THE FORTRESS PRISON

Basic layout—greater custody features
may be added for special needs

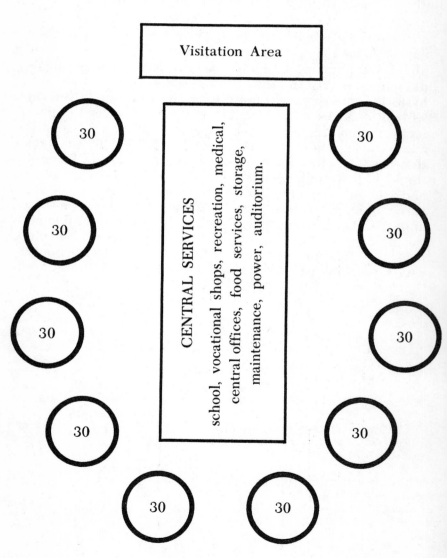

FOOTNOTES

[1]Stephen Schafer, *The Political Criminal - The Problem of Morality and Crime*, New York: The Free Press, 1974, p. 103.

[2]Paul W. Tappan, "Objectives and Methods in Correction," in Paul W. Tappan, ed., *Contemporary Correction*, New York: McGraw-Hill Book Co., Inc., 1951, pp. 4, 5.

[3]Herbert L. Packer, *Limits of the Criminal Sanction*, Stanford University Press, 1968, p. 56.

[4]*Op. cit.*, n 1, Schafer, p. 39.

[5]Norval Morris and Gordon Hawkins, *The Honest Politician's Guide to Crime Control*, Chicago: The University of Chicago Press, 1969, p. 119.

[6]Kenneth Culp Davis, *Discretionary Justice: A Preliminary Inquiry*, University of Illinois Press, 1973, p. 304.

[7]Ibid., p. 20.

[8]John Rawls, *A Theory of Justice*, Cambridge, Mass: Harvard University Press, 1972, p. 3.

[9]Edmond Cahn, *Confronting Injustice*, Boston: Little, Brown, and Co., 1966, p. 15.

[10]*Ibid.*, p. 8.

[11]Paul Keve, Book Review, in *Crime and Delinquency*, Vol. XVI, September 1970, pp. 443-444.

[12]*Op. cit.*, n 9, Cahn, pp. 10-11.

[13]*Ibid.*, p. 13.

[14]*Op. cit.*, n 2, Tappan, p. 6.

[15]Edgar Cahn and Jean Cahn, "The War on Poverty - A Civilian Perspective," *Yale Law Journal*, Vol. 73, No. 8, 1963-1964, pp. 1317-1353.

[16]Jonathan Caspar, "Criminal Justice - The Consumer Perspective," U.S. Department of Justice, Washington, D.C.: Government Printing Office (PR 72), February 1972.

[17]Philip Selznick, Introduction to Eliot Studt, Sheldon Messinger and Thomas P. Wilson, *C-Unit: Search for Community in Prison*, New York: Russell Sage Foundation, 1968.

[18]*Op. cit.*, n 9, Edmond Cahn, pp. 18-19.

[19]*Ibid.*, pp. 25-28.

[20]Marvin E. Frankel, *Criminal Sentences*, New York: Hill and Wang, 1973, p. 17.

[21]The President's Commission on Law Enforcement and Administration of Justice, *Task Force Report: Correction*, "The Legal Status of Convicted Persons," Washington, D.C.: Government Printing Office, 1967, p. 83.

[22]*Ibid.*

[23]George Bernard Shaw, *The Crime of Imprisonment*, New York: Philosophical Library, 1946, p. 63.

[24]Robert O. Dawson, *Sentencing: The Decision as to Type, Length and Conditions of Sentence*, Boston, Mass.: Little, Brown and Co., 1969, pp. 422-423.

[25]William Bennett Turner, "Establishing the Rule of Law in Prisons: A Manual for Prisoners' Rights Litigation," *Stanford Law Review*, Vol. 23, Feb. 1971, p. 473.

[26]*Op. cit.*, n 9, Edmond Cahn, p. 405.

[27]*Op. cit.*, n 20, Frankel, p. 5.

[28]*Ibid.*, p. 4.

[29]*Op. cit.*, n 24, Dawson, pp. 417-418.

[30]Daniel Glaser, Fred Cohen, and Vincent O'Leary, "Sentencing and Parole Process," in Leonard Orland, *Justice, Punishment and Treatment: The Correctional Process*, New York: The Free Press, A Division of the MacMillan Publishing Co., Inc., 1973, pp. 18-19.

[31]Sol Rubin, *The Law of Criminal Correction*, St. Paul, Minn.: West Publishing Co., 1973, p. 139.

[32]The President's Commission on Law Enforcement and Administration of Justice: *Task Force Report: The Courts*, 1967, pp. 25-26.

[33]American Friends Service Committee, *Struggle for Justice*, New York: Hill and Wang, 1971, p. 85.

[34]*Op. cit.*, n 31, Rubin, p. 164.

[35]*Op. cit.*, n 20, Frankel, p. 112.

[36]*Ibid.*, p. 113.

[37]*Ibid.*, p. 45.

[38]Annual Chief Justice Earl Warren Conference, sponsored by the Roscoe Pound-American Trial Lawyers Foundation, *A Program for Prison Reform*, June 9-10, 1972 (Caleb Foote), pp. 17-18.

[39]*Op. cit.*, n 20, Frankel, p. 45.

[40]*Op. cit.*, n 38, Annual Chief Justice Earl Warren Conference (Caleb Foote), pp. 30-31.

[41]The President's Commission on Law Enforcement and Administration of Justice: *Task Force Report: Corrections*, "The Legal Status of Convicted Persons," Washington, D.C.: Government Printing Office, 1967, p. 86.

[42]*Op. cit.*, n 6, Davis, pp. 128-130.

[43]Maurice A. Sigler, "The Courts and Corrections," (an address delivered on August 17, 1973, Kirksville, Missouri, mimeo., 8 pages), p. 6.

[44]*Op. cit.*, n 31, Rubin, p. 629.

[45]*Op. cit.*, n 38, Annual Chief Justice Earl Warren Conference (Caleb Foote), p. 34.

[46]*Ibid.*, p. 34.

[47]*Op. cit.*, n 20, Frankel, p. 103.

[48]As cited in *op. cit.*, n 20, Frankel, p. 104.

[49]*Op. cit.*, n 17, Selznick, p. ix.

[50]C. Wright Mills, *Power, Politics and People*, New York: Ballantine Books, 1963, p. 535.

[51]David F. Greenberg, "A Voucher System for Corrections," *Crime and Delinquency*, Vol. 19, No. 2, April 1973, pp. 212-217.

[52]Edward Pabon, "Voucher System," a letter to the editor, April 27, 1973, *Crime and Delinquency*, Vol. 19, July 1973.

[53]*Op. cit.*, n 17, Selznick, p. viii.

[54]James Q. Wilson, in *Harvard University Gazette*, February 27, 1974, p. 1.

[55] *Op. cit.*, n 17, Selznick, p. viii.

[56] *Op. cit.*, n 38, Annual Chief Justice Earl Warren Conference, p. 57.

[57] *Op. cit.*, n 17, Selznick, p. viii.

[58] *Ibid.*

[59] J.E. Baker, "Inmate Self-Government," *Journal of Criminal Law and Criminology*, Vol. 55, 1964, p. 39.

[60] Frank Tannenbaum, *Osborne of Sing Sing*, Chapel Hill: The University of North Carolina Press, 1933, p. 174.

[61] Harold M. Helfman, "Antecedents of Thomas Mott Osborne's Mutual Welfare League in Michigan," *Journal of Criminology*, Vol. 40, 1950, p. 598.

[62] *Ibid.*, p. 597.

[63] *Ibid.*, p. 598.

[64] *Ibid.*, pp. 598-599.

[65] *Op. cit.*, n 59, Baker, p. 42.

[66] *Ibid.*, p. 49.

[67] *Ibid.*, p. 46.

[68] *Ibid.*

[69] *Ibid.*

[70] *Ibid.*

[71] *Op. cit.*, n 17, Studt, Messinger, and Wilson, p. 160.

[72] *Op. cit.*, n 41, *Task Force Report: Corrections*, p. 49.

[73] Ernest Wenk and Rudolph Moos, "Social Climates in Prisons," *Research in Crime and Delinquency*, July 1972, (manuscript), p. 7.

[74] *Ibid.*, pp. 6-7.

[75] William D. Leeke, ed., *Riots and Disturbances*, ACA, College Park, Md., 1970, p. 7.

[76] *Ibid.*

[77] William D. Leeke, ed., *Inmate Grievance Procedure* (Collective Violence Research Project funded through the National Institute of Law Enforcement and Criminal Justice), 1973, p. 49.

[78] *Prevention of Violence in Correctional Institutions*, Criminal Justice Monograph, U.S. Dept. of Justice, LEAA, Washington, D.C.: Government Printing Office, June 1973, pp. 6-7.

[79] *Ibid.*, p. 13.

[80] *Ibid.*, pp. 22-23.

[81] *Ibid.*, p. 40.

[82] *Ibid.*, pp. 44-45.

[83] *Ibid.*, pp. 15-46.

[84] Desmond Ellis, Harold Grasmick, and Bernard Gilman, "Violence in Prison: A Sociological Analysis," *American Journal of Sociology*, Vol. 80, No. 1, July 1974, pp. 16-43.

[85] Marvin Finkelstein, *Perspectives on Prison Legal Services: Needs, Impact and the Potential for Law School Involvement*, Summary Report, U.S. Dept. of Justice, February 1972, p. 2.

[86] *Ibid.*, p. 4.

[87] *Ibid.*, p. 1.

[88] Bruce R. Jacob and K.M. Sharma, "Justice After Trial: Prisoners' Need for Legal Services in the Criminal-Correctional Process," *Kansas Law Review*, Vol. 18, 1970, pp. 493, 501.

270 / "... We Are the Living Proof ..."

[89]Comment, "Resolving Civil Problems of Correctional Inmates," *Wisconsin Law Review*, 1969, pp. 574-576.

[90]*Legal Services and Development*, University of Minnesota, (mimeo., 51 pages), p. 6.

[91]*Op. cit.*, n 25, Turner, p. 510.

[92]*Op. cit.*, n 90, *Legal Services and Development*, p. 1

[93]*Ibid.*, p. 4.

[94]*Op. cit.*, n 24, Dawson, p. 408.

[95]*Op. cit.*, n 89, "Resolving Civil Problems of Correctional Inmates," p. 578.

[96]*Op. cit.*, n 24, Dawson, p. 413.

[97]*Ibid.* p. 416.

[98]*Ibid.*, p. 401.

[99]*Op. cit.*, n 25, Turner, p. 500.

[100]*Op. cit.*, n 41, *Task Force Report: Corrections*, p. 84.

[101]*Op. cit.*, n 24, Dawson, p. 86.

[102]*Op. cit.*, n 6, Davis, pp, 98-99.

[103]George G. Killinger and Paul F. Cromwell, Jr., eds., *Penology: The Evolution of Corrections in America*, St. Paul, Minn.: West Publishing Co., 1973, p. 8.

[104]Harold L. Wilensky, *Organizational Intelligence*, New York: Basic Books, 1967, p. 171.

[105]Lance Tibbles, "Ombudsmen for American Prisons," *North Dakota Law Review*, Vol. 48, 1972, p. 386.

[106]*A Proposal to Establish an Experimental Ombudsman for the Minnesota Department of Corrections*, University of Minnesota, 1971, p. 1.

[107]*Ibid.*, p. 2.

[108]*Op. cit.*, n 105, Tibbles, p. 427.

[109]*Op. cit.*, n 6, Davis, p. 150.

[110]Enrico Ferri, *Criminal Sociology*, Boston: Little, Brown, and Co., 1917, as cited in Burt Galoway and Joseph Hudson, *Considering The Victim: Readings in Restitution and Victim Compensation*, 1975, p. 514.

[111]Lawrence W. Pierce, "Rehabilitation in Corrections: A Reassessment," *Federal Probation*, June 1974, p. 16.

[112]*OP. cit.*, n 20, Frankel, p. 101.

[113]*Op. cit.*, n 111, Pierce, p. 17.

[114]William E. Amos, "The Philosophy of Corrections: Revisited," *Federal Probation*, March 1974, p. 46.

[115]Allen F. Breed, "The Goal May Be to Make Rehabilitation Fit the Crime," *Sacramento Bee*, August 18, 1974 (the Forum Section).

[116]*Ibid.*

[117]*Op. cit.*, n 33, AFSC "The Struggle For Justice."

[118]Richard A. McGee, "A New Look at Sentencing: Part II," *Federal Probation*, September 1974, pp. 7-8.

[119]*Ibid.*, pp. 1-27.

[120]ABA and Council of State Governments, *Compendium of Model Correctional Legislation and Standards*, Part V, 11-1, July 1972.

[121]*Op. cit.*, n 20, Frankel, p. 118.

[122]*Op. cit.*, n 6, Davis, p. 135.

[123]*Op. cit.*, n 24, Dawson, pp. 383-384.

[124]*Ibid.*, p. 398.

[125]Larry I. Palmer, "A Model of Criminal Dispositions: An Alternative to Official Discretion in Sentencing," *Georgetown Law Journal*, Vol. 62, No. 1, October 1973, p. 57.

[126]*Op. cit.*, n 31, Rubin, p. 769.

[127]*Op. cit.*, n 125, Palmer, p. 18.

[128]*Op. cit.*, n 23, Shaw, pp. 61-62.

[129]*Op. cit.*, n 118, McGee, p. 8.

[130]*Ibid.*, p. 13.

[131]Abraham S. Blumberg, *Criminal Justice*, Chicago: Quadrangle Books, 1967, p. 129.

[132] Comment, "The Influence of the Defendant's Plea on Judicial Determination of Sentence," *The Yale Law Journal* Vol. 66, 1956-1957, pp. 206-207.

[133]Note, "Guilty Plea Bargaining: Compromises by Prosecutors to Secure Guilty Pleas," *University of Pennsylvania Law Review* Vol. 112, pp. 866-867.

[134]*Ibid.*, pp. 896-907.

[135]*Ibid.*, p. 907.

[136]J. D. Mabbott, "Punishment," in Frederick A. Olafson, *Justice and Social Policy*, New York: Prentice Hall, 1961, p. 46.

[137]*Ibid.*, pp. 52-53.

[138]David Rothman, "Decarcerating Prisoners and Patients," *Civil Liberties Review*, Vol. I, No. 1, Fall 1973, p. 29.

5
Hopes and Hang-Ups
The
Immediate Future

"Experience should teach us to be most on our guard to protect liberty when the Government's purposes are beneficent."

Justice Louis Brandeis

HOPES AND HANG-UPS

We have several misgivings about our model of justice in corrections. It is hard to conceive of justice retaining its vitality in the fortress prison setting. We are worried about the erosion of the justice model through a piecemeal introduction of its parts. We fear that court-harried administrators might select a portion of the model for use as "window dressing" to avoid criticism. It is even conceivable that an isolated element of this model could be used by the unscrupulous to legitimize oppressive practices. For these reasons, it is vital to reiterate our intention: the parts of the justice model must operate together if the result is to be a process of justice-as-fairness. Anything less runs the risk of being an obstruction of this process.

The justice model is not intended as a way of helping the fortress prison to survive or even making it operate more efficiently. It represents an interim strategy for the survival of the keeper and the kept — not for the prison. But we have no illusions. The prison as we know it will survive at least for the immediate future. The first task of this generation of correctional administrators should be to develop an impetus that begins the planned end of the fortress prison system.

The great irony we now face is that large numbers of prisoners not requiring maxium custody probably help maintain whatever tenuous stability we do achieve in fortress prisons. The residual offender, otherwise called the calculating, atrocious, dangerous, organized or repetitive criminal, is a troublesome case. Our sentencing plan, like others, accounts for him in a series of extended terms. We have three observations. First, the myth of the "irreducible minimum" (usually varying in estimate between 10% and 25% of prison population) has never been systematically tested for reality. Secondly, as a result, prisons over-program 100% custody (and the public retains its dim stereotype of the atrocious convict) for most who do not require such a degree of custody or even imprisonment. And lastly, unless this irreducible minimum is separated and plausibly accounted for in both senzencing and corrections, administrators will never receive the public confidence necessary to modernize the system. If probation and other forms of community-based corrections were substantially increased without something radically different in the way of handling the residual offender left in the fortress prison, we could face an even more volatile situation than now prevails. The public perceives almost all convicts as dangerous. If we continue to develop community programs without dealing safely with the residual offender, we may experience another round of Atticas, which will stiffen public resistance to the futherance of community corrections. We need, therefore, some sort of plan and public information effort that can deal sensibly with the residual offender and calm public fears. We are aware that the field is rapidly, if unsystematically, developing community-based programs. *The implication of this analysis is that we should speed up our efforts for the residual offender as a matter of first priority.* We suggest this reversal because looking down the road a bit we fear the collapse of community-based efforts as a result of mounting public fears which would follow explosive riots by resentful residual offenders left in the fortress prison.

Perhaps plans for community corrections and for residual offenders can proceed concurrently, but we see no such movement at the moment. The National Council on Crime and Delinquency rightly took a strong "moratorium on prison construction" position when it saw, for example, the opening of the Lucasville, Ohio prison. The spectacle of convicts having to be moved from the old 1834 Columbus prison to the new (fortress) prison in 1973 was testimony to the chaos of correctional planning. We now urge a *narrow easing of the moratorium* based upon our own perspective of the need to deal first with the residual offender in order to build public confidence for decriminalization, diversion, community-based alternatives, and the expansion of probation. This requires an integrated plan that maximizes the use of alternatives for the safer offender, secures rational sentencing legislation, and projects a new environment for the less safe.

We are also concerned about the humanization of the residual offender until strong justice-as-fairness safeguards are built into sentencing laws and new prison procedures. If, through rational sentencing, we successfully segregate prisoners into our proposed type of smaller, safer and more humane institutions, it may appear that we have indeed discovered the irreducible minimum. Having done so, we may not concern ourselves with such "luxuries" as justice. It may focus both resentment (producing distortion) and apathy (producing neglect) on the residual group. There are already a host of plans for dealing with what is now an amorphous group called the "repetitively violent offenders" in Illinois,[1] "special offenders" in New England and Iowa,[2] "Behavior Modification Program Units" in the Federal Bureau of Prison's plan for the new institution at Butner, North Carolina;[3] and the "Maximum Psychiatric Diagnostic Unit" in California that abortively proposed a revival of brain surgery to modify criminal behavior.[4]

Commenting on the proposed New England Project contained in the "Curran Report," Mathew Dumont of the Massachusetts Department of Mental Health wrote:

The report displays an exhilaration about the prospects of psycho-pharmacological and behaviorist technology which betrays a profound ignorance about them and an in-difference to their consequences. The 'use of drugs to control disruptive behavior' has already been suggested in every fantasy of technological fascism so that it can hardly be considered new. Tranquilizers can, indeed, be effective in the control of aggression. It has also been suggested that tranquilizers serve as chemical restraints in mental hospitals and for some patients. There has also been research and development of nonlethal weaponry utilizing tranquilizers. While they do have anti-anxiety and sedative effects which are helpful in some emotional crises, they have been out-rageously over used by physicians as if they were the answer to every human problem. Some two hundred million prescriptions are written for tranquilizers every year in this country. Some psychiatrists argue that they have done more harm than good. They have clouded over a host of emotional reactions to life and its stresses which are not only not pathological but necessary. There have been numerous instances of idiosyncratic reactions, sensitivities and side effects, including changes in the eyes, liver and nervous system, some of them irreversible and more disabling than the conditions for which the drugs were prescribed in the first place.[5]

The "special offender" population is an attractive locale for the new enthusiasts because once identified as such he is least defended,* but he is not completely undefended.[6] When the new technologies have been justified for orderliness rather than rehabilitation, the courts have reacted negatively, as in *Mackey v. Procunier,* 477 F.2d 877 (9th Cir. 1973). The court has held that the right to privacy precluded the prison from forcing drugs on a non-consenting prisoner. In Iowa, the court balked at pemitting the use of drugs, even when the purpose was "treatment," without the prisoner's consent:

> At the outset we note that the more characterization of an act as 'treatment' does not insulate it from eighth amendment scrutiny. In *Trop* v. *Dulles,* 356 U.S. 86, 95 (1958), the Supreme Court stated that the legislative classification of a statute is not conclusive in determining whether there had been a violation of the eighth amendment. Instead, the court examined the statute by an inquiry directed to the

---

*Justice Brandeis, in his dissent in *Olmstead v. United States,* 227 U.S. 438 (1928) at 478: "The makers of our Constitution undertook to secure conditions favorable to the pursuit of happiness. They recognized the significance of man's spiritual nature, of his feelings and of his intellect. They knew that only a part of the pain, pleasure and satisfactions of life are to be found in material things. They sought to protect Americans in their beliefs, their thoughts, their emotions and their sensations. They conferred, as against the government, the right to be left alone — the most comprehensive of rights and the right most valued by civilized man."

Charles Dickens (1842) also has a word on the subject: "I believe it [prison], in its effects, to be cruel and wrong. In its intention, I am well convinced that it is kind, humane, and meant for reformation; but I am persuaded that those who devised this system of prison discipline do not know what it is that they are doing . . . I hold this slow and daily tampering with the mysteries of the brain, to be worse than any torture of the body."

substance; reasoning that 'even a clear legislative classification of a statute as 'nonpenal' would not alter the fundamental nature of a plainly penal statute' . . . Here we have a situation in which an inmate may be subjected to a morphine base drug which induces vomiting for an extended period of time. Whether it is called 'aversive stimuli' or punishment, the act of forcing someone to vomit for a fifteen minute period for committing some minor breach of the rules can only be regarded as cruel and unusual unless the treatment is being administered to a patient who knowingly and intelligently has consented to it. To hold otherwise would be to ignore what each of us has learned from sad experience — that vomiting (especially in the presence of others) is a painful and debilitating experience. The use of this unproven drug for this purpose on an involuntary basis is, in our opinion, cruel and unusual punishment prohibited by the eighth amendment.[7]

We focus attention on this group of "special offenders" and the new group of enthusiasts because they could become embraced in a new wave of Orwellian distortion. One fruitful way of calling a halt to the rising clamor to treat special offenders in "new promising ways" is for the corrections establishment to forcefully declare that it knows little about changing human behavior and has even less interest in attempting it with adjudicated criminals. James Q. Wilson states (1974):

Policy analysis, as opposed to causal analysis, begins with a very different perspective. It asks not what is the cause of the problem, but what is the condition one wants to bring into being, what measure do we have that will tell us when that condition exists, and finally what policy tools does a government (in our case, a democratic and libertarian government) possess that might, when applied, produce at reasonable cost a desired alteration in the present condition or progress toward the desired condition? In this instance, the desired condition is a reduction in specified forms of crime. The government has at its disposal certain policy instruments — rather few, in fact — that it can use: it can redistribute money, create (or stimulate the creation of) jobs, hire persons who offer advice, hire persons who practice surveillance and detection, build detention facilities, illuminate public streets, alter (within a range) the price of drugs and alcohol, require citizens to install alarm systems, and so forth. It can, in short, manage to a degree money, prices, and technology, and it can hire people who can provide within limits either simple (e.g., custodial) or complex (e.g., counseling) services. These tools, if employed, can affect the risks of crime, the benefit of non-criminal occupations, the accessibility of things worth stealing, and the mental state of criminals or would be criminals. A policy analyst would ask what feasible changes in which of these areas would, at what cost (monetary and non-monetary), produce how much of a change in the rate of a given crime.[8]

We have already seen that almost all of corrections' rehabilitation programs fail and that in the absence of our ability to change behavior (rather than attitudes) we should seek, as Wilkens suggested, more simple, humanitarian, and cheaper alternatives. Wilson continues:

The criminologist assumes, probably rightly, that the causes of crime are determined by attitudes which in turn are socially derived, if not determined; the policy analyst is led to assume that the criminal acts as if crime were the product of a free choice among competing opportunities and constraints. The radical individualism of Bentham and Beccaria may be scientifically questionable, but it is prudentially necessary ... Those matters that are within the reach of policy have been, at least for many criminologists, defined away as uninteresting because they were superficial, 'symptomatic,' or not of 'causal' significance. Sociology, for all its claims to understand structure, is at heart a profoundly subjectivist discipline. When those who practice it are brought forward and asked for advice they will say either (if conservative) that nothing is possible or (if liberal) that everything is possible. That most sociologists are liberals explains why the latter reaction is more common even though the pre-suppositions of their own discipline would more naturally lead to the former.[9]

Over the last two centuries we have developed an arsenal of religious-clinical appendages around the fortress prison. George Bernard Shaw, speaking of the first prison he ever saw, said: "[it] . . . had inscribed on it 'Cease to do Evil: Learn to do Well' but as the inscription was on the outside the prisoners could not read it."[10] So it has also largely been with the many good purposes we initiated in prisons — the prisoners could not read them. Something is lost in translating social casework, psychology, education, religious ministries or psychiatry into civil service prison positions. Enthusiastic professionals arrived and in short order discovered that they could make all but the essential decisions regarding their convict-client. A few deluded themselves into thinking that the one or two therapeutic hours a week they spent with their charges could overcome, mitigate or even balance the negative effects of the other 167 hours each week spent in a cellblock. A few others may not have cared. For all the commitment, knowhow and enthusiasm brought into prisons by professionals, a slow erosion seems to have overtaken them: (1) some quit in disgust or seek a transfer to a less onerous setting within corrections or outside of it; (2) some become case-hardened through their socialization with the ideologists of the custody staff and are eventually indistinguishable morally, one from the other; or (3) some stay on in prisons, polarized from the custody staff, in a messianic overidentification with convicts. Lest this be overdrawn, a few are successfully walking a tightrope between delivering useful if not curative services and teaching usefully humane behavior to guards. But the overwhelming majority are faced with the historical fate that confronted successive armies invading China: rather than conquering China they themselves became Chinese.

Men and women from several professional disciplines have been able to enter the correctional arena, present a panacea, and capture the attention of the keeper and the kept for a time. The literature is embarrassingly replete with simplistic solutions. They represent a curious admixture of religious, moral and psychological fervor — sometimes coupled with unbridled barbarism. The introduction of the case method of psychological treatment and all its variants has always had the shadow of punishment cast over its efforts. Meanwhile, the fortress prison, in one form or another, survives, sometimes with the quality of instant obsolescence like Ohio's pastoral Lucasville. The several disciplines have used these institutions as professional playgrounds with little demonstratable gain in public safety. A voluminous literature has developed. An unprecedented polarity has occurred between the professional and the guard and between the latter and the prisoner. An economic chasm has been opened between the guard and all other criminal justice employees. Left in the fortress prison are the angry and inappropriate antagonists — keeper and kept — playing out a drama of escalating confrontations that promises to reach epic proportions.

Moderate community-based innovations will only intensify the anger of those left behind. Unless the prison's physical and social environment changes radically, we will experience unprecedented violence in the fortress prison. It is not in the interest of the correctional worker or the public safety to permit the fortress prison to operate as we now know it.

Correctional administators should begin the development of an agenda for dramatic change. We need to take hold of the reins of corrections' future and begin exerting the leadership we probably possess. We need to spell out a practical and just program for ourselves and with those over whom we are given legal sanction. We do not need still another list of innovative experiments. The Law Enforcement Assistance Administration has provided us with ample opportunity to experiment. The level of public information has never been higher, and with the report of the National Advisory Commission we have a long agenda for systematic change. What we need now is not so much a technology as much as a combined will to modernize.

As far as we can see, there is no informed opposition to correctional change, but neither is there a powerfully informed correctional position. We know what prosecutors' associations think about capital punishment. We know what the many police associations think about lengths of current sentences, probation, and community-based corrections. But the ACA, the Warden's Association, and the various trade unions have yet to project a forceful program for corrections in tune with a nation which has an unprecedented rate of crime.

Meetings of top administrative leadership in corrections tend to be wasteful sessions since there is a wide divergence in their education, training, disposition, and morality. Positions taken by them tend to be in the lowest common denominator of consensus rather than projecting five or ten years into the future. Nor are the state associations helpful since they are not deeply involved in standard setting, enforcement, the legislative process, or advanced training. As a consequence, corrections is left with a weak public image. To the public it appears tradition-oriented, defensive, and, as a result of its predominately reactive style, amoral.

It is time, as Maurice Sigler declared, that we take public leadership and call a halt to self-deception. Public apathy is not the public's fault. If it is apathetic, it is because we have not invited its participation and assistance. If legislatures are not providing enough resources, it is probably because they are tired of escalating costs and static or declining results after more than 150 years of support. Without public involvement and legislative support, we remain expensive latent volcanoes of violence with reforms destined never to outlive reformers.

We need a vision about what we are now and what we wish to become, coupled with a strategy to help us get there. With some few but notable exceptions, adult corrections can in composite be reasonably described as a two-century-old warehouse. It is staffed by a poorly paid, low status, disaffected manpower source on the periphery. The medium is the message. Steel and concrete do not mix with humaneness. Adding caseworkers or psychiatrists into this milieu does not improve the mix. Nor has it been fruitful to conceptualize current prison strife, as some prison officials are wont to do, as conspiracies perpetuated by political militants — usually black. Each disturbance usually reveals a range of contributing circumstances from neglect of massive problems to aimless escalations of minor events. The presumption underlying the conspiratorial notion is that administrators and correctional institutions in the natural order of things, should be viewed as faultless and historically stable, while increasingly troublesome sorts passing through the system cause an undue upset. A more plausible explanation is that human dignity is reaching for a new plateau which many administrators have fearfully mistaken for a widespread conspiracy brought on by a "new breed" of inmates. Our history is replete with such evasions. We should realize that we have, during the 1960's, witnessed a belated human rights explosion that promises to continue. This means more people, not less, are willing to use the system.

There is now a visible sign of change. In a rare display of candor, Maurice Sigler, Chairman of the U.S. Parole Board, said:

> We will have to agree that change has come to corrections later than for most other human endeavors. But it is now upon us, in full force. And it is very largely the courts that are setting the pace and applying pressure.
>
> I know that the 'old guard' of the corrections field has been criticized in recent years as having the mentality and resistance to reality of the so-called battleship admirals. And I guess that if anyone can be considered one of the 'old guard', I am that man. I have been in corrections longer than most people who are in it today — some 34 years.
>
> I've searched my share of cells and counted my share of inmates. I've stood my share of morning watches in remote, dark towers, which is a soul searching experience if there ever was one. I must admit that with many others who have had the same experience I found it pretty hard to adjust when the wave of change first hit corrections. . .
>
> This was a time when the courts followed a 'hands off' doctrine towards corrections . . . But corrections failed to take the cue, and the courts gradually abandoned the 'hands-off' doctrine. Today, it is about gone, at least in the federal

courts.

In the years past, I fought my share of court decisions and got licked most of the time. You know the old saying, 'if you can't lick'em join'em.' I've joined and from now on I'm going to try to stay ahead of them. I've found that it doesn't hurt a bit, and when I sit back and think about it, the decisions of the courts in the long run have strengthened rather than weakened corrections. . .

In 1946, in *Ex parte Hull*, 312 U.S. 546, the Supreme Court struck down prison regulations which said that prisoners could not send legal documents to a court unless and until prison officials determined that they were properly drawn. I remember the days when writs were often just filed away or thrown away in the institution.

And in 1969, in *Johnson v. Avery*, 393 U.S. 483, the Supreme Court held that where the stats did not provide reasonable legal service alternatives, they could not prevent inmates from assisting each other in preparing writs to be sent to the court. We used to throw 'jail-house' lawyers in the hole when we caught them helping other inmates.*

My own field is now parole, and I want to tell you that this field has not been neglected. It took a while, but the courts finally got around to us.

There was a day when parole was considered a matter of grace, and every parole board operated in its own ways which were pretty mysterious ways for most people to fathom, particularly prison inmates. Paroles were granted or revoked with very little in the way of recognizable procedure or explanation. No more. . ..

For many correctional administrators, this was brought home dramatically and painfully on February 1, 1973 when a federal judge ruled that the Corrections Director of the State of Virginia had violated the rights of three penitentiary inmates, and fined him 21 thousand 265 dollars to be paid out of his own pocket . . . The rest of America is changing, and we in corrections have to change with it. We should no longer

*For a parallel view of sorts by a convict, see Appendix II.

merely react to the pressures of the courts and the public. We should move out and take the leadership in this trend.[11]

JUSTICE WITHOUT THERAPY

Several recent developments since the first edition of this book have helped propel some of its major themes into national debate. Three jurisdictions (California, Indiana, and Illinois) have passed legislation and several others, including the federal system, are on the verge of change. Among these developments is the rapid growth of the literature related to determinate sentencing. Normally antagonistic groups have formed new political coalitions. The Law Enforcement Assistance Administration (LEAA), which sponsored the original research for this work, funded continued efforts to deepen the understanding of the implications of determinate sentencing in several related initiatives with expenditure of over two million dollars. Finally, the courts have begun escalating their concern and intervention on important issues raised in Chapter IV.

While it is not our intention to bring the emerging case law up to date (with the explosive rate of federal judicial intervention any volume is out of date by press time), attention is called to *Van Zeldern v. Kerr* (N.D. California under judicial advisement), which challenges the constitutionality of the indeterminate sentence, and *Commonwealth v. Riggins* (Pa. , 378 A.2d. 1229 [1977]) which requires the state's judiciary to articulate their reasons for sentencing rejections, the argument before it that a statement of reasons would be an "unwarranted burden." The Pennsylvania Supreme Court found this argument to be "without merit." And in *Carmona v. Ward* 436 F.Supp. 1153 (S.D. N.Y. 1977) the court declared the "Rockefeller Drug Laws" unconstitutional based on the Eighth and Fourteenth Amendments, that life imprisonment for narcotic sales in New York was grossly disproportionate to other United States jurisdictions and because the laws failed to take the degree of culpability and mitigating circumstances into consideration.

Constitutional attacks continued upon entire penal systems as

well. While Arkansas in *Holt v. Sarver,* 309 F.Supp. 362 (E.D
Ark., 1970), Alabama in *Pugh v. Locke,* 406 F.Supp. 318 (M.D
Ala., 1976), and Mississippi in *Gates v. Collier,* 501 F.2d 1291
(5th Cir., 1974), are already well known instances, federal judge
Raymond Pettine has now added Rhode Island to the list o.
states in gross violation of constitutional standards of practice. In
ordering the closing of that state's maximum custody fortress
prison (over a century old), he concluded that in addition to
being in violation of the state's law requiring efforts at prisoner
rehabilitation, it was also in violation of the Eighth Amendment
in that the pervasive atmosphere of fear and terror (largely a
result of idleness) constituted cruel and inhumane punishment
In a blistering order Judge Pettine also found that the "totality of
conditions" at both of the state's prisons violated the Fourteenth
Amendment as well. He found that the defendants had
"knowingly and recklessly permitted a reign of terror to develop
and exist at the A.C.I. [the maximum custody prison known as
the Adult Correctional Institution]." The court further detected
among correctional administrators "an attitude of cynicism,
hopelessness, predatory selfishness, and callous in-
difference. . ."*

Some corrections administrators who never betrayed a "clinical
interest," have of late taken up the "treatment" standard. The
most searing and predictably least critical review of the justice
model has come from the clinically oriented. Their argument is
that the justice model abandons treatment at a time when all the
evidence is not yet in. Wilks and Martinson, they claim, were
premature. Their data reach only to 1968**, thus not taking into
account the impact of LEAA funded rehabilitation projects
begun since that date. Also, other more promising directions in
treatment were developing. A careful reading of Chapter IV
should leave one with the clear idea that the effectiveness of
rehabilitation is not the issue. Rather we have simply been asking

Palmigiano v. Garrahy, F.Supp. (D.C. R.I. 8/10/77), 21 CrL 2489-2490. See
also federal judge Bound's findings in *Laaman v. Helgemoe,* 437 F.Supp. 269
(D.C. N.H. 1977).

**Of course these authors made superhuman efforts to point out the very
same thing.

whether it should be corrections' mission "to treat" at all, and if in this field (which Wilkins so aptly characterized as "applied mythology"[12]) we intend to pursue clinical treatment, will we continue to do so coercively, and in the face of scientific data which show no significant level of confidence in positive results?

It is, of course, becoming increasingly difficult to keep the public (and other professionals in criminal justice) convinced that *the* purpose or even a *substantial* purpose of the process of capturing, prosecuting and incarcerating the offender should be their clinical treatment or even their vocational or remedial academic education. Likewise, for the convicts in our system of criminal justice, it strains to the point of collapse the credibility of maintaining the critically overcrowded fortress prison as an appropriate site for such programs, even if they could agree that a major purpose of their imprisonment was self-improvement.

Packer has already warned us of the futility of the "leap of faith" necessary to believe that prison services alone can ever justify the length of a sentence, or that as a result of such services crime may, in the future, be substantially prevented.[13] Hans W. Mattick, from a slightly different perspective, points out in his "neutrality of knowledge" argument that education or treatment may be used to serve a variety of ends.[14] Vocational training in welding, for example, could produce better safecrackers while psychotherapy might remove the last vestige of conflict from a previously neurotically conflicted and thus perhaps unsuccessful embezzler.

Can *some* convicts improve themselves in prison? Quite likely. Can we extrapolate from some heroic individual efforts to systematic programs aimed at improving large numbers of offenders? The research convincingly demonstrates that this is quite unlikely. "Why," some ask, "should we not increase our resources and *really* try rehabilitation on a grander scale? After all, we've never had adequate financing in the past." There are two responses. First, we *have had* all sorts of adequately financed programs (smaller probation and parole caseloads, therapeutic prison communities, behavior modification adventures, classification followed by differential treatment, community-based alternatives, diversion, and a host of self-help programs especially with alcoholics and drug abusers). Most of these programs, upon careful evaluation, did not justify further expenditures.

> It is, of course, utterly unsurprising that in regard to results or 'cures', no significant relationship between prison 'treatment' programs and behavior after release from prison has been found. But to suggest, as reformists do, that those programs have failed because of the failure to invest sufficient resources in this enterprise is like saying that necromancy might solve most of our problems if only its practitioners were adequately funded.[15] (Hawkins, 1976)

Yet if we look to their post-incarcerative careers, some offenders actually do *appear* to have been helped.* But what kept them out of trouble? Was it the incarceration itself? Did they get older and wiser? Were they better equipped for the job market? Did they learn new coping skills? Or did they just not get caught again? *We simply do not know.*

But suppose we did know covincingly that 50% or even 60% of the convicts we "treated" had, as a *direct result* of such treatment, ceased criminal activity? Should we derive our policy direction from such a finding? This is the second response: if we knew that something worked more often than not, should we apply it in prison? If a scientific evaluation told us that it takes three years for the "cure" to be administered, would we release the "uncured" sooner to keep the already "cured" longer? If a prisoner were "cured" but had several more years to do (simply because of the nature of the crime) should we keep him locked up? On what basis could either action be rationalized, much less morally justified? Is a showing of, or lack of "clinical progress" or "rehabilitation" a controlling reason for shortening or lengthening a term of imprisonment? In our view it is not, and its pretention has not brought any notable increase in reformed criminals. Having failed the reformative test, indeterminate sentencing (employing the clinical method) became a custody tool: "show 'progress' or you'll stay longer". While the elastic rhetoric of the indeterminate treatment sentence permitted it to "achieve" humanitarianism, even when it fell short of cures, the plain fact is that it increased the average length of prison sentences in the last four decades in this country and England.[16]

Up to this point the reader might conclude that the writer is negatively oriented toward rehabilitation programs, but such a conclusion would be incorrect. We are, however, deeply concerned with the delivery system of clinical programs in prison, especially with the lack of credibility practioners of clinical services suffer among covict populations. Using a comparison may serve to illustrate this truth.

Some years ago Linda Singer asked a group of young lawyer-colleagues whether they could imagine themselves as prison lawyers: that is, employed by the warden to render legal services to convicts. The audience broke into derisive laughter. "How," one of them might have asked, "could we who are trained in an adversary style and in a advocacy profession possibly undertake such a role?" Imagine the same query put to a group of social workers, psychologists and psychiatrists. It would have been seen as a reasonable question, as a largely unconflicted role model for almost all of them. The lawyer could not see himself/herself as the "warden's lawyer". After all, who among the prison population would hire such "counsel"? Yet clinicians, despite a burgeoning advocacy rhetoric in their literature since the late 1960's, are still able to "fit" into a prison role much as if it were a clinic or residential treatment center. Do we still, at this late date, believe that large numbers of prisoners under the indeterminate sentence regimen seek out clinicians to assist them in honest self-improvement ventures?

Would it not be liberating for clinicians to simply withdraw from prison work unless their relationships with clients were voluntary, of an advocacy nature and when necessary, adversarial? Can the clinician be an employee of the prison and an advocate in the employ of the client at the same time? Who does the clinician "work for" in the spiritual sense of the term? The dilemma arises out of the operation of the indeterminate sentence itself. It reduces the client-treater relationship to a con game. If the clinician is the key to getting out, prisoners (as would most of us) simply play the game of acting "cured". Hans W. Mattick described the treatment-parole decision process as having transformed our prisons into great drama centers (wherein the cons are actors, the parole board serves as drama critics handing out Oscars, Emmys and paroles.)[17]

At the 1975 annual meeting of the ACA, a Catholic priest said after hearing this writer describe parole: "I'm a drama coach [at a southern prison]. All prisoners prior to going before the parole board room for a hearing pass by and drop into my office for consultation. They play their 'line' to the parole board on me first and I consult with them about the effectiveness of what they are going to tell the board." They discussed, inter alia, how to project respect, remorse, abjectness or whatever else might "work."

The indeterminate sentence requires a convict to show clinical progress to support his claim to candidacy for early release, thus determining role frames for both treater and treated. The latter must concoct a prison biography and have it captured in his "jacket" (master file) which chronologizes clinical progress. The former has to use work reports, behavior reports, tests, attendance evidence at AA, group therapy, counseling, religious meetings, etc., to "show" the parole board how his client has "progressed."

The prisoner has very limited resources to show his own progress. The prison may have only a limited range of programs shoemaking, farming or license plates. The prisoner must show his interest and growth in one or the other. Within this array he "specializes" for a period of time to convince the parole board (via his clinician) that he is prepared to be set free. Another approach is to show progressive symptom remission from earlier precipitous, volatile or explosive behavior. For example, a prisoner may deliberately punch a guard during his first segment and refrain from punching anyone again until his parole board date. The first segment assault was necessary for his "jacket" (cumulative file), otherwise he would have no base-line for a showing of symptom remission ("progress") in the last segment.*

When the release date is tied to a showing of "clinical progress" (the terminology used when the prison has clinicians), or "parolability readiness" (when the prison, as is most frequently true, is in short supply of clinicians), we have locked-in predictable responses from both the treaters and treated. *This is coercive rehabilitation.* Despite those who do become reformative accidents during their prison experience, do we still believe that the state can really hire *me* to rehabilitate *you* or *you* to rehabilitate *me* unless one of us *wants* something to happen? Under a coerced treatment regimen will we ever know?

Clinicians, though not ubiquitous, are nevertheless well rooted in the prison setting. Their numbers and effectiveness notwithstanding, the literature uncritically suggests that still larger numbers be employed. An argument for the withdrawal of their service meets two types of opposition: first, those who have a bread-and-butter problem (jobs), and secondly, those who simply cannot envisage clinical service delivery outside of its current civil service auspice — the client-prisoner. Though the justificatory rhetoric for the status quo remains altrusitic, there are many who are unable to tax their imaginations even in the service of advancing the debate.

We have already considered an example of the former "can't-let-go" type on pages 202-203 in the Greenberg-Pabon exchange. Consider, now, the 1976 ACA presidential address as it entertains the same notion of a voucher system as a service delivery system in a prison, this time as advanced by the author.

Moreover, Fogel's suggestion to allow prisoners to contract for treatment services is unrealistic. Can you imagine a professional counselor giving up his urban practice to move to Attica because 20 inmates have indicated an interest in

---

*But for the reader who believes that the above examples are too bizarre to actually occur among convicts, there are now booklets on the market written by an "ex-resident" (Bob Heise) that include convict "games" of this nature.

contracting for his services? If the prisoners change their minds, or the group itself changes, *he is out of a job.*[18]

Here again the specter is raised of being "out of a job" because of the client's will. But now the client is a prisoner and in a position of "lesser eligibility." (A free person can put his therapist "out of a job" by withdrawal but a convict is not afforded the same opportunity.) Perhaps more revealing in Mr. Keller's argument is the inability to envisage any system of service delivery other than one (he does offer the Mutual Agreement Program) which insures the civil service status of the clinician.

What at first blush sounds harsh, that is, the zero-base budgeting of clinical programs, or the withdrawal of professionals from prisons under indeterminate jurisdictions, may in the last analysis be a vehicle for freeing treatment personnel to do the job for which they were trained.* If prisoners had vouchers (or a third party contractual arrangement) and could hire clinicians as they now hire attorneys, the clinicians would be free (of many institutional restraints) to be treaters. This dilemma might be readily resolved if the release date was unhooked from a showing of progress.

This of course means voluntary treatment. How do we insure voluntariness? Perhaps we should take the "stake" out of the current treater-client relationship, namely the promise of early release. It means an end to what Dershowitz calls the ad-

---

*An assumption when applied to personnel currently employed in the field. This assumption is not shared by all:

> Moreover, the low starting salary and the elastic definitions of "professional workers" often seriously debase what it means to be a psychologist, social worker, or therapeutic counselor. A college dropout who made an unsuccessful attempt to master "English Lit. II" cannot be converted into a therapeutic counselor by undergoing an employment ritual that confers that [civil service] status. No wonder inmates see the whole enterprise as essentially fraudulent. (Mattick, "Reflections of a Former Warden", p. 309)

> It is clear that no democratic society would ever leave it to judges, administrators, or experts to decide which acts should constitute crimes. That decision is quintessentially legislative, involving, as it does, fun-

ministrative (parole board) and judicial models in answering the "basic question" in relation to the release date — "Who decides and when?" His analysis of the short-comings of both models leads him (and a growing number of scholars and practitioners) to the conclusion that in our society the legislature is a safer repository for sentencing policy.

To reiterate, determinate sentencing does not mean an abandonment of rehabilitation, but a transformation of the relationship between treater and treated. It means that we pay attention to research findings about coerced rehabilitation. More significantly it means that we accept the premise that the purpose of a prison sentence (as experienced by the client) is clearly punishment — no matter how it is rhetorically garbed. The prison sentence should be fixed, certain, definite, and liberally mitigated through day-for-day good time which is "vested" and its loss due process protected. A mandatory pre-sentence investigation report should have to demonstrate affirmatively that it sought the *least onerous* (non-incarcerative) outcome before it recommends imprisonment. The imposition of a prison sentence is thereafter guided by *statutory criteria* which must be stated on the record and is in turn *reviewable* in an appellate procedure.

We return to one of the original questions and ask it in a few slightly different ways. How do we know when someone is ready for release? As treaters do we not have an affirmative responsibility to help the offender? Can we relese an "unprepared" convict into the community? Aren't we in the prisons in a better position than the sentencing judge to make judgments about release? Is it not simply a question of sharpening our diagnostic and treatment skills until we really can increase the reliability of our assessments? All of these may contain threads of truth, but they may also be irrelevant. Can we tell what kinds of lives others actually live, much less predict the lives we believe they

---

damental questions of policy. Likewise, it should not be left to judges, administrators, or experts to determine the bases on which criminal offenders in a democratic society should be deprived lawfully of their freedom.[19] (Dershowitz, 1976)

will lead once free (having 'benefitted' from prison programs)? That, in last analysis, can only be determined historically. The rule of law clashes here with clinical predictability. As we have argued earlier, we are actors in a system of justice in a democracy and thus *simple fairness* may be a more significant goal to be sought in executing an incarcerative sentence than the criminal's cure.

The uncertainty, the disparities (for minorities and women), the whim, the caprice, the increased prison time and the injustices of the indeterminate sentence and parole release system have been documented elsewhere.[20] If we can't coercively treat with any reliability, we can at least be fair, reasonable, humane and constitutional in practice. There is a certain plausibility in the notion that a lawfully guided term of imprisonment might have some carryover effect in persuading the frequently unlawful into more frequent lawful ways of dealing with problems. Maybe this is the most we can hope to accomplish in our prisons: to get prisoners to be more law-abiding by treating them lawfully. "It is, perhaps, gratuitous to assert that those who have been convicted of breaking the law are most in need of having respect for the law demonstrated to them." (Mattick, 1972).[21] In this sense justice-as-fairness might itself be the treatment regimen.

In a democracy we should not restrict freedom except on clearly established and promulgated bases. Lengthening or shortening sentences based upon unreliable professional claims does not meet this test. Norval Morris (with characteristic parsimony and clarity), long ago (1964) suggested a path out of our moral thicket: "Power over a criminal's life should not be taken in excess of that which would be taken *were his reform not considered as one of our purposes.*"[22]

The major purpose of this book is to advance the debate concerning the constitutional quality of prison life. We have necessarily windened this area of concern as it impinges upon the everyday quality of prison life. Previous studies were, we felt, too narrowly involved in explanations of inmate cultures, riot control, management improvement and incremental privilege granting and withdrawal. We have attempted to place the prison, hence its internal human experience, in the larger environment of "evolving constitutional standards," sentencing (disparities and inequities) and parole (arbitrariness and caprice). In raising these questions (and suggesting paths to resolution) we have attempted to focus the discussion upon the "here and now." This is not to suggest the prototypical program advanced in Chapter IV as a mere panacea. Our response to the problems of lawlessness in sentencing, the degradations of prison life and the arbitrariness of parole is simply to call for the vigorous application of the rule of law in each process. But discretion can be narrowed in sentencing, prison life can be rationalized in a just manner and parole granting can be structured to reduce arbitrary discrepancy. (Admittedly the parole board may not by definition be able to survive the test of fairness when its decisions are based largely upon a point system derived from the experiences of *previous* inmate populations and applied to *future* applicants.)

Yet it is too early in the debate to fix upon solutions. In the last analysis our system of Federalism will permit several "solutions" in the next decade as several large jurisdictions experiment with different approaches toward building rational sentencing and releasing systems. These, however, are not *solutions; ends* rarely are achieved. The *means* or *process* and thus the *conscious pursuit of justice-as-fairness* is *the* purpose of the new debate.

FOOTNOTES

[1]"Planning for the Treatment of the Repetitively Violent Offender," *Conference Summary*, April 8, 1974, University of Chicago (mimeo.)

[2]Richard Shapiro and Matthew Feinberg, "The Legal Objectives to the Feasibility Study for a Proposed New England Regional Facility for Special Offenders," (a brief), *American Civil Liberities Union*, Boston, Massachusetts, February 7, 1974.

[3]William G. Nagel, *The New Red Barn: A Critical Look at the Modern American Prison*, New York: Walker and Co., 1973, p. 5.

[4]*The Free World Times*, January, 1974.

[5]Letter of Matthew Dumont, Assistant Commissioner for Drug Rehabilitation, Department of Mental Health of Massachusetts, to Lieutenant Governor Donald Dwight, dated January 7, 1974, cited in *op., cit.*, n3, Shapiro and Feinberg, p. 10.

[6]John Bowers, "Medical Research in Prisons," *Clearinghouse Review*, Northwestern University Law School, Vol VI, July 1972, pp. 148-153.

[7]*Knecht v. Gillman*, 448 F.2d 1136, 14 Cr. L.Rep. 2281 (8th Cir. 1973) cited in *op.cit.*, n3, Shapiro and Feinberg, pp. 13-14.

[8]James Q. Wilson, "Crime and Criminologists," *Commentary*, July, 1974, p. 50.

[9]*Ibid*, p. 53

[10]George Bernard Shaw, *The Crime of Imprisonment*, New York: Philosophical Library, 1946, p. 63.

[11]Maurice H. Sigler, "The Courts and Corrections," excerpted from an address delivered at Kirksville, Missouri, August 17, 1973 (mimeo.)

[12]Leslie T. Wilkins, "Directions for Corrections," *Proceedings of the American Philosophical Society*, Vol. 118, No. 3, June 1974, p. 235.

[13]Herbert L. Packer, *Limits of the Criminal Sanction*, Stanford, California: Stanford University, Press, 1968, p. 56.

[14]Hans W. Mattick, "Reflections of a Former Prison Warden", Chapter 12 in *Delinquency, Crime and Society*, Ed. James F. Short, Jr., Chicago: University of Chicago Press, 1976, pp. 299-300.

[15]Gordon Hawkins, *The Prison: Policy on Practice*, Chicago: University of Chicago Press, 1976, p. 20.

[16]*Ibid.*, p. 24. Also see John Hogarth, *Sentencing as a Human Process*, Toronto: University of Toronto Press, 1974, p. 13. Sol Rubin, *The Law of Criminal Correction*, St. Paul, 1973.

Least anyone believe that we are breaking new ground the reader may want to review Edwin H. Sutherland's classic first edition of *Criminology* (New York, 1924, p. 516-17) in which he states,

> Many accusations have been made that the indeterminate sentence has resulted in a decrease in the average period of imprisonment and therefore has tended to increase crime. The evidence, on the contrary, indicates that the average sentences have increased under the indeterminate sentence system. Sutherland compared Illinois sentences served in 1890-1894 (the last five years of the determinate sentence) with those from 1916-1920 (the first five years of the indeterminate sentence).

Comparison of the Average Time Served Under the Determinate and Indeterminate Sentence Systems, Illinois				
	Determinate Sentence		Indeterminate Sentence	
Type of Offense or Offender	Number of Prisoners Discharged	Average Time Served; Years	Number of Prisoners Discharged	Average Time Served; Years
Burglary	1483	1.64	479	2.60
Larceny...........	776	1.36	363	2.05
Robbery	286	1.77	260	2.83
Second Term......	392	2.08	172	3.89
Third or more terms	131	2.56	53	4.93

Sutherland also reports similar evidence from California, citing "California State Board of Prisons 1921", *Journal of Criminal Law*, (Vol. 12, May 1921, pp. 7-9).

Alan Dershowitz in *Fair and Certain Punishment*, (New York, 1976), pp. 122-124, 142 cites the following sources:

C.C. Van Vechten, "The Parole Violation Rate", *Journal of Criminal Law and Criminology*, (Vol. 27, 1937). Two articles by Sol Rubin, "The Indeterminate Sentence — Success or Failure?", *National Probation and Parole Association Focus*, (March 1949), p. 47, and "Long Prison Terms and the Form of Sentence", *National Probation and Parole Association Journal*, (Vol. 2, 1956), pp. 344-347.

[17]*Op. cit.*, Mattick, p. 30.
[18]O.J. Keller, "Facing the Issues", American Correctional Association Presidential Address, Denver, 8/23/76, mimeo, p. 8.
[19]*Op. cit.*, Dershowitz, p. 124.
[20]American Friends Service Committee Report, *Struggle for Justice: A Report on Crime & Punishment in America*, New York: Hill and Wang 1971, *Op. cit.*, Rubin (1973), Richard A. McGee, "A New Look at Sentencing; Part I and II", *Federal Probation* June and September, 1974, *Attica*, The Official Report of the New York Commission on Attica, (New York, 1972). Andrew Von Hirsch, *Doing Justice: The Choice of Punishment* New York: Hill and Wang, 1976.
Also see *Op. cit.*, Dershowitz, p. 142 for the following citations:
Paul Tappan, "Sentencing under the Model Penal Code", *Law and Contemporary Problems* (Vol. 23, 1958). For evidence of longer sentencing outcomes for women under indeterminate sentencing see citations in *Op. cit.*, Dershowitz, p. 142 (*Commonwealth v. Daniel*, 430 Pa. 642, 243 A.2d 400 (1968); *State v. Chambers*, 63 N.J. 287, 307 A.2d 78 (1973) and Comment; "Sex and

Sentencing," *Southwestern Law Journal*, (Vol. 26, 1972), p. 890). The New Jersey Supreme Court noted in the *Chambers* case ". . .that females are better subjects for rehabilitation, thereby justifying a potentially longer period of detention for that purpose. . ." at 82.

Op. cit., Hogarth, p. 13 cites the Stanton Wheeler *et al* study "Agents of Delinquency Control: A Comparative Analysis", *Controlling Delinquents*, (New York, 1966), pp. 31-60, which demonstrates that juvenile court judges (Boston) who identified with "treatment" philosophies also incarcerated children more frequently than those who were identified with a philosophy of punishment.

A more recent computerized study subtitled the "Demystification of the Therapeutic State" finds (in Ohio) that in relation to juvenile institutional stays under the indeterminate-parole regimen: (1) "In six of eight institutions shorter stay is associated with index offense categories" as opposed to status offenses; (2) "Institutions . . . invariably detained younger male residents longer than their older counterparts;" (3) that "Although females were committed for less serious offenses, they averaged nearly one month longer in institutions than males;" (4) Females stayed on parole longer; (5) less serious (status) offenders remained on parole longer than felony index offenders; (6) institutional bed space availability controlled length of stay, e.g., something akin to Roemer's Law in operative: "Roemer's Law states that where there exists financial incentive (pre paid medical insurance) to fill beds, they will be occupied regardless of the rate of illness in the community". Cited in Gerald R. Wheeler, "The Computerization of Juvenile Correction", *Journal of Crime and Delinquency*, April 1976, pp. 201-210.

[21]Hans W. Mattick, *The Prosaic Sources of Prison Violence*, Chicago: University of Chicago Press, 1972, p. 1.

[22]Norval Morris and Colin Howard, *Studies in Criminal Law*, (Oxford, 1964), p. 175.

POSTSCRIPT

AN INDETERMINATE SENTENCE

The history of the American prison can be visualized as a colossal fortress, a human zoo complete with steel and concrete cages into which came hundreds of thousands of America's poor, migrants, immigrants, and minorities: first we viewed them as sinners, then wayward, then ornery, then sick . . . . . we gave them Bibles, forbade them to speak, preached at them, and worked them . . . . . we introduced libraries, schools, recreation, medical services, counselling, and vocational guidance while we whipped them, maimed them, executed them, and drove some to suicide . . . . . we let them volunteer for military suicide squads and performed medical experiments on them . . . . . and when they resisted we called them militants, radicals, and revolutionaries, and gassed, maced, and shot them . . . . . doing all these things because we were told it was the right thing to do . . . . . first by Puritans, then by Quakers, then by Christians of all sorts . . . . . by educators, phrenologists, eugenicists, endocrinologists, and therapists of speech, vocational, occupational, music and dance variety . . . . . who multiplied into group counsellors, group interactionists, milieu therapists, prison community counsellors, and group psychotherapists . . . . . then came the psychologists . . . . who became clinical, confrontational, reality therapists, and transactional analysts . . . . . and they all tested, diagnosed, and classified . . . . . then there were the behavior modifiers . . . . . who divided into aversive therapists, chemotherapists, electrode implanters, and psychosurgeons . . . . and the universities sent in hoards of theorists and researchers . . . . who had formulated theories about crime and criminals, prisoners, guards, therapists, and wardens . . . . . but what they found were gorillas, bulls, rats, wolves, punks, hacks, heroes, screws, squares, squealers, gunsels, fags, queens, ball busters, toughs, politicians, merchants, and right guys . . . . . and the writers got degrees, prizes, kudos, and money . . . . . while the library shelves bulged with articles, papers, theses, dissertations, monographs, journals, and books . . . . . and occasionally they argued about the ethics of prison research . . . . . so the prison was industrialized, sociologized, then clinicized, but it was always brutalized . . . . . but no one noticed because torrents of claims ran into streams of panaceas swelling to oceans of rhetoric drowning out the tears of pain . . . . . and it's still there . . . . . and Haviland smiled at the ceremony dedicating Lucasville . . . . . and . . . . . "WE ARE THE LIVING PROOF OF ITS EXISTENCE AND WE CANNOT ALLOW IT TO CONTINUE . . . . ."

Appendix I-A
Soft on Crime? Not Prisoners

from *Committee for Prisoner Humanity & Justice Newsletter*
(Vol. 3, No. 2, 9/13/74, pp. 7-8).

One of the lesser myths about prison "reform" and the prison-abolition movement is that attempts to bring about change to criminal justice represent a soft-on-the-criminal/soft-on-crime attitude. Often the demands of prisoner groups in particular are dismissed as discontent with being in the joint in the first place. Not so. Prisoners are as much a part of our society as any group, and to the extent that crime hurts that society, it hurts them. A poll conducted by CPHJ in the prisoner edition of its last *Newsletter* suggests that prisoners are less interested in the possibility of unrealistically short terms than they are in sentences which are fair and fixed.

The poll listed more than 160 offenses for which persons were actually released by the California Department of Corrections (CDC) in the years 1965 and 1971, asking simply what respondents felt was "a fair time." Twenty-seven polls were filled out and mailed in (an average response for a mail poll), twenty-two by California prisoners, four by prisoners out-of-state, and one by a freeworld person who identified himself as an ex-guard(!?). Of the 22 CDC cons, 17 used fixed sentences in their answers, in spite of the fact that about the only persons in the CDC who are not under the Indeterminate (un-fixed) Sentence are the seven men awaiting execution in San Quentin's Death Row. While California's broad use of Indeterminate Sentencing has given the state the longest sentences in the nation, men who used it in their responses seemed neither harsher nor more lenient than those who did not.

Here are the average sentences which the 22 CDC cons would give to 27 selected crimes. Whenever an indeterminate sentence was proposed, the maximum was used here for the purposes of quantification. For comparison, median-time-served by CDC cons in 1971 are listed where possible.

301

Offense	Avg. Sentence (in months)	1971 Median Time (as rept. by CDC)
Murder 1	136.2	145
Murder 2	88.5	66
Murder 2 with firearm	94.5	--
Manslaughter	45.0	46
Manslaughter/vehicle	28.9	17.5
Robbery 1st	61.4	46
Robbery 1st with firearm	63.7	--
Robbery 2nd	46.5	37
Robbery 2nd with firearm	48.1	--
Attempted Robbery	24.9	36
Attempted Murder	50.7	--
Assault with Deadly Weapon	43.9	39
Burglary 1st	45.5	45
Burglary 2nd	28.7	27
Grand Theft Auto	16.7	23
Rape, violent	133.6	51.5
Sodomy	28.4	51
Possession of narcotics	12.0	39
Sale of narcotics	45.0	57
Possession of marijuana	1.7	2.7
Sale of marijuana	15.2	40
Arson	39.8	32
Extortion	31.8	--
Escape from Prison w/o force	19.2	--
Kidnap for ransom or robbery	88.6	111
Bribery	18.0	--
Perjury	29.1	--

The average sentence for all 27 offenses, as determined by the 22 CDC prisoner responses, is 47.6 months. The average time for the medians given for 1971 is 49.3. Keeping in mind that such a small sampling does not make for scientific precision, one could still generalize that prisoners, when they object to the sentences in California, are not objecting to their length, per se. CPHJ's interpretation is, as it has been for some time, that the real thorn is the indeterminacy of the sentences.

In a state which, in 1970, sent 1,950 men and women to prison with life maximum sentences (New York sent 67), only once in the 27 above categories did any of the 22 CDC "clients" set a life top. And only once did any call for capital punishment' for one of these crimes. The ex-guard gave out death for four crimes, plus one life top.

Note, however, how harsh the CDC responses were on rapists, and how they would lower penalties for marijuana and other drug offenses. Seventeen of the 22 would decriminalize marijuana possession altogether.

Unquestionably, the most remarkable response came from a San Quentin man, in the hole, who sent 24 pages of detailed commentary on exactly 136 separate crimes (often suggesting restitution or alternative forms of "treatment"). In a cover letter, he writes:

> I deleted every crime that deals with the use, or possession, of a firearm in, or during, the commission of said crime. I made these said deletions because I believe that more stringent laws concerning the possession of firearms should be passed. . . . Such actions would greatly reduce or completely eliminate the use of firearms in, or during, the commission of a crime. . . . [U]ntil then, the problems connected with firearms are actually of our own making. . . . I have tried to be as realistic, just and fair as possible; my comments even reflect upon myself because they would increase the amount of time I would have to remain incarcerated if they were, in fact, the law.

Our purpose in conducting the poll was to obtain as much prisoner input on the issue of sentencing as possible. Since this is going to be a major concern of anybody dealing with California's prisons in the next few years, it is important that all perspectives be heard. Especially if California follows the lead of Denmark and gets rid of the indeterminate sentence. While we would agree that California sentences are brutally long, we think that it is the uncertainty which really hurts. The results of this poll suggest that we are not alone in this opinion.

Appendix I-B
An Expression of Inmate Concern

from *Transcript of the Hearings on
The Indeterminate Sentence Law,*
The Senate Select Committee on Penal Institutions,
Sacramento, California, December 5 and 6, 1974

One of the major questions raised in the discussion of Indeterminate Sentencing is the effect a modification in this system might have on prison unrest and violence. One indication of the effects that might result can be drawn from the correspondence that the Select Committee has received from prisoners.

Recently a large number of letters were received from inmates at the California Men's Colony at San Luis Obispo, apparently the result of learning of these hearings. Of special interest was a poll conducted by the prisoners among themselves as to whether the present indeterminate sentencing system should be retained or should be rejected for a more determinate "flat-time" system. Of the 355 ballots cast and received by the Committee, all but eleven indicated an opposition to indeterminate sentencing. The eleven remaining votes consisted of three in support of the existing system and eight votes that were uncountable for various reasons. This vote represents 13.5 percent of the total of 2,630 inmates at that institution.

In addition to this, it can be mentioned that a recent, as yet unpublished, report on the prisoner correspondence program of the Select Committee, shows that nearly 29 percent of all problems brought to the Committee's attention related to term setting, parole, or other aspects of the current sentencing system. This represents correspondence from all of the California institutions. While not conclusive of any issues, it does indicate, I believe, an area of serious concern to the inmate population. Many of the letters expressed the frustration of being uncertain as to what term would be set and what future goals and plans could be developed.

Appendix II
Memoirs of a Jailhouse Lawyer Reveal a Long Hard Fight

from *Fortune News,* June 1974, p.7.

My "career" as a Jailhouse Lawyer began twenty-two years ago in a Penitentiary in the Northwestern part of these United States. I was 18 years of age, a graduate of Junior College and recently discharged from the United States Air Force, when I picked up a twenty-five-year sentence. At that time it was against the rules to "possess" a law book, much less assist one's fellow inmates in the preparation of their legal documents. Nonetheless, there were several men in the institution who took the chance of going to "The Hole" (solitary confinement) for helping their less-fortunate inmate friends and associates. Since I had a fairly good education, several men asked me to assist them with the preparation of their Habeas Corpuses and Appeals. At first I refused stating that I was no lawyer and didn't know the first thing about law. I would say, only half-way joking, "If I knew anything about law I wouldn't be here."

Finally, I became convinced that we who were somewhat literate had an obligation to assist men who couldn't help themselves. So, I began by changing the name of a petition of someone else (probably and mostly an attorney from "the streets") and using the facts of the fellow's case for whom I was preparing the pleading.

I soon found myself in the Hole for thirty days. That wasn't the end of it. Since I worked as a clerk in various departments of the institution, the officials watched me like a hawk to see that I didn't type pleadings to be smuggled out. We had a way of getting around the need of notarizing; we would swear to the facts in the petition and have two witnesses sign it, then affix our thumb print. (A practice still carried on in some places).

During the nine years I spent in that prison I was in the Hole no less than a dozen times for "Writing writs for other inmates."

As far as my own "case" was concerned; every time I would submit a Writ to the administration for filing (you had to get their prior approval), I would be told "drop your legal action and we will parole you." So, I would take a parole, stay out for anywhere from a year to three years, come back on parole violation; prepare my Writ and get paroled again. This happened five times and finally they said "file your damn Writ, that is the only way you will get out in less than twenty-five years." So, I filed and when it looked like I was going to win, they granted me a "Final Release." That is time commuted to time served.

A year after my release from Idaho I got a life sentence here in Kentucky and soon was "practicing" as a Jailhouse Lawyer. It wasn't quite as bad by then, one was allowed law books TO PREPARE HIS OWN LEGAL PLEADINGS only. It took a couple of years but eventually I went to the Hole and "Lock Up" (Segregation) for "Writing Writs for other inmates." Finally the decision of the Supreme Court in *Johnson vs. Avery*, demanding that jail house lawyers must be allowed to function. Ironically, I was the first man employed by the State to assist his fellow inmate in the preparation of his legal documents. At last it looked like I could breathe easily. I began taking LaSalle University's law course AND WAS TRANSFERRED TO THE FARM DORMITORY, FIFTEEN MILES FROM THE INSTITUTION. It seemed I was doing too good a job. From the farm I went home and attempted to continue work on the cases I started before leaving the penitentiary. However, it was impossible to communicate with the men in here because my letters would be returned to me with the inscription "not on approved mailing list."

* * *

Since my removal from the legal office I have had several threats which though subtle, were obvious. For example, the Associate Warden for Custody recently told me "you will never get out of here if you don't lay down that Ball Point Pen."

The legal office refuses (stating they have orders from "out front") to type my writs. However, there are several guys in here who are willing (with a slight charge, of course) to type the Writs after I write them. Baby you can believe I am still writing them. I turn out more pleadings alone and by hand than the five men assigned to the legal office do with all of their books and typewriters.

A man loaned me his typewriter long enough to type this article and he is here to get it back so I better close.

In closing, I want to say the only way these people are going to stop my Writ writing is to kill me. Knowing them I don't put even this past them but THEY WILL HAVE TO DO IT TO STOP ME.

William Conners, No. 24047
Kentucky State Prison

Appendix III
Plea Bargaining

from *"The Michigan Public Speaks Out on Crime,"*
Market Opinion Research, April, 1975 (mimeo., 75 pp).

A recent (1975) public opinion poll in Michigan points in the direction for the need for certainty in sentencing. On the question of plea bargaining the public apparently does not share the legal profession's enthusiasm for the practice.

"There are various ways of sentencing convicted criminals. Which one of these ways comes closest to your thoughts on sentencing?"

Table 36 (page 39)

	1974	1975	Change 1974-75
Footnote 1	45%	46%	+1
Footnote 2	38	36	−2
Footnote 3	14	14	0
Footnote 0	3	5	+2
BASE	(400)	(800)	

1 = The law should specify one single mandatory sentence, for each offense (crime or law breaking). This should get more severe for each offense after the first one. The judge would not be free to vary the sentence for different cases.

2 = The law should continue to specify minimum and maximum ranges of sentences for each crime.

3 = The judge should be free to impose any sentence he feels warranted (indeterminate sentencing).

0 = Don't know.

"Sometimes a defense lawyer and prosecutor agree to accept a guilty plea for an offense less serious than the one which led to a person's arrest. This is called "plea bargaining". Do you approve of this practice?"

Table 32 (page 35)

	1973	1974	1975	Change 1973-75
Yes, approve	21%	21%	21%	0
No, disapprove	67	69	70	+3
Don't know	12	10	9	−3

Appendix IV
A Letter from a
San Quentin Convict

The writer of this letter, at age 18, was convicted of murder and robbery. He did not pull the trigger but was correctly convicted of first degree murder according to the felony-murder statute.

San Quentin
April 22, 1975

Dearest . . . . ,

I'm so mad right now its unreal!! . . this really takes the cake!!

Today in my group (psych group) one of the guys came in from board. He went this morning and came straight to the group session from his appearance (everyone in my group has a murder charge). Anyway, he went to the board this morning and got an 18 month date. Well, that's not so surprising considering that they are giving out much shorter dates than that around here. But when you hear the circumstances, you will have a fit. Dig this.

This guy was originally sentenced to prison for a shotgun murder, for which he received the death penalty in 1967. In 1969 he went from death row back to the county jail for a new penalty trial. While in the county jail he got an escape, with force and violence on a guard, G.T.A. [Grand Theft-Auto] and kidnap and while out on the escape he got 2 first degree robberies. He was caught, brought back to the county jail, tried and convicted on each of those new charges, and sentenced on each of them, with the sentences to run concurrent with his death penalty sentence. In 1972 he was commuted to life imprisonment from death row because of the Supreme Court ruling abolishing the death penalty. Now, with all that shit against him, he went to the board this morning and took them

[sic] only 7 years 10 months and they gave him an 18 month date!!! Altogether he will be serving only 9 years 4 months on all that shit!

Are you still there? Yeah, I know what you're saying to yourself right now. I've been saying the same thing since he told me about it. Here is a dude with everything I have and then some and he gets a date like that while I get another 7 years. Do you realize that I have ALREADY DONE all but 3 months of all the time he has to do?! He has 2 concurrent 1st degree robberies where I have only one. His escape is with force and violence on a GUARD, while I have no force of violence in my escape at all. And he has a kidnap with his G.T.A., while I didn't. Plus the fact that he was on death row a little less than 3 years ago and only got off because of the blanket Supreme Court ruling abolishing the death penalty and not because of any particular circumstances in his murder conviction. He told me they gave him only 96 months on the murder?!! That's the typical time. The fact that he was on death row should have been sufficient to aggravate it to the maximum. No one else from death row has gotten any kind of date—PERIOD!! Plus those 2 1st degree robberies, WHILE ON ESCAPE, should have been enough to aggravate his time. But it didn't. He is doing a total of 112 months on all that shit. I *brought* them 108 months!!

But I'm glad we have this example. "P" [the Parole Board Chairman] doesn't have a leg to stand on now to back up his claim that the time for my murder/robbery "wasn't too aggravated" in his opinion. This guy who got the date today HAD *NO CRIME PARTNERS* IN *ANY* OF HIS ACTS!! There wasn't even anyone else they could say was responsible for influencing him, or that he was just an accomplice. He was ALONE on all his crimes!!

This isn't all though. There was another guy who went to the board yesterday, took 3½ years on 2 second degree murders, one of which was the shooting death of a *baby*, and they gave him a 5 year date. He had two 5 years to life sentences running concurrently for the murders. He is doing a total of only 8½ years for them! And I believe they found him guilty of having done the shooting. I will have to go and get the details of his case. I already have the details of the other case I described . . . .

. . . From this it can be seen that the board members are doing exactly what they want to do in each individual case, rather than going by any sort of guidelines . . . .

Baby, I still can't really adjust to the fact that that guy really got an 18 month date. He DID get it, but it's just so hard to conceive that they could use such extremes in cases. His case and mine are similar in many respects. Yet, they want me to do 6 years 6 months more than him when he not only has more, and more serious, concurrent sentences than I do but also was the principle actor in *ALL* of his crimes. They *are* going to have to straighten what they did to us out *real* quick!! There's just no two ways about it.

. . . My patience with these stupidass people here is being tested to the maximum!! And impatience is beginning to win out. I feel myself getting mad, so I'll close here until I get back together.

. . .

Appendix V

Excerpts from *The Official Report of the New York State Special Commission on Attica*, 1972

Correction personnel and some older inmates tended to take a conspiratorial view of the uprising, calling it the work of left-wing radicals and "troublemakers" among the inmate population and insisting that it was planned in advance. That view was expressed in a report dated October 7, 1971, prepared for Executive Deputy Commissioner Walter Dunbar by a group of parole officers who were assigned to investigate the uprising, essentially by interviewing the hostages. The parole officers' report concluded that the disturbance was the result of a "long thought-out, well-organized plot, conceived and implemented by a group of hard core radical extremists—mostly from the New York City area." (p. 104)

* * *

Contrary to these popular views, the Attica uprising was neither a long-planned revolutionary plot nor a proletarian revolution against the capitalist system. After talking with inmates, correction officers, administrators, observers, and experts, and after much reflection, the Commission has concluded that:

Rather than being revolutionary conspirators bent only on destruction, the Attica rebels were part of a new breed of younger, more aware inmates, largely black, who came to prison full of deep feelings of alienation and hostility against the established institutions of law and government, enhanced self-esteem, racial pride, and political awareness, and an unwillingness to accept the petty humiliations and racism that characterize prison life.

Like the urban ghetto disturbances of the 1960s, the Attica uprising was the product of frustrated hopes and unfulfilled expectations, after efforts to bring about meaningful change had failed.

The uprising began as a spontaneous burst of violent anger and was not planned or organized in advance; the relative ease with which the inmates took control of large areas of the prison was due not to a preconceived plan but to a combination of fortuitous circumstances, including the failure of the central Times Square gate and an outdated communications system which prevented the authorities from quickly mobilizing force to quell the disturbance.

The highly organized inmate society in D block yard developed spontaneously, after a period of chaos, rather than by prearrangement; in the hours following the initial violence the leaders of political and religious groups with preexisting structures, and inmates who were politically motivated, well versed in the law, or otherwise respected by their peers, emerged as spokesmen and took the lead in organizing the yard and drafting demands.

In reaching these conclusions concerning the causes of the uprising, the Commission nevertheless condemns the taking of hostages as a means of bringing about changes in society, even where peaceful efforts at reform have failed. Whether carried out in a commercial jetliner, or in a prison, the holding of human lives for ransom is wrong and only leads to more violence and to a backlash that makes change more difficult. (pp. 105-106)

＊ ＊ ＊

It is clear, therefore, that the Attica uprising was not planned in advance by a group of militant inmates. To continue to blame the uprising solely on a group of political "radicals" and "revolutionaries" merely perpetuates the dubious policy of isolating and transferring a few suspected "troublemakers" in response to mounting tensions, which prevailed prior to the uprising. It also fails to focus on the real reason why inmates were able to take over Attica so easily: insufficient manpower on the correction staff, lack of a plan for dealing with large-scale uprisings, and a completely inadequate internal communications system.

More fundamentally, if future Atticas are to be avoided, correction personnel must stop looking for individual scapegoats and concentrate on major efforts to train officers to understand and deal with the new breed of inmates, to eliminate the petty harassments and root out the racist attitudes which these inmates will never tolerate, and accelerate programs to make prisons—as long as they must exist—more humane environments for men to live in. (pp. 112-113)

Appendix VI
The Effect of Flat Time Sentences on Time Served*

I. OBJECTIVE OF ANALYSIS:

To determine if flat time sentencing would increase/decrease the average time served for persons convicted of felonies in each of five, all inclusive, felony classes and to determine the aggregate effect of flat time sentencing on man-years served by a given releasee population, yielding respectively some relative measures of the punitive and economic impact of flat time sentencing.

II. METHODOLOGY

A. The releasee population selected for study was that released from the Illinois Department of Corrections in 1973 and 1974. This was felt to be a reasonable basis for comparison as:

  i. The available data base was most complete for these years.

  ii. Current release trends would more likely be reflected by the events of the recent rather than distant past

B. The approximately 20,000 active and inactive (i.e., no longer under supervision) cases available in the data base were searched for records exhibiting non-institutional status codes (e.g., paroled, mandatory release, etc.), and these records, for which the period of custody could be calculated (custody = release date minus initial custody date), served as the basis for the analysis.

---

*The data base used in this analysis was obtained from the Illinois Department of Corrections' Correctional Information System in December 1974, an automated statewide system that has maintained approximately 20,000 offender records since December 1971.

C. The records were further classified as to crime set, where crime set was defined to be a unique offense combination (i.e., burglary, burglary-burglary, burglary-robbery).

D. For each crime set an average custody-to-release-date was calculated. Note that "custody" refers to initial custody thus including credit for jail time.

E. The crime sets were then aggregated into felony classes according to the most serious offense in the crime set. A robbery-murder, for example, was a Class 0 (murder = Class 0). The assignment of offenses to felony classes was governed by the schedule employed by the Administrative Office of the Illinois Courts.

F. The following average-time served figures were then calculated for each felony class yielding the following results:

Class	0	1	2	3	4
Average-Time Served (yrs.)	11.7	4.3	2.2	1.8	1.7

G. The following flat-time sentences, commonly used as a benchmark in the entire series of flat-time analyses and simulations, were selected for a comparison test:

Class	0	1	2	3	4
Statutory Flat-Time Sentences (yrs.)	25	8	5	3	2

H. It was assumed that "good time" would be earned on a one-day for one-day-served basis, and only 90% of all available good time would actually be earned. It was further assumed that two (2) months (fractionalized at .167) jail time would be credited towards the statutory sentence. Thus effective-sentences were calculated for each felony class according to the following formula:

$$Se_i = Sf_i - .90 [.50 \times Sf_i] - .167$$

where: i = class (0, 1, 2, 3, 4)
        Se = effective flat-time sentence
        Sf = statutory flat-time sentence

yielding the following results:

Class	0	1	2	3	4
Statutory Flat-Time Sentence (yrs.)	25	8	5	3	2
Effective Sentence (yrs.)	13.6	4.3	2.6	1.5	.9

III. RESULTS

A. The flat-time sentences, in comparison with the December 1971 to December 1974 actual averages, had the effect of *lengthening* the custody period of the *more serious* felons and *reducing* that of the *less serious* felons, as follows:

A. Class	0	1	2	3	4
B. Flat-Time Effective Sentence	13.6	4.3	2.6	1.5	.9
C. Average Time Served	11.7	4.3	2.2	1.8	1.7
D. Difference (B-C)	1.9	0	.4	-.3	-.8

B. Assuming the December 1971 to December 1974 averages apply uniformly to the intervening three years, the difference in time served for each felony class, weighed by the number of releasees from the Illinois Department of Corrections in each of two years (1973 and 1974)*, indicates that, in the aggregate, flat time sentencing *would not* have had a dramatic effect on total man-years served by the respective releasee populations:

---

*Release figures for 1973 and 1974 were obtained from published reports of the Illinois Department of Corrections.

1973

1. Class	0	1	2	3	4	TOTAL
2. Number of Releasees	81	615	1300	455	562	3013
3. Flat-Time/ Actual Time Difference (yrs.)	1.9	0	.4	-.3	-.8	
4. Effect (2 x 3) (man-years)	153.9	0	520.0	-136.5	-449.6	87.8

Net flat-time effect = +87.8 man years
Per person flat-time effect = +.03 man years (87.8/3013)

1974

1. Class	0	1	2	3	4	TOTAL
2. Number of Releasees	101	508	1606	488	570	3273
3. Flat-Time/ Actual Time Difference (yrs.)	1.9	0	.4	-.3	-.8	
4. Effect (2 x 3) (man-years)	191.9	0	642.4	-146.4	-456.0	231.9

Net flat-time effect = +231.9
Per person flat-time effect = +.07 man-years (231.9/3273)

C. An examination of results A and B above indicates that flat-time sentencing, for the population examined, would have had the effect of *redistributing* total man-years served from the *less serious* to the *more serious* felons without significantly increasing the *total* man-years served and hence the associated incarceration costs.

D. Man-years and cost under flat time sentencing can be significantly adjusted according to the flat time sentence scheme employed. For example, by changing the statutory flat time sentence for felony Class 2 (43% of the 1973 releasee population and 49% in 1974) from five (5) years to four (4) years, with all other factors unchanged, the effective flat time sentence becomes 2 years less than the December 1971 to December 1974 average, yielding a net flat time effect for the 1973 and 1974 populations under flat time sentencing of -692.2 and -731.9 man years respectively. Similarly, the per person flat time effect becomes -.22 per and -.19 man year per person respectively.

BIBLIOGRAPHY

American Bar Association, Project on Standards for Criminal Justice, *Standards Relating to Sentencing Alternatives and Procedures*, New York, N.Y., 1969.

American Bar Association, Resource Center on Correctional Law and Legal Services, *The Minnesota Correctional Ombudsman*, Washington, D.C., 1974.

American Bar Association and Council of State Governments, *Compendium of Model Correctional Legislation and Standards*, (including: American Bar Association, "Standards Relating to Appellate Review of Sentences," 1968; National Council on Crime and Delinquency, "Model Sentencing Act," 1972; American Law Institute, "Model Penal Code," 1963 August, 1963.

American Correctional Association and Chamber of Commerce of the United States, "Community Corrections: A Cheaper and More Humane Approach, Marshalling Citizen Power to Modernize Corrections," 1971.

American Friends Service Committee, *Struggle for Justice*, New York: Hill & Wang; 1971.

Amos, William E., "The Philosophy of Corrections: Revisited," *Federal Probation*, March 1974.

Annual Chief Justice Earl Warren Conference sponsored by the Roscoe Pound-American Trial Lawyers Foundation. *A Program for Prison Reform*, June 9-10), 1972.

Atkins, Burton M., and Glick, Henry R., *Prisons, Protest and Politics*, Englewood Cliffs, New Jersey: Prentice-Hall, Inc. 1972.

Attica, The Official Report of the New York State Commission on Attica, New York: Bantam Book, 1972.

Bailey, Walter C., "Correctional Outcome: An Evaluation of 100 Reports," *Journal of Criminal Law, Criminology and Police Science*, Northwestern University School of Law, Vol. 57, No. 2, 1966.

Balch, Robert W., Ph. D., "Deferred Prosecution: The Juvenilization of the Criminal Justice System," *Federal Probation*, June 1974.

Baker, J.E., "Inmate Self-Government," *Journal of Criminal Law, Criminology and Police Science*, Vol. 55, No. 1, 1964.

Bancroft, H.H., *History of the Pacific States of North America*, Vol. XXI, "Popular Tribunals," San Francisco: History Company, 1887.

Bennett, James, *I Choose Prison*, New York: Alfred A. Knopf, Inc., 1970.

"Beyond the Ken of the Courts: A Critique of Judicial Refusal to Review the Complaints of Convicts," *Yale Law Journal*, Vol. 72.

Black Caucus Report of the California Assembly, "The Treatment of Prisoners at California Training Facility at Soledad Central," California, 1970.

Blumberg, Abraham S., *Criminal Justice*, Chicago: Quadrangle Books, 1967.

Bowers, John, "Medical Research in Prisons," *Clearinghouse Review*, Northwestern University Law School, Vol. VI, No. 3, July 1972.

Breed, Allen F., "The Goal May Be to Make Rehabilitation Fit the Crime," *Sacramento Bee* (The Forum Section), August 18, 1974.

Brodsky, Stanley L., Ph.D., "A Bill of Rights for the Correctional Officer," *Federal Probation*, June 1974.

Cahn, Edgar and Cahn, Jean, "The War on Poverty - A Civilian Perspective," *Yale Law Journal*, Vol. 73, No. 8, 1963-64.

Cahn, Edmond, *Confronting Injustice*, Boston, Mass.: Little, Brown and Co., 1966.

California Senate Select Committee on Penal Institutions, "The Indeterminate Sentence Law," *Transcript of Hearings*, Sacramento California, Dec. 5-6, 1974.

Campbell, James P., et al., *Law and Order Reconsidered*, Task Force on Law Enforcement, National Commission on Causes and Prevention of Violence, Washington, D.C.: United States Government Printing Office, 1969.

Carter, Robert M., Glaser, Daniel and Wilkins, Leslie T., *Correctional Institutions*, New York: J.B. Lippincott Company, 1972.

Caspar, Jonathan D., "Criminal Justice - The Consumer Perspective," U.S. Department of Justice, Government Printing Office, February, 1972.

Chambers, Clarke A., *Seedtime of Reform: American Social Service and Social Action, 1918-1933*, Ann Arbor: University of Michigan Press, 1963.

Chambers, Howard W., *Phrenology for the Millions*, Los Angeles, California: Sherbourne Press, 1968.

Clemmer, Donald, *The Prison Community*, New York: Holt, Rinehart and Winston, 1966.

Cloward, Richard A., et al., *Theoretical Studies in Social Organization of the Prison*, Social Science Research Foundation, 1960.

Comment, "The Influence of the Defendant's Plea on Judicial Determination of Sentence," *The Yale Law Journal*, Vol. 66, 1956-1957.

Comment, "Resolving Civil Problems of Correctional Inmates," *Wisconsin Law Review*, 1969.

The Committee for the Study of Incarceration Report, (forthcoming, 1975).

Conference Summary, "Planning for the Treatment of the Repetitively Violent Offender," April 8, 1974, University of Chicago (mimeographed 15 pages).

"Constitutional Status of Solitary Confinement," *Cornell Law Review*, 1972.

Cooper, H.H.A., "Toward a Rational Doctrine of Rehabilitation," *Crime and Delinquency*, April 1973.

Council of Europe, *European Committee on Crime Problems, I Collected Studies in Criminological Research*, 1967.

Crinimal Justice Monograph, "The Classification of Criminal Behavior", U.S. Department of Justice Law Enforcement Assistance Administration, Washington, D.C., U.S. Government Printing Office, June 1973.

Criminal Justice Monograph, "The Classification of Criminal Behavior," U.S. Department of Justice Law Enforcement Assistance Administration, Washington, D.C., U.S. Government Printing Office, June 1973.

Criminal Justice Monograph, "Prevention of Violence in Correctional Institutions," U.S. Department of Justice Law Enforcement Assistance Administration, Washington, D.C.: U.S. Government Printing Office, June 1973.

Davis, Kenneth Culp, *Discretionary Justice: A Preliminary Inquiry*, University of Illinois Press, 1973.

Dawson, Robert O., *Sentencing: The Decision as to Type, Length, and Conditions of Sentence*, Boston, Mass.: Little, Brown and Co., 1969.

"Declaration of Principles of Prison Discipline," Albany, New York: Weed & Parsons, 1870.

Denfield, Duane, *Streetwise Criminology*, Cambridge, Mass.: Schenkman Publishing Co., 1974.

Earle, Alice Morse, *Curious Punishments of Bygone Days*, Rutland, Vermont: Charles E. Tuttle Co., 1972.

Ellis, Desmond, Grasmick, Harold and Gilman, Bernard, "Violence in Prison: A Sociological Analysis," *American Journal of Sociology*, Vol. 80, No. 1, July 1974.

Esselstyn, T.C., "The Social System of Correctional Workers," *Crime and Delinquency*, April 1966.

Feinberg, Mathew, DSQ., & Shapiro, Richard, ESQ., *The Legal Objections to the Feasibility Study for a Proposed New England Regional Facility for Special Offenders*, prepared for the New England Governor's Conference, February 1974.

Ferri, Enrico, *Criminal Sociology*, Boston, Mass.: Little, Brown and Co., 1917.

Finkelstein, Marvin, *Perspectives on Prison Legal Services: Needs, Impact and the Potential for Law School Involvement*, Summary Report, U.S. Department of Justice, Government Printing Office, February 1972.

Fitzharris, T.C., *The Desirability of a Correctional Ombudsman*, California Assembly, Sacramento, 1973.

Fogel, David, Galoway, Burt and Hudson, Joseph, "Restitution in Criminal Justice: A Minnesota Experiment," *Criminal Law Bulletin*, Vol. 8, No. 8, October 1972.

Fox, Vernon, "Why Prisoners Riot," *Federal Probation*, March 1971.

Frankel, Marvin E., *Criminal Sentences*, New York: Hill & Wang, 1973.

Free World Times, January 1974.

Fried, Joan and William, *The Uses of the American Prison*, Lexington, Mass.: Lexington Books, 1974.

Galoway, Burt and Hudson, Joseph, *Considering the Victim: Readings in Restitution and Victim Compensation*, (forthcoming 1975).

Galoway, Burt and Hudson, Joseph, "Issues in the Correctional Implementation of Restitution to Victims of Crime," *American Society of Criminology*, New York, November 1973.

Geis, Gilbert and Edelherz, Herbert, "California's New Crime Victim Compensation Statute," *San Diego Law Review*, Vol. 11, 1974.

Gill, Howard B., "A New Prison Discipline: Implementing the Declaration of Principles of 1870," *Federal Probation*, June 1970.

Glaser, Daniel, "The Prison of the Future," *Crime in the City*, Harper and Row Publishers, 1970.

Glueck, Sheldon and Glueck, Eleanor, *Five Hundred Criminal Careers*, New York: Knopf, 1930.

Glueck, Sheldon and Glueck, Eleanor, *Later Criminal Careers*, New York: Commonwealth Fund, 1937.

Goldfarb, Ronald and Singer, Linda, "Redressing Prisoner Grievances," *Washington Law Review*, Vol. 34, 1970.

Greenberg, David F., "Much Ado About Little: the Correctional Effects of Corrections," *Final Report of the Committee for the Study of Incarceration*, June 1974.

Greenberg, David F., "A Voucher System for Corrections," *Crime and Delinquency*, Vol. 19, No. 2, April 1973.

Griffith, Stanley, "A Training Experience as a Pseudo-Guard," 1974 (unpublished manuscript, 50 pages plus appendices).

Group for the Advancement of Corrections and the Ex-Prisoners Advisory Group, "Toward a New Correctional Policy: Two Declarations of Principles," Columbus, Ohio: Academy for Contemporary Problems, July 1974.

Guenther, Anthony L., and Guenther, Mary Quinn, "Screws vs. Thugs," *Transaction: Social Science and Society,* Vol. 11, No. 5, July-August 1974.

Harvard Center for Criminal Justice, "Judicial Intervention in Prison Discipline," *Journal of Criminal Law, Criminology and Police Science,* Northwestern University School of Law, Vol. 63, No. 2, 1972.

Harvard University Gazette, February 27, 1974.

Hayner, Norman S., "Attitudes Toward Conjugal Visits for Prisoners," *Federal Probation,* March 1972.

Helfman, Harold M., "Antecedents of Thomas Mott Osborne's 'Mutual Welfare League' in Michigan," *Journal of Criminal Law,* Vol. 40, 1950.

Hermann, Michele and Haft, Marilyn, *Prisoner Rights,* New York: Clark Boardman Co., 1973.

Hirschkop, Philip J. and Milleman, Michael A., "The Unconstitutionality of Prison Life," *Virginia Law Review,* Vol. 55, No. 5, June 1969.

"Historical Perspective: The Evolution of Prisoner Rights," *New England Journal on Prison Law,* Vol. 1, No. 1, 1974.

Hood, Roger and Sparks, Richard, *Key Issues in Criminology,* New York: McGraw-Hill, 1970.

Irwin, John, *The Felon,* "The Prison Experience: The Convict World," Englewood Cliffs, New Jersey: Prentice-Hall, Inc., 1970.

Jacob, Bruce R. and Sharma, K.M., "Justice After Trial: Prisoners' Need for Legal Services in the Criminal-Correctional Process," *Kansas Law Review,* Vol. 18, 1970.

Jacobs, James B. and Grear, Mary P., "Dropouts and Rejects: An Analysis of Turnover Among Stateville Guards," 1975 (unpublished manuscript).

Jacobs, James B. and Retsky, Harold G., "Prison Guard," *Urban Life and Culture,* Vol 4, No. 1, April 1975.

Jaffray, Julia K., *The Prison and the Prisoner,* Boston, Mass.: Little, Brown and Co., 1917.

Johnson, Elmer, *Crime, Correction and Society,* Homewood, Illinois: The Dorsey Press, 1968.

Keve, Paul, Book Review in *Crime and Delinquency,* Vol. XVI, September, 1970.

Killinger, George G. and Cromwell, Paul F., Jr., eds., *Penology: The*

Evolution of Corrections in America, St. Paul, Minn.: West Publishing Co., 1973.

Knight, Etheridge, *Black Voices from Prison*, Pathfinder Press, Inc., 1970, p. 63.

Kohlberg, Lawrence, Kaufman, Kelsey, Scharf, Peter and Hickey, Joseph, "Just Community . . . Approach to Corrections: A Manual," Parts I and II, Moral Education Research Foundation, 1974.

Kohlberg, Lawrence, Scharf, Peter, and Hickey, Joseph, "The Justice Structure of the Prison - A Theory and An Intervention," *Prison Journal*, Vol. 51, No. 2, Autumn-Winter, 1972.

Leeke, William D., ed., *Inmate Grievance Procedures*, (Collective Violence Research Project funded through the National Institute of Law Enforcement and Criminal Justice), 1973.

Leeke, William D., ed., *Riots and Disturbances*, College Park Maryland: American Correctional Association, 1970.

"Legal Services and Development," University of Minnesota, (mimeo., 51 pages).

Lewis, W. David, *From Newgate to Dannemora*, Ithaca, New York: Cornell University Press, 1965.

Lubove, Roy, "The Professional Altruist," Cambridge, Mass.: Harvard University Press, 1964.

Mabry, James, "Alternatives to Confinement," *Criminal Justice Monographs*, Vol. 1, No. 2, 1969.

McGee, Richard A., "A New Look at Sentencing; Part I," *Federal Probation*, June 1974.

McGee, Richard A., "A New Look at Sentencing; Part II," *Federal Probation*, September 1974.

Machiavelli, Niccolo, *The Prince*, Thomas B. Bergin, ed., New York: Appleton-Centure-Crofts, 1947.

Mannheim, Hermann, ed., *Pioneers in Criminology*, London: Stevens & Sons Limited, 1960.

Martin, John Bartlow, *Break Down the Walls*, New York: Ballantine Books, 1951.

March, James, ed., *Handbook of Organizations*. Chicago: Rand McNally, 1965.

Martinson, Robert, "What Works? - Questions and Answers About Prison Reform," *The Public Interest*, No. 35, National Affairs, Inc., 1974.

Mattick, Hans W., *The Prosaic Sources of Prison Violence*, Chicago: Occasional Papers from the Law School, The University of Chicago, 1972.

"Michigan Public Speaks Out On Crime,"[1] Market Opinion Research, April, 1975 (mimeo., 75 pp.)

Miller, Walter B., "Ideology and Criminal Justice Policy: Some Current Issues," *The Journal of Criminal Law and Criminology*, Northwestern University School of Law, Vol. 64, No. 2, 1973.

Mills, C. Wright, *Power, Politics and People*, New York: Ballantine Books, 1963.

Mills, Michael and Morris, Norval, "Prisoners as Laboratory Animals," *Transaction: Social Science and Society*, Vol. 11, No. 5, July-August 1974.

Mitford, Jessica, *Kind and Usual Punishment*, New York: Knopf, 1973.

Morris, Norval, *The Future of Imprisonment*, Chicago: University of Chicago Press, 1975.

Morris, Norval, "Impediments to Penal Reform," *The University of Chicago Law Review*, Vol. 33, No. 4, Summer 1966.

Morris, Norval and Hawkins, Gordon, *The Honest Politician's Guide to Crime Control*, Chicago: University of Chicago Press, 1969.

Morris, Norval and Hawkins, Gordon, "Rehabilitation: Rhetoric and Reality," *Federal Probation*, December 1970.

Morse, Wayne, gen. ed., "State Prisons in America 1787-1937," *The Attorney General's Survey of Release Procedures* (1940).

Nagel, William G., *The New Red Barn: A Critical Look at the Modern American Prison*, New York, N.Y.: Walker & Co., 1973.

National Advisory Commission on Criminal Justice Standards and Goals' Report, Washington, D.C.: U.S. Government Printing Office, 1967.

National Association of Attorneys General, *Special Report on Corrections*, January 18, 1974.

New York City Board of Corrections' 1971 Annual Report, "Crisis in the Prisons: New York City Responds: A Commitment to Change," New York, N.Y., 1972.

New York State Citizens Inquiry on Parole and Criminal Justice Summary Report, 845 Fifth Ave., New York, N.Y., 1974.

Note, "Guilty Plea Bargaining: Compromises By Prosecutors to Secure Guilty Pleas," *University of Pennsylvania Law Review*, Vol. 112, 1964.

Ohlin, Lloyd E., "Current Aspects of Penology: Correctional Strategies in Conflict," *American Philosophical Society*, Vol. 118, No. 3, June 1974.

Olafson, Frederick, *Justice and Social Policy*, New York: Prentice-Hall, 1961.

Orland, Leonard, *Justice, Punishment, and Treatment: The Correctional Process,* New York: The Free Press, A Division of MacMillan Publishing Co., Inc., 1973.

Osborne, Thomas Mott, *Prisons and Common Sense,* Philadelphia: J.B. Lippincott Co., 1924.

Osborne, Thomas Mott, *Society and Prisons,* New Haven: Yale University Press, 1916.

Osborne, Thomas Mott, *Within Prison Walls,* New York: D. Appleton and Co., 1915.

Pabon, Edward, "Letter to the Editor," *Crime and Delinquency,* Vol 19, No. 3, July 1973.

Packer, Herbert L., *Limits of the Criminal Sanction,* Stanford, California: Stanford University, 1968.

Paddock, Arthur L. and McMillin, James, "Final Report Vienna Staff Training Project," Southern Illinois University, Carbondale, June 30, 1972 (mimeo, 18 pages, plus 11 tables).

Palmer, Larry I., "A Model of Criminal Dispositions: An Alternative to Official Discretion in Sentencing," *Georgetown Law Journal,* Vol. 62, No. 1, October, 1973.

Perdman, H.S. and Allington, T.B., *The Task of Penology,* Lincoln, Neb.: University of Nebraska Press, 1969.

Pierce, Lawrence W., "Rehabilitation in Corrections: A Reassessment," *Federal Probation,* June 1974.

Piliavin, Irving, "Social Work, Rehabilitation in Corrections, and Social Justice," (unpublished manuscript, University of Wisconsin).

President's Commission on Law Enforcement and Administration of Justice, *Task Force Report: Correction,* Washington, D.C.: U.S. Government Printing Office, 1967.

"A Proposal to Establish an Experimental Ombudsman for the Minnesota Department of Corrections," Law School, University of Minnesota, 1971.

Radzinowicz, Leon and Wolfgang, Marvin E., ed., *Crime and Justice,* Vol. 3, "The Criminal Confinement," New York: Basic Books Co., 1971.

Rawls, John, *A Theory of Justice,* Cambridge, Mass.: Harvard University Press, 1972.

"Report and Recommendations," Task Force to Study Violence, California Department of Corrections, 1974.

Resource Center on Correctional Law and Legal Services, *The Minnesota Correctional Ombudsman,* American Bar Association, Washington, D.C., 1974.

Rothman, David, J., "Decarcerating Prisoners and Patients," *Civil Liberties Review*, Vol. I, No. 1, Fall 1973.

Rothman, David J., "Decarcerating Prisoners and Patients," *Civil Liberties Review*, Vol. I, No. 1, Fall 1973.

Rothman, David J., *The Discovery of the Asylum: Social Order and Disorder in the New Republic*, Boston, Mass.: Little, Brown and Co., 1971.

Rubin, Sol, "Developments in Correctional Law," *Crime and Delinquency*, April 1973.

Rubin, Sol, "The Impact of Court Decisions on the Correctional Process," *Crime and Delinquency*, Vol. 20, No. 2, 1973.

Rubin, Sol, *The Law of Criminal Correction*, St. Paul, Minn.: West Publishing Co., 1973.

Rudovsky, David, *The Rights of Prisoners*, New York: Discus Books, 1973.

Schafer, Stephen, *The Political Criminal - The Problem of Morality and Crime*, New York: The Free Press, 1974.

Sellin, Thorsten, "The Origin of the 'Pennsylvania System of Prison Discipline,'" *Prison Journal*, Vol. L, No. 2, Spring-Summer 1970.

Sellin, Thorsten, "The Philadelphia Gibbet Iron," *Journal of Law, Criminology and Police Science*, Vol. 46, 1955.

Shaw, George Bernard, *The Crime of Imprisonment*, New York: Philosophical Library, 1946.

Sigler, Maurice H., "The Courts and Corrections," (an address delivered on August 17, 1973, Kirksville, Missouri) (mimeographed, 8 pages).

Singer, Linda and Keating, J. Michael, "Prisoner Grievance Mechanisms," *Crime and Delinquency*, July 1973.

Smith, Joan and Fried, William, *The Uses of American Prisons*, Lexington, Mass.: Lexington Books, 1974.

Sparks, Richard, "Research on the Use and Effectiveness of Probation, Parole and Measure of After-care," Council of Europe, European Committee on Crime Problems, III *Collected Studies in Criminological Research*, 1968.

Strange, Heather and McCrory, Joseph, "Bulls and Bears on the Cell Block," *Transaction: Social Science and Society*, Vol. 11, No. 5, July-August 1974.

Steele, Eric H., *A Model for the Imprisonment of Repetitively Violent Criminals*, Chicago: Center for Studies in Criminal Justice, 1974.

Studt, Eliot, Messinger, Sheldon and Wilson, Thomas, *C-Unit: Search for Community in Prison*, New York: Russell Sage Foundation, 1968.

Sutherland, Edwin H. and Cressey, Donald R., *Criminology*, 9th ed., Philadelphia, Pa.: J.B. Lippincott Co., c1974.

Sykes, Gresham, *The Society of Captives: A Study of Maximum Security Prisons*, Princeton, New Jersey: Princeton University Press, 1958.

Tannenbaum, Frank, *Osborne of Sing Sing*, Chapel Hill: University of North Carolina Press, 1933.

Tappan, Paul W., ed., *Contemporary Correction*, New York: McGraw-Hill Book Co., Inc., 1951.

Taugher, B., "A Penal Ombudsman," *Pacific Law Journal*, Vol. 3, No. 166, 1972.

Teeters, Negley K., *Cradle of the Penitentiary: Walnut Street Jail at Philadelphia 1773-1835*, for the Pennsylvania Prison Society, 1955.

Teeters, Negley K., "State of Prisons in the United States: 1870-1970," *Federal Probation*, December 1969.

Theoretical Studies in Social Organization of the Prison, Social Science Research Council, 230 Park Ave., New York, N.Y., March 1960.

Tibbles, Lance, "Ombudsmen for American Prisons," *North Dakota Law Review*, Vol. 48, 1972.

Trecker, Harleigh B., ed., *Goals for Social Welfare, 1973-1993: An Overview of the Next Two Decades*, New York: Associated Press, 1973.

Turner, William Bennett, "Establishing the Rule of Law in Prisons: A Manual for Prisoners' Rights Litigation," *Stanford Law Review*, Vol. 23, February 1971.

The Village Voice, September 10, 1970.

Walker, Nigel, Wilmer, Michael and Carr-Hill, Roy, *Sentencing in a Rational Society*, New York: Basic Books, Inc., 1969.

Wenk, Ernest and Moos, Rudolph, "Social Climates in Prisons," *Journal of Research in Crime and Delinquency*, July 1972, (manuscript).

Wilensky, Harold L., *Organizational Intelligence*, New York: Basic Books, 1967.

Wilkins, Leslie T., "Variety, Conformity, Control and Research: Some Dilemmas of Social Defense," *International Review of Criminal Policy*, No. 28, United Nations, New York, 1970.

Wilsnack, Richard and Ohlin, Lloyd E., "Prison Disturbances" (Winter 1973-74) (draft chapter unpublished, Harvard Law School, Center for Criminal Justice), 1974.

Wilson, James Q., "Crime and Criminologists," *Commentary*, July 1974.

INDEX

(References are to page numbers)